CHINESE SMALL PROPERTY

Small properties provide living space to about eight million migrant workers, office space for start-ups, grassroots police stations, and primary schools; their contribution to the economic growth and urbanization of a city is immense. The interaction between the small property sector and the formal legal order has a long history and small property has become an established engine of social and legal change. *Chinese Small Property* presents vivid stories about how institutional entrepreneurs worked together to create an impersonal market outside of the formal legal system to support millions of transactions. Shitong Qiao uses an eleven-month fieldwork project in Shenzhen – China's first special economic zone that has grown to a mega city with over 15 million people – to demonstrate this. A thorough and detailed investigation into small property rights in China, *Chinese Small Property* is an invaluable source of new information for students and scholars of the field.

SHITONG QIAO is Assistant Professor of Law at the University of Hong Kong and NYU Global Associate Professor of Law. Qiao graduated from top Chinese and US law schools with numerous prizes, including the Top Academic Prize from Peking University and the Judge Ralph K. Winter Prize from Yale University. He advises government agencies, inside and outside China, on the Chinese land regime. His publications on property and social norms have appeared in leading English and Chinese law journals.

CHINESE SMALL PROPERTY

The Co-Evolution of Law and Social Norms

SHITONG QIAO
The University of Hong Kong

CAMBRIDGE
UNIVERSITY PRESS

CAMBRIDGE
UNIVERSITY PRESS

University Printing House, Cambridge CB2 8BS, United Kingdom

One Liberty Plaza, 20th Floor, New York, NY 10006, USA

477 Williamstown Road, Port Melbourne, VIC 3207, Australia

4843/24, 2nd Floor, Ansari Road, Daryaganj, Delhi – 110002, India

79 Anson Road, #06–04/06, Singapore 079906

Cambridge University Press is part of the University of Cambridge.

It furthers the University's mission by disseminating knowledge in the pursuit of education, learning, and research at the highest international levels of excellence.

www.cambridge.org
Information on this title: www.cambridge.org/9781107176232
DOI: 10.1017/9781316810095

First published 2018

Printed in the United Kingdom by Clays, St Ives plc

A catalogue record for this publication is available from the British Library.

Library of Congress Cataloging-in-Publication Data
Names: Qiao, Shitong, 1985-
Title: Chinese small property : the co-evolution of law and social norms / Shitong Qiao, the University of Hong Kong.
Description: Cambridge [UK] ; New York : Cambridge University Press, 2017. | Includes bibliographical references and index.
Identifiers: LCCN 2017019534| ISBN 9781107176232 (hardback : alk. paper) | ISBN 9781316628737 (pbk. : alk. paper)
Subjects: LCSH: Property–China. | Land tenure–Law and legislation–China. | Right of property–China.
Classification: LCC KNQ640 .Q53 2017 | DDC 346.7304/3–dc23 LC record available at https://lccn.loc.gov/2017019534

ISBN 978-1-107-17623-2 Hardback

CONTENTS

FIGURES

TABLES

ACKNOWLEDGMENTS

First, I would like to thank Professor Robert Ellickson for his invaluable guidance and his supervision of this project, including, but not limited to, discussions on the choice of topic and design of my research in 2009, grammatical corrections, the substance of particular arguments and broad discussions on the limits of social sciences. His dedication and patience, for which I am deeply grateful, have made this project possible. He helped me find solid ground in exploring the complicated swamp of Chinese land reform. He is my Confucius.

Professor Susan Rose-Ackerman introduced me to the legal studies of property in the United States in her course "Corruption, Economic Development and Democracy" in the fall of 2009. From then on, I have benefited tremendously and continuously from her guidance, discussions, suggestions, and detailed comments on various drafts of my chapters. Professor Paul Gewirtz and his China Law Center provided invaluable support to my study and research, in particular my fieldwork in China.

I also greatly appreciate the administrative support from the graduate program of the Yale Law School, in particular Maria Dino; research support from the Lillian Goldman Law Library of Yale Law School, in particular Evelyn Ma and Cha Chi Hung, and financial support from the Oscar M. Ruebhausen Fund, the Kauffmann Summer Fellowship and the Streicker Fund of Yale Law School.

I finished a big chunk of this book during my stay at NYU in the 2013–14 academic year. I would like to thank Professors Frank Upham, Jerry Cohen, and Ira Belkin for providing me with a fellowship, enabling me to benefit from the rigorous research on Chinese law, property law, and urban governance at NYU, in particular, Professor Vicki Been's Land Use Regulations course and Professor Richard Epstein's Water Law course. Professor Upham has been a great mentor, friend, and "comrade of rogue law and economics," providing extremely helpful support, guidance, and suggestions at every stage of my career development.

Second, I would like to thank those I met in Shenzhen who shared with me their personal lives and their love, enthusiasm, passion, and knowledge of Shenzhen, "the city of reform." In particular, I thank Zhang Ganfu, Xie Zhikui, Wu Dan, and Lv Peng who opened doors to different sectors of the city for me. Professor Jeffrey Lehman, then Dean of the Peking University School of Transnational Law, and Professor Francis Snyder provided a base for my fieldwork in Shenzhen, and were extremely supportive to my research during my visit there. I am also grateful to Professor Zhou Qi'ren and his colleagues at the Peking University National School of Development for accepting me as a member of their land research group, allowing me to participate in their fieldtrips in Shenzhen in April and June of 2012 and many stimulating discussions within the group.

Third, this book has also benefited from comments and suggestions from numerous workshops and conferences, a complete list of which would be too tedious. Predecessors of Chapters 1, 2, 3, and 4 have been published by the *Columbia Journal of Asian Law*, *Canadian Journal of Law and Society*, the *American Journal of Comparative Law*, and as a book chapter in *Law and Economics of Possession*, respectively. I thank their publishers for permission to use substantial parts of the original publications in this book. I would also like to express my special gratitude to Yun-chien Chang, editor of *Law and Economics of Possession*, and Mariana Valverde, editor of *Canadian Journal of Law and Society*, for their help and advice much beyond their roles as editors.

Many other people have helped me in various ways. They are Bruce Ackerman, Benito Arruñada, Abraham Bell, Anya Bernstein, Eleanor Brown, Ray Campbell, Jianlin Chen, Ruoying Chen, Jinhua Cheng, Jacques deLisle, Monica Eppinger, Lee Fennel, Tom Ginsburg, Xuan Gui, Derek Hall, Su Lin Han, Yu Han, Henry Hansmann, Xin He, Jamie P. Horsley, Fenglong Huang, Christine Jolls, Daniel Klerman, Maximo Langer, Daphna Lewinsohn-Zamir, Saul Levmore, Lixing Li, Gary Libecap, Benjamin L. Liebman, Weici Ling, Han Liu, Xiaotang Liu, Yu Luo, Noelle Lyle, Xiang Ma, Ji Ma, Neysun Mahboubi, Thomas Merrill, Noah Messing, Randal Picker, Katharina Pistor, Eric Posner, Jeffrey Prescott, Michael Reisman, Carol Rose, Jacqueline E. Ross, Kim Lane Scheppele, Jingxia Shi, Henry Smith, Thomas Ulen, Zhiqiang Wang, Zewei Wen, Linfei Xia, Xiaohong Xu, Zhaofeng Xue, Tian Yan, Jie Yang, John K. Yasuda, Qingyong Zhang, Taisu Zhang, Wei Zhang, Jiaxin Zhong, and Mo Zhou. All their help is greatly appreciated.

I would also like to thank Tian Lei, Chen Jian, Qiao Qi, and Li Xiaoshan for providing a sympathetic ear to my anxieties and bouts of writer's block in the past years.

Last but not least, this book is dedicated to Carol and my parents for their unwavering support and love.

Introduction

I.1 A Market without Legal Titles?

Can a real estate market form in the absence of a supportive property law system? If so, how, and by what means does it operate? What would be the legal responses to such an extralegal market? How would the legal responses influence the evolution of the extralegal market and the underlying property arrangements?

The answer to the first question has conventionally been no. "Where do we record the relevant economic features of assets, if not in the records and titles that formal property systems provide? Where are the codes of conduct that govern the use and transfer of assets, if not in the framework of formal property systems?"[1] Hernando de Soto, by posing these rhetorical questions, implies that life in informal settlements, where formal property rights are absent, is nasty, brutish, and poor.[2] For example, according to a study on informal settlements in Lima, Peru, one adult must occupy the house twenty-four hours a day in order to prevent others from taking possession of it.[3] The presumption is that informal property rights must be uncertain and insecure, and, thus, transactions must be very limited. In de Soto's seminal works on the relationship between informal property rights and a market economy, *The Other Path* and *The Mystery of Capital*, de Soto discussed real estate transactions in seven pages in the former and not at all in the latter.[4] In the following years, most academic research has focused on calculating the value of legal titles – including topics such as how titling programs have increased tenure security, promoted investment, and

[1] Hernando de Soto (2000). *The Mystery of Capital: Why Capitalism Triumphs in the West and Fails Everywhere Else* 46.

[2] *See* Hernando de Soto (1989). *The Other Path*, 17–57, 133–172.

[3] Winter King (2003). Illegal settlements and the impact of titling programs, 44 *Harv. Int'l L.J.* 433.

[4] De Soto, *supra* note 2, at 25, 30–33, 35, 54 (discussing illegal real estate transactions).

increased the value of the property.[5] In "Hernando de Soto and Property in a Market Economy," a book consisting of essays by leading property law scholars, the editor writes in the introduction that,

> [I]t is important to distinguish between the two types of arguments that De Soto makes about property. *De Soto's arguments that formal property systems are* ***necessary*** *to the proper functioning of a market economy receive little, if any criticism.* In contrast, de Soto's apparent argument that property formalization is sufficient to bring the benefits of a market economy to the poor has received sustained criticism.[6] [emphasis added]

Real estate is the primary form of property and probably the most valuable asset to most individuals. Scholars assume that a real estate market cannot operate, nor even form, without property rights.[7] As a result, development scholars have seldom studied exchanges of untitled real property. To my knowledge, one significant exception is Annette M. Kim, who examines the housing market in Ho Chi Minh City, Vietnam, where the vast majority of private titles in urban areas had still not been distributed by the state.[8] Even this rare exception focuses on the value of a legal title, rather than the mechanism of property rights and market in the absence of a supportive legal system.

However, a well-functioning property law system should be the end – not the beginning – of discussions of property rights and economic development. Most developing countries are struggling to build a well-functioning property law system. Thus, it is crucial to explore how a market economy and the underlying property arrangements work in the absence, rather than the presence, of a well-functioning property law system.

[5] *See, e.g.*, Lee J. Alston, Gary D. Libecap and Robert Schneider (1996). The determinants and impact of property rights: Land titles on the Brazilian frontier, 12 *J.L. Econ & Org.* 25; Lee J. Alston, Gary D. Libecap and Robert Schneider (1995). Property rights and the preconditions for markets: The case of the Amazon frontier, 151 *J. Institutional & Theoretical Econ.* 89; Timothy Besley (1995). Property rights and investment incentives: Theory and evidence from Ghana, *J. Pol. Econ.* 903; Erica Field (2005). Property rights and investment in urban slums, 3 *J. Eur. Econ. Ass'n* 279; Erica Field (2007). Entitled to work: Urban property rights and labor supply in Peru, 122 *Q.J. Econ.* 1561; Sebastian Galiani and Ernesto Schargrodsky (2010). Property rights for the poor: Effects of Land titling, 94 *J. Pub. Econ.* 700.

[6] *Hernando de Soto and Property in a Market Economy* 2 (D. Benjamin Barros, ed.) (2010).

[7] Andrzej Rapaczynski (1996). The roles of the state and the market in establishing property rights, 10 *J. Econ. Perspectives* 87, 96–98.

[8] Annette M. Kim (2004). A market without the 'right' property rights – Ho Chi Minh City, Vietnam's newly-emerged private real estate market, 12 *Econ. Transition* 275–305.

A real estate market can form in the absence of a supportive property law system. According to the Chinese Ministry of Land and Resources, by 2007, Chinese farmers had built over 6.6 billion square meters of houses in evasion of the legal prohibition on private rural land development and transfer, resulting in a huge market of illegal houses. By way of comparison, in 2007, the total floor space of housing sold on the legal housing market was 0.76 billion square meters.[9] People in China call these illegal buildings "small-property houses" (*xiaochanquan* in Chinese)[10] because their property rights are "smaller" (weaker) than those on the urban/formal housing market, which have "big" property rights protected by the government. Shenzhen is the city with the highest ratio of small-property houses, which make up 47.57 percent of the city's total floor space, compared to 30 percent in Xi'An and 20 percent in Beijing.[11] These

[9] 小产权房存量66亿平米相当于十年房产成交量[Small-Property Houses total 6.6 Billion Square Meters, almost the same amount of Legal Housing Transactions within a Decade] www.china.com.cn/info/txt/2008-11/17/content_16779899.htm (last visited May 6, 2014).

[10] There is no general consensus on the translation. Fennel uses "small title" to describe the phenomenon; Chen use "housing with a petit title;" some others use "small property rights housing," "minor property rights," or "limited property housing." As this research shows, it is not a simple "title" problem, but a phenomenon we need to understand from the perspective of the evolution of the Chinese property system. "Property" is a more precise word than "title" because of its more encompassing meaning. People might worry about the conflation of *physical* property and property *rights* when I use "small property" as the translation. Here I refer to Alchian and Demsetz: "In its original meaning, property referred solely to a right, title, or interest, and resources could not be identified as property any more than they could be identified as right, title, or interest." Armen A. Alchian and Harold Demsetz (1973). The property right paradigm, 33 *J. Econ. Hist.* 16, 17. Under this understanding of the term "property," the word "rights" becomes superfluous. Accordingly, I use "small property" to depict the general phenomenon, and "small-property buildings," "small-property houses," or "small-property constructions" to refer to the physical constructions built under the general phenomenon. Also, "small" is more direct and neutral than "minor" or "limited." *See* Wang Lanlan, Tieshan Sun and Sheng Li, *Legal title, tenure security, and investment – An empirical study in Beijing*, HOUSING STUD.1 (2014); Li Lixing (2012). Land titling in China: Chengdu experiment and its consequences, 5 *China Econ. J.* 47; Wang Qianyi, Miao Zhang and Kee-Cheok Cheong (2014). Stakeholder perspectives of China's land consolidation program: A case study of Dongnan Village, Shandong Province, 43 *Habitat Int'l* 172; Lee Anne Fennell (2012). Options for owners and outlaws, 1 *Brigham-Kanner Prop. Rts. Conf. J.* 239; Ruoying Chen, Informal Sales of Rural Housing in China: Property, Privatization and Local Public Finance (2010) (unpublished Ph.D. dissertation, University of Chicago) (on Proquest).

[11] 宋林飞（全国政协委员、江苏省政府参事室主任）："小产权房没有转正"特区"，"人民论坛" 2012年7月4日[Song, Linfei, *No Special Economic Zone for Legalization of Small-Property Houses*, PEOPLE'S FORUM, July 4, 2012], http://theory.people.com.cn/n/2012/0704/c112851-18443279.html (last visited February 15, 2013).

illegal buildings, lacking legal titles and concentrated in 320 intracity villages, host most of the eight million migrant workers in Shenzhen and are the main livelihoods of the more than 300,000 local villagers. The market has developed in step with China's continuing struggle for a formal property regime, an effort that is still unfinished. According to an official at the Shenzhen Real Estate Ownership Registration Center, "Nobody cares whether they have legal titles or not. You say they are illegal, dare you void the contracts? You say they are legal, are you to grant them legal titles? The contracts are there – to void them, could you do that? It is a huge number of transactions – you say farmers cannot sell, it is illegal, but they do it privately with little ado. Are you to tell them whether it is legal or illegal?"[12]

The object of my study is the co-evolution of property law and norms in the formation, operation, and institutionalization of the small-property market in Shenzhen. This book is based on my eleven-month fieldwork in Shenzhen, during which I observed small-property transactions firsthand; interviewed real estate brokers, lawyers, buyers, sellers, and government officials and judges whose work was related to small-property houses; and participated in the formation of government policies addressing small-property houses. I collected government investigation reports, court files, village maps and records, transaction documents, and news reports that addressed small-property houses to further my research.

I.2 The Market: A Bird's Eye View

I.2.1 Chinese Property Law Reform and Small Property Nationwide

In the early 1980s, the communist prohibition on land alienation proved to be inadaptable to a market-oriented economy with the experimentation and implementation of the "reform and opening-up" policy under the leadership of Deng Xiaoping. This inadaptability was most acute in the urban area, where both urban construction and cooperation with foreign investors could benefit greatly from land development and transfer. As a result, in 1988, China amended both the Constitution and Land Administration Law ("LAL"), stating that use rights to both state-owned and collective-owned land could be transferred "according to law."

[12] Interview with a city government official, in Futian District of Shenzhen City (June 7, 2012).

On May 19, 1990, the State Council promulgated detailed rules governing the sales of *urban* land use rights from the government and the transfer among land users.[13]

This urban land use reform not only built the legal basis for China's urban real estate market but also made land the most important source of revenue for Chinese local governments, which can requisition rural land at compensation equal to its agricultural value and sell the same land on the urban land market at fifty times or more of that value.[14] As a result, the more the urban real estate market develops, the more unlikely it is that the central and local governments would liberalize rural land development and transfer, since this would jeopardize their monopoly over land.[15]

Unsurprisingly, the corresponding legal authorization for the transfer of rural land use rights has never been promulgated. Instead, the Chinese government made a comprehensive revision to LAL that excluded the possibility of the transfer of rural land use rights in 1998. The 1998 revision also made it clear that rural-urban land conversion could only be legally achieved through requisition by the state.[16]

However, the rural land has not been insulated from the booming urban real estate market. The boom in China's urban real estate market began in 1998, when the central government decided to replace its housing allocation system with a housing market.[17] According to official statistics, from 1998 to 2007 the annual nationwide sales of residential houses grew tenfold.[18] Under such circumstances, rural land, especially land located near urban areas, has become attractive. Therefore, local governments have great incentives to seize rural land. The general mechanism is that the government requisitions rural land, converts it to urban

[13] For the history of Chinese property law, *see* Chapter 1.

[14] Compensation for the requisitioned rural land is mainly based on its agricultural output, but the government transfers it at urban land market prices. Chinese laws do say that land requisition should be "for the need of public interest." *See* art. 10 of the Chinese Constitution and art. 42 of the Chinese Property Law. However, as rural land requisition is the main legal way to satisfy the vast need for construction land in China's urbanization process, the above public interest requirement has been essentially moot. *See* Chapter 1 for a more comprehensive explanation.

[15] *See* Chapter 1. [16] *Id.*

[17] *See* 陈杰："中国住房事业六十年：回顾与反思" [CHEN JIE, SIX DECADES OF CHINA'S HOUSING AFFAIRS], www.chps.fudan.edu.cn/cn/content.asp?id=50 (last visited February 3, 2014).

[18] 国家统计局："2008年二季度经济述评：市场不支持高房价" [*Economic Review of the Second Quarter of 2008: Market Does Not Support High Housing Price*, XINHUA NET], http://news.xinhuanet.com/fortune/2008-08/05/content_8974798.htm (last visited December 10, 2009).

land (thereby qualifying it for various construction purposes), and then sells it to commercial land developers. Millions of acres of rural land have been urbanized in this way in China since the 1980s, creating more than 40 million landless farmers.[19]

One way Chinese farmers have responded to this unjust law is by evading legal prohibitions on rural land development and transfer. Farmers living in the periurban[20] areas of big cities often face large incentives to transfer their houses to urban residents who cannot afford a house in the urban area. While they cannot sell houses at prices comparable to those on the formal market due to the illegality of the transfer, they can still get much more profit than they could from using the land for agricultural purposes. Their illegal transfers of land for non-agricultural uses have created a huge informal real estate market in China.

The prices of small-property apartments are significantly lower than those of legal apartments, ranging from 20 percent to 60 percent of the price.[21] For better or worse, small-property houses have become a serious option for many Chinese residents. According to an investigation in 2011, 60.3 percent of the respondents viewed small-property apartments as an option for buying a house.[22]

I.2.2 ***Small-Property Market in Shenzhen***

Shenzhen, a city in the southern part of southern China's Guangdong Province and situated immediately north of Hong Kong, has been the literal and symbolic heart of the Chinese economic miracle.[23] In many ways, Shenzhen epitomizes China's recent economic development: It is

[19] 新华网： "委员称失地农民超4000万人　过半人生活困难" ，2011年3月9日 [*A CPPCC Member Revealed that There Were over 40 Million Landless Farmers, Over Half of Them Live in Hard Times*, XINHUA NET (March 9, 2011)], http://news.qq.com/a/20110309/001085.htm (last visited February 18, 2013).

[20] "Periurban" is defined as areas where the dynamic, interactive and transformative urbanization is happening and mixed features of the rural-urban spectrum are present in the background of developing countries. *See, e.g.*, David L. Iaquinta and Axel W. Drescher, *Defining Periurban: Understanding Rural-Urban Linkages and Their Connection to Institutional Contexts* (Paper presented at the Tenth World Congress of the International Rural Sociology Association, Rio de Janeiro, August 1, 2000).

[21] REICO工作室："我国小产权房问题研究：现状与出路" [INVESTIGATION REPORT OF SMALL-PROPERTY CONSTRUCTIONS 12–13, REICO (2012)] (on file with author).

[22] 袁业飞： "禁？放？小产权房路在何方？——聚焦走到十字路口的小产权房" ，"中华建设" ，2011年第5期，6–15页[Yefei Yuan, *Whither Is Small Property?*, CHINA CONSTRUCTION, 2011(5): 6–15.]

[23] *See, e.g.*, Howard W. French, Chinese Success Story Chokes on Its Own Growth, *N.Y. Times* (December 19, 2006), www.nytimes.com/2006/12/19/world/asia/19shenzhen.html.

the starting point of China's transition to a market economy, the birthplace of China's urban land-use reform and modern real estate industry, and the city with the highest ratio of small-property houses in China. It is the ideal case study of the relationship between property rights and the market economy in China.

In 1980, Deng Xiaoping, the then-supreme leader of China, designated Shenzhen – then named Bao'An and a small agricultural county – as a "special economic zone" (SEZ) for piloting market-oriented reforms.[24] Within this SEZ, investment from overseas Chinese and foreign companies would be permitted and used for urban construction.

Since the establishment of the SEZ, Shenzhen has experienced miraculous economic growth and urbanization. In 1979, the urban population in Shenzhen was no more than 30,000, and all of the remaining population of 284,100 was rural.[25] Agriculture was the county's main and nearly only industry in 1979. There was no decent public infrastructure – not even a sewage system. From 1979 to 2010, the annual average growth rate of gross domestic product ("GDP") in Shenzhen was 25.3 percent.[26] The population of Shenzhen has grown from 314,100, of whom 312,600 have local *hukou* (household registration) in 1979 to 10,372,000 in 2010, of whom only 2,510,300 have local *hukou*.[27] Shenzhen ranked fourth in GDP and first in GDP per capita among mainland Chinese cities in 2009.[28] In 2010, the GDP of Shenzhen was over 958 billion RMB (1 RMB = 0.16 USD).[29] Shenzhen has ranked first since 1993 in the total value of exports among all mainland Chinese cities.[30] Moreover, the economies of Shenzhen and Hong Kong are closely interconnected; an integration plan has even been officially proposed.[31] More than half of the foreign direct investment in Shenzhen has been from Hong Kong.[32]

[24] *See, e.g.*, 江潭瑜主编："深圳改革开放史"，人民出版社2010年版 [THE HISTORY OF REFORM AND OPENING-UP IN SHENZHEN (Jiang Tanyu, ed., 2010).]

[25] 深圳市统计局、国家统计局深圳调查队："深圳统计年鉴（2011）"，中国统计出版社[SHENZHEN STATISTICAL Y.B. 2011, STATISTICS BUREAU OF SHENZHEN CITY & SHENZHEN SURVEY OFFICE OF THE STATE STATISTICS BUREAU 4, (2011).]

[26] *Id.* at 5. [27] *Id.* at 4.

[28] 乐正主编："深圳之路"，人民出版社2010年版，第16页[ZHENG LE, THE ROAD OF SHENZHEN 16(2010)]

[29] SHENZHEN STATISTICAL Y.B. 2011, *supra* note 25, at 5. [30] Le, *supra* note 28, at 121.

[31] Vaudine England, *Mega-City Plans for Hong Kong*, BBC NEWS (September 17, 2007), http://news.bbc.co.uk/2/hi/asia-pacific/6989473.stm.

[32] In 1986, 78.86% of foreign investment in Shenzhen came from Hong Kong; 63.47% in 1988; 64.49% in 1992; 71.69% in 1998; 53.91% in 2001; 53.05% in 2005; 63.75% in 2008. SHENZHEN STATISTICAL Y.B. 2011, *supra* note 25, at 284.

Three decades ago, most of the land in Shenzhen was rural and collectively owned by the farmers of the respective villages. Urban (state-owned) land made up a little more than three square kilometers in Shenzhen in 1980. The Shenzhen government has since converted most of the rural land to urban land under its jurisdiction. Villages that used to be located on the outskirts of the city are now surrounded by urban buildings, many of which are skyscrapers. In the urbanization process, the Shenzhen government requisitioned most of the rural land (mostly farmland) and converted it to urban land, preserving only the rural land on which residential homes and village factories had been built because of the higher social and economic costs of requisitioning those plots. These remaining villages are called "intracity villages" (*chengzhongcun* in Chinese). Though located in the midst of the urban area, land in intracity villages is still rural, which makes it subject to the legal prohibition on rural land development and transfer. Among the total 1,993 square kilometers of land in Shenzhen, the government failed to convert over 300 square kilometers of rural land to urban land, on which there have been 356,852 illegally-built buildings, totaling 392 million square meters and making up 47.57 percent of the total floor space of Shenzhen (Table I.1).[33]

In the periurban area, the actual problem is not to find a small property, but to find a legal property. Small-property buildings were intended for a variety of residential and industrial uses, as well as for use as shopping malls, offices, and public facilities such as primary

Table I.1 *Illegal buildings in Shenzhen*[34]

	Number of buildings	Total floor area
Illegal Buildings	356,852	392 million
Total Buildings	620,800	824 million
Illegal Buildings (% of Total Buildings)	57.49	47.57

33 Shenzhen City Gov., Investigation Report on Illegal Buildings in Shenzhen 26 (2010) (on file with the author).

34 *Id.* at 11.

schools, hospitals, and even government buildings. This differs from the conventional view of informal settlements presented by de Soto and many others. In a report on small property in Shenzhen, a journalist found that even an official building of a sub-district government had no legal titles.[35] Table I.2 shows the different uses of small-property buildings the information of which has been reported to the government–that is 348,400 of the 356,852 buildings.[36]

Many of these small-property buildings are of decent quality and are not "small" at all. According to an official from the Bureau of Construction of the Shenzhen city government, "The illegal buildings built after 2000 were designed and built under professional supervision; they also used high-quality steels; the qualities of these buildings

Table I.2 *Uses of small-property buildings in Shenzhen*[37]

Uses	Number of buildings	Ratio (%)	Total floor space (millions of square meters)	Ratio (%)	Land area (millions of square meters)	Ratio (%)
Residential	234100	67.19	149	38.70	33	25.58
Industrial	83400	23.94	166	43.12	70	54.26
Commercial or Office	9400	2.70	20	5.19	12	9.30
Public Facilities	4300	1.23	6	1.56	4	3.10
Multiple Uses	10400	2.99	41	10.65	8	6.20
Other Uses	6800	1.95	3	0.78	2	1.55
Total	348400	100.00	385	100.00	129	100.00

35 庄浩滨："深圳违建一线报告:旧改诞生十几个亿万富翁"，《南方日报》2009年7月10日[Zhuang Haobin, *Frontier Report of Illegal Buildings in Shenzhen*, NANFANG DAILY, July 10, 2009], http://news.dayoo.com/shenzhen/200907/10/67208_9881497.htm (last visited September 10, 2013).

36 Shenzhen City Gov., *supra* note 33, at 13.

37 *Id.* at 38.

Table I.3 *Number of floors of small-property buildings in Shenzhen*[38]

Number of floors	Number of buildings	Ratio (%)	Total floor space (millions of square meters)	Ratio (%)	Land area (millions of square meters)	Ratio (%)
1 or unknown	94100	27.02	21	5.51	29	22.65
2–4	118600	34.03	121	31.35	53	41.35
5–6	69500	19.95	104	27.04	25	19.05
7–10	58500	16.77	94	24.54	15	11.73
11–14	5800	1.67	23	5.95	5	3.47
15 or more	1900	0.56	22	5.61	2	1.74
Total	348400	100.00	385	100.00	129	100.00

are above the median."[39] As shown in Table I.3, many small-property buildings are typically five to ten floors high. The tallest may reach fifteen floors or higher.

De Soto suggests, with no empirical backup, that both the selling and the renting of the illegal buildings would be limited because of the lack of legal titles.[40] Below, I present some statistics from the Shenzhen government to discuss the scale of the market, which is not limited to exchanges between villagers and their acquaintances.

For residential buildings, about 34 percent of the current owners were not original villagers, the only category of legal owners. For non-residential buildings, 60.75 percent of the current owners were not village co-ops, the only category of legal owners.[41] Regarding the land used for small-property buildings, for residential buildings, over 43 percent of the land had been transferred to non-villagers. For non-residential buildings, over 30 percent of the land had been transferred to non-villagers (Table I.4).[42]

The Shenzhen government also investigated small-property high-rises, buildings of fifteen floors or more that were mostly built after 2000 in

38 Shenzhen City Government, *supra* note 33, at 70.
39 Interview with a city government official, in Bao'An District of Shenzhen City (June 29, 2012).
40 De Soto, *supra* note 2, at 25.
41 Shenzhen City Gov., *supra* note 33, at 66–67.
42 *Id.*

Table I.4 *Illegal transactions of land and buildings*[43]

	Owner	Land
Residential Buildings	34% were not original villagers	43.53% had been transferred to non-villagers
Non-Residential Buildings	60.75% were not original village co-ops	30.2% had been transferred to non-villagers

response to the high demand for residential housing in Shenzhen. The total floor area of these buildings totaled 21,598,800 square meters,[44] about one-third of the total area of legally developed residential houses for sale built in Shenzhen from 2000 to 2009.[45] The Shenzhen Urban Planning and Design Institute conducted a questionnaire survey of small-property apartments in these high-rises. Among 334 buyers, 278 used their apartments for self-living; 56 used their apartments for renting or investment.[46] Regarding the size of their apartments, 36 were less than 70 square meters; 96 were between 70 and 90 square meters; 172 were between 91 and 140 square meters, and 30 were more than 140 square meters.[47]

There is no comprehensive data available on the total number of small-property transactions, but according to a government official in Bao'An, one district of Shenzhen, the number of illegal sales of small-property apartments was about half that of sales of legal/ big-property apartments (there were about 1,400,000 sales of legal apartments in 2011 in that district).[48] These transactions are not limited to villagers and their personal contacts; rather, they happen daily between strangers. Village co-ops, real estate brokers, land developers, and other stakeholders have formed a network to support this small-property market.[49] Small-property apartments can be used and rented freely, sold and mortgaged subject to some constraints, and

[43] *Id.* at 49, 65. Some sold land directly; some sold buildings and the land was not sold.

[44] *Id.* at 77.

[45] From 2000 to 2009, the official market of residential houses supplied 59,220,000 square meters of housing in total. 黄珽主编："深圳房地产年鉴（2011）"，海天出版社，第151页[SHENZHEN REAL ESTATE YEAR BOOK 2011 151 (Huang Ting, ed. 2011).].

[46] SHENZHEN URBAN PLANNING & DESIGN INSTIT., SURVEY ON UNIFIED-CONSTRUCTED BUILDINGS (2012), on file with the author.

[47] *Id.*

[48] Interview with a city government official, in Bao'An District of Shenzhen City (June 26, 2012).

[49] *See* Chapter 2 for more details.

compensated according to comparable standards of big-property apartments when requisitioned by the government.[50]

I.3 Piercing the Market: Structure of the Book

Chapter 1 investigates the history of land use reform in China and reveals that the so-called rural land problem is the consequence of China's partial land use reform. In 1988, the Chinese government chose to conduct land use reform sequentially: first urban and then rural. It was a pragmatic move because it would focus the reform and would provoke much less resistance. A consequence was that local governments in China became the biggest beneficiary and supporter of the partial reform. However, as a beneficiary of partial reform, local governments do not necessarily support further reform because of the excessive rents available between the market of urban real estate and the government-controlled rural land system.[51] The central government, in particular its agency in charge of land administration (the former Bureau of Land Administration, which has been elevated to the Ministry of Land and Resources), also has interests embedded in this regime. In contrast, Chinese farmers and other relevant groups have no voice or power in the political process of the reform, which makes it difficult for the central government to achieve an agenda that balances the interests of all parties.

However, this is not to say that a country, even without a democratic political structure, would necessarily be trapped in the partial reform equilibrium. In the China case, Chinese farmers challenged the existing system by forming a huge small-property market, around which social groups disadvantaged by the partial reform, mainly Chinese farmers and the middle-and-low income urban population, present their interests and their capacity to counteract the goals the central and local governments hope to achieve through the existing system. This has led to adaptive policy changes. Recent news demonstrates that Chinese land reform is moving in a direction that would address Chinese farmers' concerns, though much work is still needed to unify the small-property market and the legal real estate sector.

[50] *Id.*

[51] Under the current dual land system, which is the result of this partial reform, the government can requisition rural land at compensation equal to its agricultural value (because rural land sector is not liberalized for construction or commercial uses) and sell the same land on the urban land market (which is monopolized by the government) at prices according to its construction or commercial value, which is often fifty times or higher of the agricultural value. *See* Chapter 1 for a comprehensive discussion.

Based on my fieldwork in Shenzhen, Chapter 2 presents the factual situations and mechanisms of the small-property market in Shenzhen. The main participants in the market are legitimate and include village co-ops, real estate brokers, lawyers, a local bank, and even the local government branches and agencies, which from time to time choose to acquiesce to the development of the small-property market. Although they are legitimate actors, they are not constrained by legalities. They have developed a network to support the operation of the small-property market. The formal property law has been ambiguous and subject to change and inconsistent enforcement, and, thus, it has had limited prohibitive force.

Chapter 3 models the formation and operation of the small-property market as coordination games and demonstrates that a focal point of rural land development and transfer coordinates players' expectations to converge on the same equilibrium. It investigates the historical, political, and other contextual factors that not only structure the interactions of relevant parties but also influence their expectations.

Chapter 4 focuses on the Shenzhen government's policies addressing small-property houses. To demolish them has proven an impossible mission. To legalize them would encourage more illegal buildings. I frame this small-property conundrum as an adverse possession question and resolve it by utilizing the optional law framework developed by Professor Ian Ayres. I find that in an effort to grandfather in existing small-property constructions and deter further development of small property, the Shenzhen government has spent the last three decades adopting land use policies that can be neatly categorized into the five rules of legal entitlements under the optional law framework. The only missing rule, Rule 5, also provides a solution to a certain type of cases. Evidence from my fieldwork shows that Rule 2, the liability rule in which entitlement is assigned to the government, subject to taking by residents willing to pay the government, is most successful. I make a general argument in this chapter that the allocation of initial options matters as much as the allocation of initial entitlements and that options should be granted to parties with the best information to make decisions, which in the small-property case, are the individual owners rather than the government.

Chapter 5 explores two distinct outcomes for small-property villages. Some villages successfully gain government recognition of their real estate business by making use of various government policies created in response to the widespread small-property constructions. In contrast, other villages have given up any legal dialogue with the official system and resorted mainly to bribes and even violence to maintain their small-property business. One reason for these vastly different outcomes is the layering and fragmentation of the legal system, which makes the choice of different social control systems more nuanced than the existing theories portray. Built on a multiple-network evolution model, I investigate the three identities of village co-ops in the triple-system of social control (market, community and law) and how the three identities influence each other and the systems in which they are embedded and ultimately lead to each village's outcome.

Chapter 6 examines the Chinese judiciary's responses to small property. Despite variations across courts in different parts of the country, represented by Beijing and Shenzhen, this chapter reveals that Chinese courts share the same bottom line: make no changes to the status quo or minimize the negative impacts of illegality when it must be confirmed. This chapter supplements the argument that social norms are more responsive to social development than is the law by extending the discussion from property laws and regulations to judicial decisions. It concludes that the Chinese judiciary is reactive and responsive to social change rather than leading it. It thus represents neither a hindrance to nor engine of social change.

The last chapter concludes with a critique of the residual legal centralism embedded in the existing research on law and social norms and argues that property norms can precede property law in the context of market transition and serve as a catalyst for legal change, which would be achieved through a reconstitution of law and social norms. It also clarifies that the focus of my research is the co-evolution and interaction mechanism of property law and norms, different from de Soto's focus on the formalization of informal property systems.

I.4 Property Law and Norms in Temporality

A well-functioning property law regime, albeit beneficial to the development of a market economy, may be a long time in coming for many transitional countries. Through this original case study, I propose a theory that provides an option for transitional countries during their long march toward rule of law:

- Stage I: Property law reform trapped in partial reform equilibrium;
- Stage II: A network of institutional innovators invented a market under the focal point of market transition;
- Stage III: Pragmatic/ad hoc legal responses;

- Stage IV. Reconstitution of layered and fragmented law in local communities, which in turn can be catalyst for legal change.

This unique case study can shed some light on the evolution of property rights. In his 1967 path-breaking work *Toward a Theory of Property Rights*, Demsetz offered before-and-after snapshots of the evolution of property rights, but left the actual process that leads from one state to another as a black box.[52] The Demsetz thesis is very concise: "[P]roperty rights develop to internalize externalities when the gains of internalization become larger than the cost of internalization." This portrays the evolution of property rights as happening automatically in response to new cost-benefit possibilities, regardless of the social and political processes. This is, of course, oversimplified. Comparing to Demsetz's solo emphasis on economic constraints, Ostrom focused on the communal settings in which resources are governed.[53] In recent years, there has been increasing interest in the political process of property rights. Levmore argues that "the prevailing arrangement of property rights may be the product of politics and interest-group activity."[54] According to him, interest groups, including coordinators and beneficiaries of emerging property rights, such as entrepreneurs, play a key role in the evolutionary process of property rights. Anderson and Hill, Epstein, and Banner arrive at similar conclusions through their separate case studies.[55] Wyman emphasizes the political character of property rights by studying the case of New York taxicab medallions[56] and the evolution of individual tradable rights in US coastal fisheries.[57] China's market transition provides an opportunity to observe the co-evolution of property law and norms, which are shaped by economic constraints, communal settings, and interest group

[52] *See* Thomas W. Merill (2002). Introduction: The Demsetz Thesis and the evolution of property rights, 31 *J. Legal Stud.* S331, S336.

[53] *See* Elinor Ostrom (1990). *Governing the Commons: The Evolution of Institutions for Collective Action.*

[54] Saul Levmore (2002). Two stories about the evolution of property rights, 31 *J. Legal Stud.* S421, S427.

[55] Terry L. Anderson and Peter J. Hill (2002). Cowboys and contracts, 31 *J. Legal Stud.* 489; Richard A. Epstein (2002). The allocation of the commons: Parking on public roads, 31 *J. Legal Stud.* S515; Stuart Banner (2002). Transitions between property regimes, 31 *J. Legal Stud.* S359.

[56] Katrina M. Wyman (2013). Problematic private property: The case of New York taxicab medallions, 30 *Yale J. on Reg.* 125.

[57] Katrina M. Wyman (2005). From fur to fish: Reconsidering the evolution of private property, 80 *N.Y.U. L. Rev.* 117.

politics, calling for an integrated theory about the evolution of property rights.

Moreover, by revealing the dynamic process of the evolution of property rights in China, in particular considering the bottom-up institutional exploration, this research can contribute to resolving the so-called China problem – why China has enjoyed almost four decades of rapid economic growth with a weak legal system.[58]

Lastly, this research also has broad implications for research on law and economic development. It treats an informal (bottom-up) market economy as a positive change toward a modern market economy, not simply as an anomaly. Therefore, rather than focusing on the lack of or need for legal property rights, a focus on the mechanics of informal markets could shed light on the way forward for transitional market economies. Scholars have referred to exchanges of untitled real property in their studies of Chinese Rural Land Reform,[59] property reform in Vietnam,[60] squatters in Hong Kong,[61] the Brazilian Amazon,[62] and the US frontier history.[63] Systematic case studies of informal real estate markets around China and the world would greatly enrich our understandings of law and economic development.

[58] *See, e.g.*, Victor Nee & Sonja Opper, *Capitalism from Below: Markets and Institutional Change in China* (2012); Donald C. Clarke (2003). Economic development and the rights hypothesis: The China problem, 51 *Am. J. Comp. L.* 89; Frank K. Upham (2010). From Demsetz to Deng: Speculations on the implications of Chinese growth for law and development theory, 41 *N.Y.U. J. Int'l L. & Pol.* 551.

[59] Chen, *supra* note 10. [60] Kim, *supra* note 8.

[61] *See* Alan Smart (1986). Invisible real estate: Investigations into the squatter property market, 10 *Int'l J. Urb. & Regional Res.* 29.

[62] *See* Lee J. Alston, Gary D. Libecap and Bernardo Mueller (1991). *Titles, Conflict, and Land Use: The Development of Property Rights and Land Reform on the Brazilian Amazon Frontier.*

[63] Terry L. Anderson and P. J. Hill (1978). An American experiment in anarcho-capitalism: The not so wild, wild west, 3 *J. Libertarian Stud.* 9, 19.

1

The Evolution of Land Law in China

Partial Reform, Vested Interests, and Small Property

This chapter investigates the history of land use reform in China and argues that the so-called rural land problem is the consequence of China's partial land use reform. In 1988, the Chinese government chose to conduct land use reform sequentially: first urban and then rural. It was a pragmatic move because it would focus the reform and provoke much less resistance. It also made local governments in China the biggest beneficiary and supporter of the partial reform.[1] However, a beneficiary of partial reform does not necessarily support further reform because of the excessive rents available between the market of urban real estate and the government-controlled system of rural land development and transfer. The central government, in particular its agency in charge of land administration (the former Bureau of Land Administration, which has been elevated to the Ministry of Land and Resources (the "MLR")), also has interests embedded in the current regime with the explicit goal of preserving agricultural land. In contrast, Chinese farmers and other interested groups have no voice or power in the political process of the reform, which makes it difficult for the central government to achieve an agenda that balances the interests of all parties.[2]

[1] Land sales revenue became an important source of Chinese local governments. In some Chinese cities, half of local government finance is from land sales revenue. Thus, it is not that particular individuals or constituencies benefited from land sales, or at least not directly. Of course, there are beneficiaries of government-dominated rural-urban land conversion, including real estate developers, and the department of land administration, which is able to maintain its budget and importance within the government system due to the existence of such a system. In general, land sales revenue has been in the *public* pocket of local governments, rather than in particular individuals or constituencies. The revenue has been used in maintaining the operation of the government and in various city public infrastructure projects.

[2] The influence of the partial reform on farmers is complicated. On one hand, it does give local governments incentives to grab farmers' land, which would not be so strong if there was no such a reform. On the other hand, thanks to the reform, local governments can afford to pay higher compensation to farmers than they could otherwise. In a more general way, urban land use reform was crucial to China's market transition and has greatly

However, this is not to say that a country, even without a democratic political structure, would necessarily be trapped in the partial reform equilibrium. In the China case, Chinese farmers challenged the existing system by forming a huge small-property market, through which social groups disadvantaged by the partial reform, mainly Chinese farmers and members of the middle-and-low income urban population, present their interests and display their capacity to counteract the goals of the central and local governments. This has led to adaptive policy changes. Recent news shows that Chinese land reform is moving in a direction that would address Chinese farmers' concerns, though much work is needed to unify the small-property market and the legal real estate sector.

My historical investigation builds not only on my systematic examination of national laws and landmark resolutions of the Chinese Communist Party ("CCP") but also on government documents generated in their drafting processes, ordinances, regulations, notices, communications between the central government and local governments, and memoirs of retired national leaders and senior government officials who participated in the reform. This chapter is organized as follows. Section 1.1 introduces the dual land ownership system in China. Sections 1.2 and 1.3 investigate the urban land use reform and rural land use reform, respectively. Section 1.4 explores how Chinese farmers have promoted policy changes through their illegal land uses.

1.1 Dual Land Ownership and Rural-Urban Land Conversion

Article ten of the current Chinese constitution reads that urban land is owned by the state and rural land is owned by collectives (except those owned by the state according to law). This is what dual land ownership means. *The most important character of this dual land ownership is the dominating role of the state landowner over the collective landowner, with the former's monopoly over rural-urban land conversion.* Throughout this book, "urban land" and "rural land" are legal terms regardless of the physical characteristics of the land. Rural land can be near the city center, such as that in some intracity villages, and urban land can be far away from the city center, such as those remote villages that were requisitioned by the government in recent years. In the following section, I discuss the origin and structure of dual land ownership in China.

facilitated China's urbanization process, from which farmers have benefited a lot. One example would be job opportunities for farmers who work in cities as migrant workers.

1.1.1 State Ownership of Urban Land

The undisputed moment at which private land ownership in China was abolished was the passage of the 1982 Constitution, which, for the first time in the history of the People's Republic of China, declared that urban land is state-owned without exceptions. Although several letters solicited from the populace on the draft of the 1982 Constitution addressed the state-ownership of urban land, this clause faced little dispute within the amendment committee.[3] The 1982 Constitution recognized the *de facto* demise of private land ownership caused by the Cultural Revolution for two reasons. First, in the ideological struggle between market and planned economies, the latter still prevailed. The orthodox Marxist understanding of property was strictly followed and, thus, there was no need to deny the nationalization of urban real estate in the Cultural Revolution. It was not until two years later in 1984 that the CCP finally achieved consensus on building a commercial economy with planning (*you jihua de shangping jingji*). Second, it was widely regarded that state ownership of urban land would serve the purposes of state-dominated economic development, as demonstrated by the proposal to nationalize rural land described in Section 1.1.2.

1.1.2 Collective Ownership of Rural Land

The CCP's promise to reallocate landlords' land to millions of peasants contributed to the civil war victory over the Nationalist Party in 1949. The Common Program of the Chinese People's Political Consultative Conference (which was passed in September 1949 and served as the temporary constitution of the People's Republic of China until 1954) made a system of "peasant land ownership" a goal of the new Communist government and protected the private property of "workers, peasants, the petty bourgeoisie and the national bourgeoisie."[4]

However, this did not last long. The CCP began to promote the establishment of farmers' co-ops (*hezuohua*) in rural areas in 1951, which led to the establishment of the people's commune system

[3] 程雪阳："城市土地国有规定的由来"，"炎黄春秋"2013年第6期[Xueyang Cheng (2013). The origin of state ownership of urban land, 6 *Yan Huang Chun Qiu Mag.*], www.21ccom.net/articles/zgyj/ggzhc/article_2013061085334_3.html.

[4] "中华人民共和国共同纲领"第三条[THE COMMON PROGRAM OF THE CHINESE PEOPLE'S POL. CONSULT. CONF., Article 3].

in 1958.[5] The people's commune consisted of three echelons: the commune, the production brigade, and the production team.[6]

Since the early 1980s, the Household Responsibility System (hereinafter "HRS") has replaced the people's commune system as the main rural land institution. Under the HRS, the collective should contract collectively owned land to individual households. Individual households, as contractors of rural land, are free to use the contracted land for agriculture. In the past three decades, the contract rights have gradually matured to quasi property rights due to the extension of the contract period from 15 years to "permanency" (*changjiu bu bian*)[7] and the establishment of measures to protect rural households' contract rights from the interference of rural collectives.[8] Rural land is categorized into three types: residential land; agricultural land, and public construction land. The permitted uses of different categories of rural land are strictly controlled, and farmers are prohibited from diverting land to any other urban use – which encompasses any use not listed among the three categories above.

[5] 陈锡文等："中国农村制度变迁60年"，人民出版社2009年版[Xiwen Chen et al., *Six Decades of the Evolution of Chinese Rural Institutions, People's Publ'g House* 10–16 (2009).]

[6] *See* Peter Ho (2001). Who owns China's land? Policies, property rights and deliberate institutional ambiguity, *166 China Quart.* 394, 404–405.

[7] *See*, 中国共产党第十七届中央委员会第三次全体会议公报（2008年10月12日中国共产党第十七届中央委员会第三次全体会议通过）[Gazette of Third Plenary Session of the 17th Central Committee of the CCP), promulgated October 12, 2008.]

[8] The last nationwide reallocation of rural land happened in 1998. In 2002, the central government passed the Rural Land Contract Law ("RLCL"), which stipulates that farmland tenure security must be maintained for at least 30 years. The third plenary session of the seventeenth Party congress also decided that the current land contract system "should not be changed for a long time." (*changjiububian*). Thus under the current law and policy, village collectives have no right to change or revoke the contract. Under very exceptional situations, such as natural disaster, adjustment of the land contracts should be agreed by two-thirds majority of villager representatives approved by the local government. *See, e.g.*, Article 27 of RLCL. Farmers can seek conciliation by local governments, special arbitration, and litigation for rural land contract disputes. *See* Article 51 of RLCL. However, failure to allocate land to the newly increased population often induced conflicts among village members if the above law and policy were strictly implemented. Administrative land reallocations then still continued in some villages to accommodate demographic changes in these places. Land requisition is another reason for land reallocation. According to a 2005 seventeen-province survey, 30.3% of the villages carried out land reallocation after 1998. *See* Zhu Keliang et al. (2006). The rural land question in China: Analysis and recommendations based on a seventeen-province survey, *38 N.Y.U. J. Int'l L. & Pol.* 761, 794; *see also* Hui Wang, et al. (2011). To reallocate or not: Reconsidering the dilemma in China's agricultural land tenure policy, *28 Land Use Pol'y* 805.

1.1.3 Structure of Chinese Local Government and Rural-Urban Land Conversion

In 1982, the Standing Committee of the NPC passed the Regulations on the Requisition of Land by the State for Construction ("RRLSC"). Article Two of the Regulations said that:

> When the state conducts economic, cultural and national defense construction and social public affairs, it should requisition collective-owned land according to this regulation. All direct or covert buying or renting of land from rural people's communes and production brigades by any unit shall be forbidden. Rural people's communes and production brigades shall not participate in the business operations of any enterprise or institution by contributing land as shares.

It was clear from the RRLSC that all land use must be consistent with the State's economic plan. Rural land was supposed to be used for agriculture and the livelihood of farmers, and it could only be used for "construction" if it was approved under the economic plan. State requisition is the only legal way of converting collectively owned land, which could only be used for agricultural and related uses, to state-owned land, which could be used for various construction projects.

Which level of the government represented the state in these types of conversions? According to Article Seven of the RRLSC, the city and county-level governments were responsible for selecting sites and requisitioning land for specific projects. Land requisition was subject to the approval of the provincial or central government, and decisions were made according to the size of the land requisitioned. City and county-level governments were able to approve requisition of land of no more than three *mu* of arable or garden land, ten *mu* of forestry or grassroots land, and twenty *mu* of other kinds of land. Although often subject to the approval of upper level governments, city and county-level governments were the actual managers of the state ownership of land.

Why were county and city governments responsible for land management? In contrast with the United States, China is a unitary state, meaning that all powers of local governments are delegated by the central government. Generally speaking, Chinese local governments are divided into four levels: province, city, county, and township, as shown in Figure 1.1.

Chinese provinces tend to be too large as an economic development unit and townships tend to be too small. Cities and counties, on the other hand, tend to be of an efficient scale for economic management.

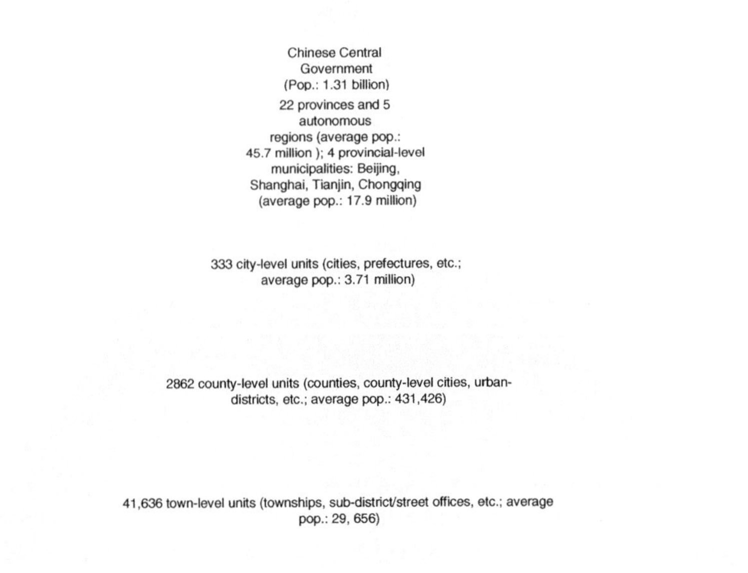

Figure 1.1 The structure of the Chinese government
Source: Xu Chenggang, *The Fundamental Institutions of China's Reform and Development*, Journal of Economic Literature 2011, 49:4, 1076–1151, 1084.

In China's economic reform process, cities and counties have become the administrative units that actually manage the economy.[9] Naturally, city/county governments are the real managers of land within their jurisdictions. In the United States, land use power is also within the hands of the city or county governments.

Taking a Chinese city/county as an example, the structure of land ownership is as shown in Figure 1.2.

However, the boundary between urban land and rural land is not static. City/county governments can change this boundary by requisitioning rural land and converting it to urban land. The two kinds of land ownership, state ownership of urban land and collective ownership of rural land, are not equal. The organizational hierarchy of the Chinese

[9] 张五常："中国的经济制度"，中信出版社2009年版[Steven N.S. Cheung, *The Economic System of China*, CITIC Press Group (2009)] (concerning inter-county competition in China).

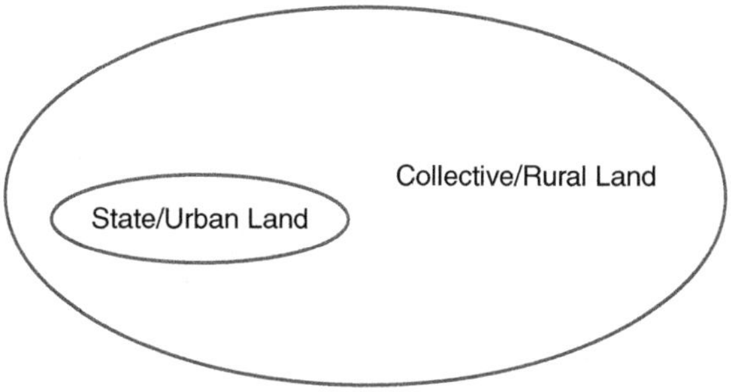

Figure 1.2 Dual land ownership in China

government and the county and city governments' legal power to requisition rural land for urban construction made it easy for city and county governments to encroach upon the collective ownership of rural land.

The former people's commune consisted of three echelons: the commune, the production brigade, and the production team.[10] The people's communes were under the direct control of county or city governments. The reforms initiated in 1978 by Deng Xiaoping dismantled the communes and granted individual households the right to use the land. Generally, the township (*xiang/zhen*) replaced the commune, the village (*cun*) replaced the brigade, and the villagers' group (*cunmin xiaozu*) replaced the production team, as shown in Figure 1.3.[11] However, the political structure of local government did not change fundamentally. Townships were still under the direct control of the city/county governments. Village-level self-governance organization, under the leadership of the party branch, also remains a puppet of the local government.[12]

Moreover, at the policy level, city and county governments represented the interests of all units and individuals under their jurisdictions in the national political arena, including the rural sector. Villagers do not have direct access to the political process of policy making. Even in exceptional situations where the villagers' leaders are selected to serve as members of the NPC, their voices and influence were subject to and inferior to that of city and county government leaders.

[10] *See* Ho, *supra* note 6, at 404–405. [11] *Id*, at 405.
[12] Shitong Qiao (2012). Governing the post-socialist transitional commons, 24 *Colo. J. Int'l Envtl. L. & Pol'y* 115, 146–148.

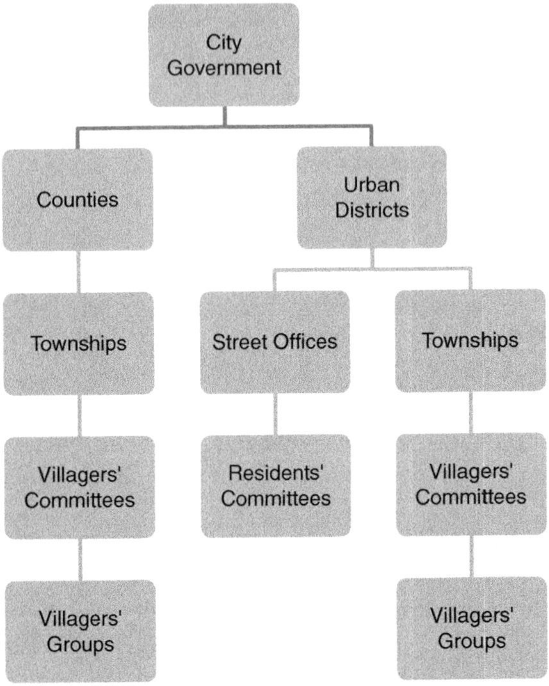

Figure 1.3 Chinese government structure under the city-level after 1978

Thus, politically speaking, Chinese farmers still do not have their own "autonomous organizations" that can represent their interests in national policy making. Their rights to use the land contracted to them are easily encroached upon by the city and county governments' power to requisition land. The relationship between owners of urban land and rural land is the key to understanding the land use reform discussed in the following parts.

1.2 Urban Land Use Reform

Urban land use reform was initiated and captured by Chinese city governments. An urban land use market provided Chinese city governments with the financial resources urgently needed for urban construction and public investment, and has been a main engine for urbanization and economic development in China. Chinese local governments' pursuit of financial interests forced the central government to concede most of the land revenue to them and has deeply shaped the Chinese land regime.

1.2.1 *The Creation of Land Use Rights: From Shenzhen Experiment to Constitutional Amendment*

Before 1979, land was controlled by the state and used by various government units for free in accordance with Marxist principles stating that the price mechanism was inapposite after abolishing private property. However, with the implementation of the reform and opening-up policies, state ownership of land must be given a richer understanding than under Marxist orthodoxy.

The cities at the frontier of reform and opening up blazed a trail of land use reform. On December 31, 1979, the Director of the Shenzhen City Construction Commission signed a contract with a Hong Kong investor, according to which the Shenzhen city government contributed land, the Hong Kong investor financed the land development and shared a fixed percentage of the profits.[13] On December 5, 1980, the Shenzhen City Construction Commission signed the first "land use fee" contract with a Hong Kong investor, which included the essential contents of today's standard contracts of assignment of state-owned land use rights between local governments and real estate developers, including the term (30 years in this contract) and price of the land use (HKD 5000 per square meter).[14]

Lawmaking and the practice of land use fees discussed above could be considered a prologue because of their limited scale, which ultimately served as the beginning of a norm cascade.[15] Shenzhen, the first special economic zone ("SEZ") of China, went a step further. In November 1981, the Shenzhen government extended the charging of land use fee from foreign investors to domestic investors.[16]

However, without a land market, the standard land use fee was arbitrarily fixed by law and was applied to all construction projects.[17] Users who valued the land most did not have an opportunity to reveal

[13] 冯杰："深圳土地管理二十年"，"深圳特区报"2006年6月22日[Jie Feng, Two Decades of Shenzhen Land Administration, *Shenzhen SEZ Daily*, June 22, 2006], www.szpl.gov.cn/xxgk/gzdt/zwdt/200908/t20090825_46190.html.

[14] *Id.*

[15] *See* Robert C. Ellickson (2001). The market for social norms, *3 Am. L. & Econ. Rev.* 1–49; Cass R. Sunstein (1996). Social norms and social roles, *96 Colum. L. Rev.* 903, 903–968.

[16] "深圳经济特区土地管理暂行规定"（广东省人大常委会，1981年12月24日）[Interim Regulations on Land Administration in Shenzhen Special Economic Zone, art. 19] (promulgated by The People's Cong. of Guangdong Province, December 24, 1981).

[17] Feng, supra note 13.

their willingness to pay higher prices. Shenzhen, as the first city to charge land use fees, first felt the constraints of the land use fee. After studying crown land sales in Hong Kong[18] carefully, the Shenzhen government sensed the money-generating power of a land market. It wanted to sell land, and it created a slogan in response to the CCP's call to build a "commercial economy with planning." The slogan was: "No land market, no complete commercial economy." This reform faced an ideological challenge from Marxism: Should a socialist country that abolished private property sell land? In response to this challenge, reformers separated land use rights from land ownership. A local reformer checked the classics by Marx and Engels page by page and cited words from Engels as support. Engels wrote that, "[A]bolishing private ownership of land does not require abolishing land rents; rather it requires submitting land rents to the society."[19] Thus selling land use rights would not challenge state land ownership in China and would allow the state to utilize land rents.

Shenzhen eventually held the first public auction of transferrable land use rights in the history of the PRC on December 1, 1987, in direct conflict with the then effective Land Administration Law ("LAL") and Constitutional Law.[20] The public defiance led to the legal authorization of transfer of land use rights by the People's Congress of Guangdong Province (the province where Shenzhen was located) on January 3, 1988, and more importantly, the Chinese Constitutional Amendment that allows the transfer of land use rights on April 12, 1988,[21] and a similar amendment to the LAL on December 29, 1988.[22]

The 1988 amendments of the Constitution and LAL removed the legal barrier against selling land use rights for local governments. On May 19, 1990, the State Council promulgated detailed rules governing the sales of land use rights from the government and the transfer among land users, i.e., the Interim Regulations of the People's Republic of China

[18] *See* Roger Nissim, *Land Administration and Practice in Hong Kong* (2008).

[19] Feng, *supra* note 13. [20] *Id. See also* Chapter 3, Section 3.1.2 for more details.

[21] "中华人民共和国宪法修正案"（1988年4月12日第七届全国人民代表大会第一次会议通过，1988年4月12日第七届全国人民代表大会第一次会议主席团公告第八号公布施行）[*See* Article Two of the 1988 Constitutional Amendment].

[22] "全国人民代表大会常务委员会关于修改<中华人民共和国土地管理法>的决定"（1988年12月29日第七届全国人民代表大会常务委员会第五次会议通过 ，1988年12月29日中华人民共和国主席令第十二号公布 自公布之日起施行）[1988 LAL Revision] (promulgated by Nat'l People's Cong., December 29, 1988).

Concerning the Assignment and Transfer of the Right to the Use of the State-owned Land in the Urban Areas, which is still in effect today.[23] It confirms that the transfer of land use rights is the responsibility of city and county governments.

1.2.2 The Central-Local Distribution of Land Sales Revenue

The 1988 amendments were silent as to the distribution of land sales revenue. However, as land use reform was implemented by city governments, they initially controlled land sales revenue and could use them for their own purposes. This situation soon changed when the central government, as the ultimate owner of state land, promulgated a notice on May 12, 1989, providing that 40 percent of land sales revenue should be submitted to the central government.[24]

Local governments, who not only tried to hide their land sales revenue from the central government but also threatened to stop land use reform if they gained little from it, resisted this promulgation. Due to the large number of cities engaging in land use reform, the central government had no way of knowing how much land sales revenue each city had collected. As a result, one year later on September 26, 1990, the Chinese Ministry of Finance promulgated another notice that stipulated that the central government would return its share of land sales revenue to local governments for urban construction.[25] The reasons for the central government's concession were clear: "to promote the transfer of state-owned land use rights and to consider the practical situation of local governments."[26] A more fundamental change came on December 15, 1993, when the State Council promulgated a decision that redivided the tax power of the central government and local governments in an effort to

[23] 中华人民共和国城镇国有土地使用权出让和转让暂行条例（中华人民共和国国务院令第55号，1990年5月19日）[the Interim Regulations of the People's Republic of China Concerning the Assignment and Transfer of the Right to the Use of the State-owned Land in the Urban Areas].

[24] 国务院关于加强国有土地使用权有偿出让收入管理的通知（国发[1989]38号，1989年5月12日）[Notice on Strengthening Management of Revenue from Transfer of State-Owned Land Use Rights] (promulgated by the State Council, May 12, 1989).

[25] "关于国有土地使用权有偿出让收入上缴中央部分有关问题的通知"（（90）财综字第111号，1990年9月26日）[Ministry of Finance Notice on the Revenue of Transfer of State-Owned Land Use Rights Submitted to the Central Government] (promulgated by the Ministry of Finance, September 26, 1990).

[26] *Id.*

benefit the central government's finances.[27] Taxes since then have been divided into state taxes and local taxes. The central government established its own tax collection agencies all over the country. Land sales revenue, which had proved hard to collect without the assistance of local governments, was completely conceded to local governments.[28]

This was not the end of bargaining over the distribution of land sales revenue between the central and local governments.[29] On April 15, 1997, in a notice jointly issued by the Central Committee of the CCP (CCCCP) and the State Council on the preservation of agricultural land, the central government decided that *all* revenue from the increased construction land (i.e., urban construction land converted from rural land) should be submitted to the central government and used in the development of land for agricultural use.[30] It hoped that by decreasing the incentive for local governments to requisition agricultural land, it could achieve its goal of agricultural land preservation.[31] This move by the central government led to another round of bargaining between central and local governments in the 1998 LAL revision.

The 1998 LAL revision was the direct product of the above notice. However, in the first draft of the LAL revision (*songshen gao*), which was submitted by the SBLA (State Bureau of Land Administration) to the Bureau of Legal Affairs of the State Council ("BLA") on August 18, 1997, the proposal was changed so that *40 percent* of the revenue from rural-urban land conversion should be submitted to the central government. The reason was that, after the SBLA submitted the first draft to the BLA, the latter solicited comments from local governments, other departments of the central government, legal experts, and other groups. Under the prevalent opposition of local governments, the BLA made the above

27 "国务院关于实行分税制财政管理体制的决定"（1993年12月15日）[Decision on Implementing Tax Division in Finance Administration] (promulgated by the State Council, December 15, 1993).

28 *Id.*

29 Throughout this research, "local government" is used as distinct from "central government," and can refer to any level of the provincial, city, county, or township government. The most relevant local governments in this research are the city- and county-level governments. I use "local government" in a general way when there is no need to specify or the behaviors of the city/county governments cannot be distinguished from those of the lower levels of the government; otherwise I specify the particular level of the government according to the specific situations.

30 "中共中央、国务院关于进一步加强土地管理切实保护耕地的通知"（1997年4月15日）[Notice on Strengthening Land Administration and Preserving Agricultural Land] (promulgated by the State Council and the Central Comm. of the CCP, April 15, 1997).

31 *Id.*

change.[32] The BLA then submitted the revised draft to the National People's Congress, which publicized the draft for public comments. Again, according to the official interpretation of the 1998 LAL, edited by Bian Yaowu, the then deputy director of the Committee of Legal Affairs of the Standing Committee of the National People's Congress (NPC) "The ratio of the central-local distribution of the revenue from increased construction land was quite controversial in the discussions."[33] Local governments suggested that the ration submitted to the central government should be lowered for various reasons. Nevertheless, in the third meeting of the Standing Committee of the Ninth National People's Congress on June 24, 1998, the Committee of Legal Affairs suggested keeping the ratio at 40 percent for the purposes of more efficient use of urban land and the preservation of agricultural land.[34] However, in the fourth meeting two months later, this ratio was finally lowered to 30 percent as a result of suggestions from some local governments and members of the Standing Committee of the NPC.[35] The 1998 LAL revision proved that local governments had substantial control and bargaining power over the distribution of land revenue. This is because the central government is forced to rely on local governments, mainly city and county governments, to manage state-owned land, which gives local governments great leverage in formulating national land laws and policies. With regard to daily land administration, the central government also faces frequent challenges from local governments.

1.2.3 Regulating Local Governments' Land Use Power

Even before the 1988 constitutional amendment that allowed the transfer of land use rights, illegal land use by local governments was a problem. Local governments always had incentives to requisition more land than they needed because land could be requisitioned at relatively low prices. This problem became more significant after the legal authorization of a land use market in 1988 that provided local governments more incentives to requisition land due to the profits from land sales.

[32] 张清勇："纵向财政竞争、讨价还价与中央-地方的土地收入分成——对我国20世纪80年代以来土地收入的考察" Zhang Qingyong, *Vertical Fiscal Competition, Bargaining, and the Land Revenue Sharing Relationship between Central and Local Governments in China*, www.unirule.org.cn/xiazai/200711/69.pdf.

[33] 卞耀武主编："中华人民共和国土地管理法释义"，法律出版社1998年版[Bian Yaowu, Interpretation of PRC Land Administration Law, *Legal Press* (1998)].

[34] Zhang, *supra* note 32. [35] *Id.*

The central government's control over land use was confronted with two serious challenges. First, though China allowed the transfer of state-owned land use rights, it did not abolish the land assignment system, in which different kinds of government agencies and institutes, including state-owned enterprises, could obtain land for free. Once there was a market for land use rights, all these players could profit by transferring their rights to use state-owned land. They continued to apply for state-owned land under the guise of their own uses, but such application was actually for future profit-making transfers. Second, as collective-owned land could be requisitioned and converted to state-owned land, various government agencies requisitioned rural land without clear authorization. City and county governments did not bother to seek approval from upper level governments in many situations.

When the value of land use rights was recognized and there was no clear definition and enforcement of state land ownership, a rush to grab and develop state-owned land occurred. State-owned land includes land that was originally collectively owned by farmers and then requisitioned by the government. This resulted in a rapid decrease in the amount of agricultural land.

In numerous notices and regulations, the SBLA emphasized that it must "strengthen the high monopoly of transfer of land use rights," ("*jia qiang dui tu di chu rang de gao du long duan*") and "approval of land requisition with only one pen" ("*yi zhi bi shen pi*").[36] The SBLA devoted many resources to building a system that centralized the control of the use of state-owned land within the government system and did not tolerate land use outside of the system it was endeavoring to build. This has greatly impacted the rural land use reform discussed here.

1.3 Rural Land Use Reform

Chinese farmers' spontaneous transfer of rural land has occurred at the early stage of China's market transition, but a rural land use market

[36] "国家土地管理局关于进一步加快土地使用制度改革的通知"（1992年6月25日）[Notice on Further Promoting Land Use Reform] (promulgated by State Bureau of Land Administration, June 25, 1992); "国家土地管理局关于严格依法审批土地的紧急通知"（1992年7月31日）[Emergent Notice on Strictly Approving Land Use] (promulgated by State Bureau of Land Administration, July 31, 1992); "国家土地管理局关于对房产开发公司建商品房出售行为的定性及法律适用问题的请示的答复"（1992年10月16日）[Reply on Legal Issues Regarding Commercial Real Estate Development] (promulgated by State Bureau of Land Administration, Oct. 16, 1992).

would jeopardize local governments' monopoly over land supply. Compared with local governments' strong bargaining power in the making of central government laws and policies, farmers could only be represented rather than represent their own interests, and were basically voiceless. As a result, spontaneous market transactions did not lead to legalization of rural land use transfer, but "the strictest land use control system in the world," emphasizing the government monopoly over rural-urban land conversion.

1.3.1 Rural Land Transfer Is Nothing New

The first decade of China's economic reform began with the establishment of the HRS, which liberated households from the people's communes and greatly increased agricultural productivity. The need for better housing came immediately after satisfying the need for food. In the early 1980s, farmers all over the country began to devote their savings to building houses. The saying was that "each family was in preparation; each village was under construction." (*jiajia beiliao, cuncun dongtu*).[37] In 1980, the total floor area built was 500 million square meters and in 1981 it was more than 600 million square meters.[38] Within only two years, Chinese farmers built one square meter for each person in China.

China had no specialized land administration agency before 1986. Building rural houses was outside of the state economic plan and, thus, it flew under the radar of local governments. Generally, local governments saw no need to regulate rural housing construction – as quoted in the second rural affairs conference of the central committee of the CCP, some local government leaders said "farmers used their own money to build houses, so what would be wrong with that?"[39] Local government officials also joined this trend and became a main force in rural housing development. Under the central housing planning system, even a city mayor could not afford a spacious apartment.[40] It would take several

[37] "国务院批转第二次全国农村房屋建设工作会议纪要的通知"（1982年1月7日）[Summary of Minutes of the Second Rural Affairs Conference] (promulgated by State Council and Central Comm. of CCP 1982).

[38] *Id.* [39] *Id.*

[40] "国务院办公厅转发城乡建设环境保护部关于福建省晋江地区狠刹乱占耕地建房风的简报的通知"（1982年9月17日）[Forwarded Notice of the Ministry of Urban and Rural Construction and Environmental Protection on the Rural Housing Fever in Jinjiang of Fujian Province] (promulgated by the Office of the State Council, September 17, 1982).]

years to reform the urban housing sector and provide enough apartments for employees of the government and other state sectors. This unmet demand for housing could only be remedied by rural housing development. The central government publicly acknowledged that the leading role of local government officials was one main reason for this "rural housing fever" (*nongcun jianfang re*).[41] On February 18, 1982, the Office of State Council (OSC) circulated an investigation report among departments of the State Council. According to this report, six central government agencies rented 310 rooms from rural hotels, 16 agencies bought or rented about 60,000 square meters of other rural housing. These houses had been used for offices, training space, dormitories, and many other uses.[42] Such transactions, although prohibited, constituted a real estate market.[43]

This market was not a result of intentional reform. The 1982 RRLSC stipulated that rural land *must be requisitioned* to be used in urban construction and prohibited any form of buying or renting rural land.[44] On March 21, 1986, the State Council promulgated a notice, creating the SBLA, whose main purpose was to regulate land use and prevent the waste of agricultural land.[45] In the same year, the NPC passed the first comprehensive LAL in China, which took effect in 1987. The 1987 LAL, on one hand, restated the prohibition on the alienation of land. On the other hand, it permitted rural collective organizations to use rural land to cooperate with urban enterprises.[46] This measure seemed to imitate urban land use reform, which began by allowing state-owned land as a form of investment in Sino-foreign joint enterprises.[47] The 1987 LAL also permitted urban residents to build houses in rural area, subject to the

[41] "国务院批转第二次全国农村房屋建设工作会议纪要的通知"（1982年1月7日）[Summary of Minutes of the Second Rural Affairs Conference (1982)] (promulgated by the State Council, January 7, 1982).

[42] "国务院办公厅转发国务院机关事务管理局<关于一些国家机关、事企业单位租用招待所和购租社队房地产问题的调查报告通知>"（1982年2月18日国办发[1982]15号）[Forwarded Notice of the Bureau of Agencies on Renting and Buying of Rural Real Estate by Some Central Government Agencies] (promulgated by Off. of the State Council, February 18, 1982).

[43] *Id.* [44] RRHCA, art. 2.

[45] "中共中央、国务院关于加强土地管理、制止乱占耕地的通知"（1986年3月21日）[CCP Central Comm. and State Council Notice on Strengthening Land Administration and Stopping Developing Arable Land (March 21, 1986).]

[46] Land Administration Law, art. 36 (passed on June 25, 1986, effective January 1, 1987).

[47] *See* Section 1.2.1

approval of the county government and the payment of fees according to the standards of governmental land requisition.[48]

In the initial period of China's economic reform, Chinese farmers and their collectives developed and transferred rural land to realize its potential use and commercial value, which was not much different from Chinese city governments' experiments with the commodification of urban land. Land commodification in both urban and rural areas challenged the old legal and ideological systems, but there was reason to believe that China would achieve land commodification, both in the urban and rural areas. Both the central government (as revealed in the exceptions made in the 1987 LAL) and the local governments (as revealed through their involvement with rural land development and transfer) showed willingness to tolerate farmers' development and transfer of rural land, particularly when this was done to address legitimate social and economic needs.

1.3.2 Rural Land Transfer Is Not Legalized

In 1988, the NPC passed amendments to the Constitution and the LAL. Both laws removed the prohibition on land rents and added a clause permitting the transfer of land use rights, essentially a form of land renting. The amendment to the 1988 Constitution said land use rights could be transferred according to law. The 1988 amendment to the LAL stated it more clearly – rights to use both state land and *collective* land could be transferred according to law and the State Council would make specific regulations on the transfer of land use rights. However, the added Section V, Article II of the LAL said only that the state implemented "*compensated* use of state-owned land" (*guoyou tudi youchang shiyong*) and did not mention the "*compensated* use of collective-owned land." (*jiti tudi youchang shiyong*). In the report to the Standing Committee of NPC, the Deputy Commissioner of the CLANPC Lin Jianqing, revealed the reason:

> Regarding the use of collective land with compensation, some central government departments and local governments raised that the main task of deepening rural reform was perfecting the household responsibility system (HRS); implementing use of collective land with compensation might alter the HRS and also raises all kinds of concrete questions;

[48] 1987 LAL, art. 41.

> different regions are at different levels of development and have different land management systems, which makes it hard to settle down the details of use of collective land with compensation. We could firstly experiment with collective land use reform in some places and leave the laws untouched. In this way, we can further explore and accumulate experiences to deepen rural reform.[49]

This reasoning against rural land use reform is understandable. HRS was the focus of rural reform, and perhaps overall economic reform, through the 1980s. It is widely believed that China's economic reform began with villagers' experimentation with the HRS in Xiaogang, Anhui, in 1978.[50] It was first incorporated into the first No. 1 Document (*yi hao wen jian*) of the CCCCP in 1982.[51] The HRS gives individual rural households relatively secure rights to farm the land they contracted from the rural collectives, and this practice has rid China, a country that experienced 30 million deaths in the famine of the Great Leap Forward, of the threat of hunger.[52] The great increase of agricultural productivity also boosted the rise of township-village enterprises and built the foundation of reform in the urban area. Using the words of the CCP – "First to eat; second to construct" (*yi yao chi fan, er yao jian she*). Therefore, the Chinese government placed a very high priority on the security of the HRS. Even in the late 1990s, the central government promulgated several regulations to protect the security of the HRS.[53] Going back to 1988, during which time the HRS had only been formally recognized for less

[49] 林涧青："全国人大法律委员会对<中华人民共和国土地管理法修正案（草案）>审议结果的报告"（1988年12月23日在第七届全国人民代表大会常务委员会第五次会议上）[Lin Jianqing, The Committee of Legal Affairs of the NPC Review Report of the Draft of the Land Administration Law, promulgated at the The Fifth Meeting of the Standing Comm. of the Seventh NPC, December 23, 1988).]

[50] Qu Futian, Nico Heerink, and Wanmao Wang (1995). Land administration reform in China: Its impact on land allocation and economic development, *12 Land Use Pol'y* 193–203.

[51] "1982年1号文件：全国农村工作会议纪要"（1982年1月1日）[No. 1 Document of 1982: Summary of the National Annual Conference of Rural Affairs (January 1, 1982)].

[52] Kung, James Kai-sing, and Justin Yifu Li (2003). The Causes of China's Great Leap Famine, 1959–1961, *52 Econ. Dev. Cult. Change* 51–73.

[53] "国务院批转农业部关于稳定和完善土地承包关系意见的通知"(1995年3月28日) [Notice of the Ministry of Agriculture on Maintaining and Improving Land Contracting Relationships] (promulgated by the State Council, March 28, 1995); "中共中央办公厅、国务院办公厅关于进一步稳定和完善农村土地承包关系的通知"（1997年8月27日）[Notice on Further Maintaining and Improving Rural Land Contracting Relationships] (promulgated by the Off. of the Central Comm. of the CCP and Off. of the State Council, August 27, 1997).

than six years, villagers' rights to the contracted land were still often violated by village collectives despite the central government's strict prohibition against such a breach. Villagers were further concerned about the credibility of the central government's commitment to protecting their rights. To the Chinese government, land use reform meant land rentals by the owner. In the urban areas, the owner was the state and in the rural areas, the owner was the village collective. Implementing land use reform in rural areas would mean granting village collectives the right to transfer use rights for the rural land, most of which had been granted to individual households through the HRS. Thus rural land use reform would necessarily cause a rearrangement of rural land rights in the direction of strengthening the control of the village collectives, which would jeopardize the security of the villagers' rights to farm the contracted land. This was a risk the central government would not take.

1.3.3 The Incompatibility of Rural Land Use Reform with Urban Land Use Reform

Although the 1988 amendments of the constitution and the LAL legalized the transfer of urban land use rights, the Chinese government still needed to build a functioning land administration system. When the old system of land use in the planned economy collapsed without a clear definition of property rights or a delineation of land administration power, rural land became a limited-access commons for interested parties to grab.[54] The chaos impacting the whole land use system was demonstrated during the 1992–1993 real estate bubble.[55] Different types of public agencies and institutions were rushing into the real estate business. The main source of the land was rural land. Any public agency or institution could fake a need for construction, which would serve as the basis to requisition rural land, and then devote the acquired land to the real estate sector. Of course, farmers and their collectives did not hesitate to develop their land when there were profit-making opportunities.

Against this background, the SBLA and local governments tried to centralize the land administration power within their hands and eliminate any

[54] *See* Carol M. Rose (1998). The several futures of property: Of cyberspace and folk tales, emission trades and ecosystems, *83 Minn. L. Rev.* 129, 155 (A limited access commons is common on the inside, but private on the outside).

[55] *See* e.g., Zarathustra W., China: The Forgotten Real Estate Bubble Of The 1990s, http://www.businessinsider.com/china-the-forgotten-real-estate-bubble-in-1990s-2011-3.

use of land outside of their control. This effort was due to both their desire to have a functioning land administration system and their financial incentives.

Local governments acutely sensed the need to monopolize land use supply. For example, early in 1989, the Fujian provincial government emphasized in a notice that city and county governments must monopolize the primary market of land use rights. In other words, rural collective-owned land must be requisitioned and converted to state-owned land in order to be transferred.[56] In 1992, the Jilin Provincial government emphasized that the land administrative agency was representative of state land ownership for the same-level government and was in charge of the requisition and transfer of rural land. All other agencies and institutions, including rural collective economic organizations, should not transfer land use rights directly.[57]

To cool the 1992–1993 real estate bubble, the SBLA promulgated an emergency notice on July 31, 1992, emphasizing that the transfer of land use rights must be highly monopolized. On November 4, 1992, the State Council promulgated a notice, providing that collectively owned land must be officially converted to state-owned before being transferred.[58] This stipulation attempted to close the door that the 1988 constitutional amendment had opened for the transfer of use rights of collectively owned rural land.[59] From this notice, we can see that there is a direct link between rural and urban land use reforms. The choice was whether to allow farmers to sell rural land use rights, or to require rural land to be requisitioned before being transferred. There was no middle ground or time for delay, as once the transfer of urban land use rights created a market of land use rights, buyers would be interested in both urban and rural land. The more the urban land market grew, the more demand and speculation there would be for rural land transfer. As a result, in 1992, the State Council was forced to clarify that collectively owned rural land

56 "福建省人民政府关于出让和转让国有土地使用权试点工作的通知"（1989年9月5日福建省人民政府文件闽政[1989]37号发布）[Notice on Experiments on the Assignment and Transfer of State-Owned Land Use Rights], (promulgated by Fujian Province People's Gov., September 5, 1989).

57 "吉林省人民政府转发省土地管理局关于进一步加强划拨国有土地使用权管理报告的通知"（1992年5月3日吉政发[1992]15号）[Notice on Strengthening Management of Assigned State-Owned Land Use Rights], (promulgated by Jilin Province People's Gov., May 3, 1992).

58 "国务院关于发展房地产业若干问题的通知"（国发＜1992＞61号，1992年11月4日 (*State Council on the Development of Real Estate Industry*, promulgate by the State Council, Guofa No. 61 (1992), November 4, 1992.)

59 *Id.*

must be requisitioned before being transferred. Clearly, the State Council was not ready to allow the transfer of rural land use rights.

On July 26, 1993, about one month after the burst of the real estate bubble,[60] the SBLA promulgated another notice emphasizing the *monopoly* of land sales. According to the SBLA, without the strong monopoly on land sales by the government, the use of land for construction would greatly exceed the planned quota.[61] The 1993 notice clarified that the government must requisition rural land before it could be transferred.[62] It also emphasized that the development of agricultural land must be strictly controlled.[63] In 1994, the State Council promulgated the Regulation on Protection of Basic Agricultural Land, which required local governments to mark some land as basic agricultural land and made stricter approval procedure for developing this kind of land.[64]

The efforts to protect agricultural land,[65] to build a uniform land administration system, and to monopolize land supply led to the comprehensive revision of the LAL in 1998.

1.3.4 1998 LAL Revision: "The Strictest Land Use Control System in the World"

In 1997, the CCCCP and the State Council decided to freeze nonagricultural uses of agricultural land for one year to finish the revision of

[60] China Property Net, *supra* note 69.

[61] 国家土地管理局关于加强宏观调控管好地产市场的通知（[1993]国土[办]字第120号1993年7月26日）[SBLA Notice on Strengthening Macro Regulation of Real Estate Market] (promulgated by the State Bureau of Land Admin., Off. of the SBLA, No. 120 (July 26, 1993).

[62] *Id.* [63] *Id.*

[64] *See* 基本农田保护条例(1994年8月18日)[Regulation on Protection of Basic Agricultural Land], (promulgated by the State Council, August 18, 1994, effective October 1, 1994).

[65] Central government leaders and policy-makers were genuinely concerned about preservation of agricultural land, which is based on the consideration that food self-sufficiency is a national security strategy that must be followed. Lester Brown's book, "Who Will Feed China? Wake-Up Call for a Small Planet," caught widespread attention and discussion in China after its publication in 1995. *See* 蒋亚平、张亚莉："土地管理三大制度改革回顾及期待——访原国家土地管理局第一任局长王先进"，"中国国土资源报"2008年12月5日[Jiang Yaping & Zhang Yali, Review of Three Major Reforms of Land Administration: Interview with the First Director of the former State Land Administration Bureau, *China Land & Res. Daily*, Dec. 5, 2008.]; 杨慧萍："变化中国：田凤山后的土地'变法"，"今日东方"2003年12月1日[Yang Huiping, Changing China: Land Law Reform after Tian Fengshan, *Today's East*, December 1, 2003 (an interview with Professor Yan Jinmin who participated in the 1998 amendment of the LAL.).] *See also* Gan, *infra* note 124.

the LAL.[66] According to the deputy director of the revision team, the purpose was to build "the strictest land use control system in the world" to preserve agricultural land.[67] Under the supreme goal of preserving agricultural land, the 1998 revision left little room for the transfer of rural land use rights. It revised Article II of LAL from initially reading, "[U]se rights to the state-owned land and collective-owned land can be transferred according to law" to reading, "[L]and use rights can be transferred according to law." The intentional deletion of "collective-owned land" signaled a change of tone. The pre-revised Article II was pro-transfer of rural land use rights, subject to further legal reform, while the revised version removed that option. Furthermore, Article 43 of the 1998 LAL states:

> [A]ny unit or individual that needs to use land for construction must apply for the use of state-owned land in accordance with law; however, use of collectively owned rural land for township and village enterprises, construction of village residences, or public facilities is allowed subject to approval according to law.

This article makes the *transfer* of rural land use rights for nonrural uses impossible according to law, despite the still effective 1988 constitutional amendment on land use rights. Under this article, there are only three situations in which collectively owned land can be used for construction: township and village enterprises, construction of village residences, and public facilities.

Article 63 of the 1998 LAL was even clearer, stating that, "The right to use land collectively owned by farmers shall not be assigned, transferred or rented out for non-agricultural construction."

The official interpretation of this article clearly states the purposes of the prohibition on rural land transfer:

> First, allowing collectively owned rural land into the market would influence state-owned land use reform. As a land market was just established in our country, the government's regulation of the market

66 "中共中央、国务院关于进一步加强土地管理切实保护耕地的通知（1997年4月15日中发[1997]11号）" [CCCCP and State Council on Strengthening Administration and Protection of Agricultural Land, promulgated by the Central Committee of the CCP and the State Council, *Zhongfa* No. 11 (1997), April 15, 1997].

67 甘藏春："重温<土地管理法>的全面修訂"，"中国法律发展评论" 2011年第6期 [Gan Cangchun (2011). The comprehensive revision of land administration law, 6 *China L. Dev. Commentary* 38] (Gan Cangchun led the 1998 revisions of the Land Administration Law).

> is yet well- functioning; the real estate fever and development zone fever in previous years have created much vacant unused land; allowing collectively owned land into the market would convert more of them into construction land, creating more vacant land, which would make state-owned land use reform difficult to proceed. Second, it is for the purpose of preserving agricultural land. Township and village cadres are very enthusiastic about real estate development; without strict control there would be tons of agricultural land converted into construction land, making our purpose of preserving agricultural land difficult to achieve.[68]

This interpretation clarifies why top-down rural land use reform did not lead to transferrable land use rights for farmers. The basic purposes of the land administration system, including preserving agricultural land and land supply monopoly, are in direct conflict with individual or decentralized property rights. The parties who would benefit from individual or decentralized property rights, such as villagers and their collectives, were the silent majority in the process of the top-down rural land use reform. In the making of national laws and policies, their opinions had little weight. During the 1998 LAL revision, the NPCSC solicited public comments on the revision draft for the first time since 1978, making it a precedent to "open-door" legislation in post-1978 China.[69] In the report to the Standing Committee, suggestions on the transfer of rural land use rights were divided into two main types:

> Some mass suggest that allowing the transfer of rural land use rights is consistent with what's happening in reality and the market demand. Some mass think that we should not allow the transfer of rural land use rights; otherwise a lot of agricultural land would be converted to construction land and farmers' interests would be grabbed by a few people. The Committee of Legal Affairs holds that allowing rural land into the market is a very complicated issue and needs serious research and suggests we maintain the current prohibition.[70]

68 Interpretation of Article 63 of the 1998 Land Administration Law; *see* Bian, *supra* note 61.

69 Gan, *supra* note 124; "全国人大常委会办公厅关于公布土地管理法（修订草案）征求意见的通知"（ 1998年4月29日）[Notice on Soliciting Public Opinions on the Draft of the Land Administration Law] (promulgated by the Off. of the Standing Comm. Nat'l People's Cong., April 29, 1998).

70 李伯勇："全国人大法律委员会关于<中华人民共和国土地管理法（修订草案）>初步审议情况的汇报"（1998年6月24日在第九届全国人民代表大会常务委员会第三次会议）[Li Boyong, *The Report of the Committee of Legal Affairs on the Review of the Draft of the Land Administration Law*, taken from the Third Meeting of the Standing Comm. of the Ninth NPC, June 24, 1998).

Overall, Chinese farmers' interests in the transfer of rural land use rights were not represented in the making of national laws and policies. They remain characterized as "the masses" (*qunzhong*) who are never allowed to take care of their own interests, but whose interests should be taken care of. Compared to the local governments' overwhelming influence in making national laws and policies (as seen during the bargaining over the distribution of land revenue between the central government and local governments), Chinese farmers' influence and voices were too weak to play a role.

In the market transition, partial reforms generated arbitrage opportunities arising from rent-seeking between the liberalized sectors of the economy and those still coordinated by nonmarket mechanisms.[71] Beneficiaries of partial reform often attempt to block specific advances in the reform process that threaten to eliminate the remaining market distortions upon which their special advantages are based. Instead of forming a constituency in support of advancing reforms, these short-term winners have often sought to stall the economy in a partial reform equilibrium that generates concentrated rents.[72]

In the case of Chinese land reform, Chinese local governments benefited from partial land use reform, i.e., a liberalized urban land market and an unreformed rural land regime. The overall purpose of land use reform was to have a unified liberalized land market, as indicated in the 1988 constitutional amendment and other official documents. Starting reform from the urban area made sense in the context of the historical background: Local governments needed money for urban construction and the focus of rural reform was the household responsibility system. It was important to convince the most powerful stakeholders of the land regime – local governments – to support the reform. However, the winners of this partial reform, local governments, sought to prolong the period of partial reform because taking land from the unreformed rural sector and selling it on the liberalized urban sector were too profitable to be given up easily.

The central government and the SBLA, in particular, were concerned about the preservation of agricultural land and a unified land administration system. Local governments successfully prolonged the period of partial reform by threatening the central government with the potential loss of agricultural land and the chaos of land administration that might

71 Hellman, J. (1998). Winners take all: The politics of partial reform in postcommunist transitions. World Politics, 50(2), 203–234, at 219.

72 *Id.* at 204.

be caused by a liberalized rural land market. These concerns, though not necessarily accurate, were well grounded and easily accepted by a central regulator. Millions of farmers did not have a say in the reform process and did not have a chance to address these concerns of the central regulator. They are disadvantaged in this partial reform, and their share of benefits is lower than in the case of complete reform. This situation begs the question: Is there a way for politically weak farmers to drive this reform forward against the opposition of local governments?

1.4 "Weapons of the Weak:"[73] Increasing Illegality and Institutional Adaptation

The 1998 LAL revision consolidated the government's monopoly on land, from which the government accumulated a huge amount of wealth. Since then, land finance (*tu di cai zheng*) became more and more important to the Chinese government.[74] Revenue from land sales became a major source of local government finance. From 2003 to 2012, the Chinese governments requisitioned 37,400 square kilometers of rural land at an average price of about 30,000 to 40,000 RMB per *mu*, which was calculated according to the agricultural value of the land. The total amount of revenue from selling this land on the urban market was 15.2 trillion RMB, which supported China's rapid urbanization over the past years.[75]

However, at the same time, land conflicts became the top reason behind large-scale mass incidents (*da gui mo qun ti shi jian*) in China, making headlines in both Chinese and international media. This pressed the Chinese central government to change its land regime. Most attention has been on the reform of the eminent domain regime, including specifying the definition of "public interest" for which rural land can be requisitioned and enhancing the compensation standard in rural land requisition. In 2010, the State Council promulgated the Regulations on

[73] *See* James Scott, *Weapons of the Weak: Everyday Forms of Peasant Resistance* (1985).

[74] 袁志刚：《土地财政的功与过》[Yuan Zhigang, *The Success and Failure of Land Finance*, Yuan Zhigang Caixin Blog, Apr. 12, 2010], http://yuanzhigang.blog.caixin.com/archives/3015.

[75] 郑振源：新型城镇化与中国土地制度改革，4月23日（周二）晚7-9点；地点：北京大学法学院凯原楼模拟法庭 [Zheng Zhenyuan, *New Urbanization and China's Land Reform*, taken from lecture minutes from Zheng Zhenyuan, April 23, 2013, 7:00 pm–9:00 pm, Moot Court Room of Peking Univ. L. School] (on file with the author). Zheng Zhenyuan is a former senior official of the State Bureau of Land Administration.

the Requisition of Real Estate on State-Owned Land, while a corresponding regulation on the requisition of rural real estate was said to be under discussion. The effect of such efforts is still subject to the test of time.

Mass protests, however, are only a rare form of resistance that Chinese farmers take to contest for their property rights. An arguably more significant everyday form of Chinese farmers' contestation for property rights – illegal rural land development and sales – has received scant attention. This section seeks to highlight the daily illegal property arrangements Chinese farmers developed to deal with the formal land administration system and to explain how this increasing illegality jeopardizes the normal functioning of the Chinese land administration system and causes policy adaptation at both the local and central levels. The following articulates two specific camouflages Chinese farmers have taken to develop and transfer rural land.

1.4.1 Township and Village Enterprises ("TVEs")

Township and village enterprises (*xiang zhen qi ye*) emerged from the market rather than from law. Originally, it was the township and village economic organizations that got involved in agriculture-related industries, such as the processing of agricultural produce. Later, their activities extended into other industry areas, such as family electronics, and beyond. Their organization and ownership structure has never been clearly defined. It used to be the township and village economic organizations that provided initial capital and equipment and organized production. Later, that control fell into the hands of individuals, mostly managers who were village cadres. TVEs were viewed as a form of socialist enterprise and were thus recognized and protected by law. Many Chinese entrepreneurs built their own enterprises under the auspices of TVEs.[76]

TVEs, due to their more flexible management structure, were more attuned to market demand and had a great advantage against the State-Owned Enterprises in the market for daily goods. TVEs were the main force of China's economic growth from the mid-1980s to 1990s. Even the 1998 LAL revision, which was intended to implement the strictest control of land use in the world, made land use by TVEs an exception to the prohibition on nonagricultural use of rural land. TVE land is not allowed

[76] *See, e.g.*, Wenhong Chen (2007). Does the colour of the cat matter? The red hat strategy in China's private enterprises, *3 Mgmt. & Org. Rev.* 55.

to transfer except in the cases of merging enterprises and bankruptcy. The central government made this legal exception to promote the development of TVEs, but it has become a main way for local practices to access rural land development and transfer.

Under the TVEs, a large amount of rural land has been developed and devoted to commercial and industrial uses, and even illegally transferred to users outside of villages, resulting in huge markets for rural land.[77] Through illegal transactions, villagers were able to break the government monopoly of the land market, and promote a bottom-up institutional change. For a few Chinese local governments which experimented with granting farmers the right to transfer rural land, the prevalence of illegal transactions was a common motivation for their adaptive changes.

1.4.2 Agricultural Construction

As Article 63 of the 1998 LAL states that rural land use rights shall not be assigned, transferred, or rented out for *non-agricultural* construction, many rural real estate businesses in China take the form of *agricultural* construction. One typical form of small-property construction is called Greenhouse-Farm Houses (in Chinese, "*da peng fang*," "GFH" hereinafter). In this type of project, part of the greenhouse farms are built for storage and housing for farm employees. It is possible to get this kind of project approved by the government as the Chinese government has promoted agricultural investment in recent years. In Beijing, the city government has publicized over a dozen small-property neighborhoods under the name of agricultural buildings, which are called GFH, Chicken Farm Dorm (*yangjichang zhuzhailou*), Berry Garden (*caomeiyuan*), Plantation Base (*zhongzhi jidi*), Fruit-Picking Orchard (*caizhai yuan*), and so on.[78]

Article 43 of the 1998 LAL provides that the construction of village residences is allowed as an exception. This became another way to

[77] 国土资源部土地利用司调研组："创新制度　规范流转：集体建设用地流转调研报告"，"国土资源通讯2002年第3期，第25页[Ministry of Land Resources Bureau of Land Use, Investigation Team of the MLR Bureau of Land Use, Innovate Institutions and Regulate Transfers: Investigation Report on Transfer of Rural Construction Land, State-Owned Land Letters, *State Land Res. Dispatch* NO. 3, at 25 (2002).]

[78] "北京公布108个"小产权房" 已拆25个"[Beijing Publicized 108 Small-Property Neighborhoods and Already Demolished 25, *People's Daily*, reprinted on Soho.com, December 5, 2013], http://roll.sohu.com/20131205/n391313180.shtml.

camouflage small property, called uniformly constructed buildings ("tong jian lou," TJL hereinafter). Recently, the MLR has called for farmers to live in uniformly constructed buildings, rather than individual residential houses, as a way to preserve farmland. It is also consistent with local governments' interests because they do not want to use their quota of construction land to build houses for farmers. Thus, village collectives often applied for construction projects under the name of TJL. But these projects provided more than enough apartments for their villagers to live in. A small portion of these units was allocated or sold at very low prices to local villagers and the rest of the units were sold to outsiders. TLJ has become one of the main forms of small property in Shenzhen.[79] In Beijing, reports have disclosed a similar form of small property, which is called resettlement housing ("*huiqian fang*").[80] In some government-approved projects, farmers whose land was requisitioned are authorized to build a building to be used as resettlement housing. Farmers often make use of such opportunities to expand their projects and sell apartments to make money.

1.4.3 *Policy Resistance and Adaptation*

This huge small-property market involves millions of farmers, middle-and-low income buyers, various kinds of real estate developers, and grassroots-level governments because small property has promoted economic development of particular districts where it is located and has contributed to business taxation[81] of the grassroots-level governments. For city and central governments, small-property houses also relieved them of the responsibility of providing public housing and public facilities in the peripheral area of cities, where most of the middle-and-low income population live. These combined interests make small property a serious challenge to the current land system in China.

The central government's initial response was to enforce the law. On May 6, 1999, the Office of the State Council promulgated a notice to

[79] *See* Chapter 2.

[80] 赵莹莹："小产权房变身"生态庄园" 以租代售继续钻营"，"北京晚报" 2012年9月10日 [Zhao Yingying, Small-Property Sales in the Camouflage of Ecological Gardens, *Beijing Evening Newspaper*, September 10, 2012], http://news.xinhuanet.com/house/2012-09/10/c_123696561.htm.

[81] Companies, convenience stores, and factories that use small-property houses as their official locations need to pay business taxes. Grassroots-level governments do not collect property tax from small-property owners.

provincial governments and central government agencies, pointing out that illegal transactions of collectively owned land had become a serious problem and many such transactions were conducted in the name of orchards and farms. This notice states very clearly that:

> Farmers' residential houses cannot be sold to urban citizens; nor to allow urban citizens to buy collectively owned land to build residential houses . . .
>
> Any units or individuals should not sign land use agreements with rural collective economic organizations privately. . .
>
> Agricultural and forestry projects should use land strictly according to the approved use; change to real estate development use is strictly prohibited; for legitimate needs of accompanying facilities, approval for construction land use must be obtained according to law.[82]

This notice also requires provincial governments to investigate illegal land transactions and halt approvals of orchards, farms, or tourism agricultural projects until finishing the investigation.

The responses to this notice were poor. In the following years, the central government emphasized the strict implementation and enforcement of land administration laws again and again in many notices. On December 30, 2007, the OSC promulgated a notice on the strict implementation of rural collective construction land laws and policies. It also used the term "small property" for the first time in central government notices, marking the first official recognition of the term coined by small-property market participants. It provides that "urban citizens should not buy rural residential land, farmers' residential houses, or 'small-property houses;' units and individuals should not rent or occupy land collectively owned by farmers for real estate development."[83] The No. 1 Document of the CCP Central Committee of 2008, promulgated on December 31, 2007, also referred to the term "small property house" and reiterated the same prohibition as the OSC had the previous day.[84] Since 1980, the CCCCP has devoted its first annual official documents to agricultural

82 "国务院办公厅关于加强土地转让管理严禁炒卖土地的通知"（国办发[1999]39号，1999年5月6日）[OSC on Strengthening Land Administration and Prohibition of Land Speculation, promulgated by the Off. of the State Council, Guoban Fa No. 39 (1999), May 6, 1999.]

83 *Id.*

84 "中共中央、国务院关于切实加强农业基础建设进一步促进农业发展农民增收的若干意见"（2007年12月31日□中发[2008]1号）[CCCCP and State Council Opinions on Strengthening Rural Infrastructure Construction and Promoting Agriculture

policy, called No. 1 Document, laying down the agenda and policies for a new year. The appearance of the term "small property" in such an important document was an indication and confirmation that it had become a national phenomenon that top policy makers could not ignore.

Meanwhile, policy reflection and change were under discussion. On January 16, 2003, the CCCCP required local governments to encourage TVEs to use land more efficiently through transfer of collectively owned construction land and other methods.[85] A similar stipulation appears in the State Council Decision on Deepening Reform and Strictly Administering Land, which was issued on October 21, 2004.[86] On April 4, 2005, the State Council promulgated the Opinions of the State Council on Deepening Reform of Economic Institutions, which calls for further exploration of the market entry of rural collective-owned land use rights.[87]

In early October 2008, at the Third Plenary Session of the 17th CCCPC, the rural land use reform passed a new milestone. For the first time in the history of land use reform in the PRC, 20 years after the 1988 amendments of the Constitution and the LAL, the Chinese central government proposed to "gradually unify the construction land use markets in urban areas and rural areas" and that "legally-acquired rural collectively-owned construction land has equal rights to state-owned land."[88] It also emphasized that rural land use rights must be transferred through a unified and *visible* market in a *public* way, a clear indication of the central government's concern with the *invisible* and *hidden* small-property market.[89]

Development, promulgated by the Central Comm. of the CCP and State Council, Zhongfa No. 1 (2008), December 31, 2007.]

85 "中共中央国务院关于做好农业和农村工作的意见"（2003年1月16日，中发[2003]3号）[CCCCP and State Council Opinions on Agricultural and Rural Affairs, promulgated by the Central Comm. of the CCP and State Council, Zhongfa No. 3 (2003), January 16, 2003.]

86 "国务院关于深化改革严格土地管理的决定"（国发[2004]28号，2004年10月21日）[State Council on Deepening Reform and Strictly Managing Land, promulgated by State Council, Guofa No. 28 (2004), October 21, 2004.]

87 "国务院关于2005年深化经济体制改革的意见"（2005年4月4日□国发[2005]9号）[State Council Opinions on Deepening Reform of Economic Institutions, promulgated by the State Council, Guofa No. 9 (2005), April 4, 2005.]

88 "中共中央关于推进农村改革发展若干重大问题的决定"（ 中发[2008]16号，2008年10月15日）[CCCCP Decision on Several Crucial Questions about Promoting Rural Reform, promulgated by the Central Comm. of the CCP, Zhongfa No. 16 (2008), October 15, 2008.]

89 *Id.*

This proposal was reiterated and reformulated as two points in the decision of the Third Plenary Session of the 18th CCCPC, promulgated on November 12, 2013: (1) establishing a unified construction land market, thus allowing rural collective construction land to be transferred in a similar manner as state-owned land; (2) granting more property rights to farmers by selecting several experimental sites and cautiously promoting the lien, mortgage, and transfer of farmers' property rights to their residential houses.[90]

Through the review of the policy change, we can see that the small-property market has caused formal institutional change by demonstrating the great interests embedded in a market of rural land use rights. Transferrable rural land use rights not only serve Chinese farmers' interests but they also serve the interests of central and local governments and of society overall. It is not to say that central and local governments' endowed interests in the existing land system, including preservation of agricultural land and local government finance, do not matter anymore. The lack of voice and political power of Chinese farmers and their collectives was the main reason that land use reform in China has remained partial and has only benefited the winners of this reform, mainly local and central governments. This section suggests that *farmers and their collectives challenge this formal system through their everyday resistance (i.e., illegal development and transfer of rural land), sometimes under the camouflage of legal projects, and have influenced the policy agenda of land use reform. Small property is the weapon of the Chinese farmers. They are powerful because they greatly increased the costs of the whole land administration system, and they eventually proved the legal prohibition on rural land development and transfer costly to implement.* The central government had no other choice but to reform the current system.

90 "中共中央关于全面深化改革若干重大问题的决定"（2013年11月12日中国共产党第十八届中央委员会第三次全体会议通过）[Decision of the CCCCP on Several Crucial Questions about Comprehensively Deepening Reform, promulgated by the Central Comm. of the CCP, passed during the Third Plenary Session of the Eighteenth CCCCP, November 12, 2013.]

2

Planting Houses in Shenzhen

Based on my fieldwork in Shenzhen, this chapter presents the factual situation and mechanisms of the small-property market. The main participants in the market are legitimate and include village co-ops, real estate brokers, lawyers, a local bank, and even local government branches and agencies, which from time to time chose to acquiesce to the development of the small-property market. Although they are legitimate actors, they are not constrained by legal boundaries. They have developed a network to support the operation of the small-property market. The formal property law has been ambiguous and subject to change and inconsistent enforcement, and thus has had limited prohibitive force.

This chapter proceeds as follows: Section 2.1 introduces the historical background of the small-property market and discusses rural land development amidst the legal ambiguity of China's market transition. Section 2.2 discusses the number of small-property constructions and the scale of small-property transactions, which are mostly impersonal exchanges; explores the network of institutional innovators that supports this market, including village co-ops, real estate brokers, a local bank, and lawyers, all of which are legitimate organizations or professionals; and examines how this network reduces the contract risks of small-property transactions. Section 2.3 investigates the confrontation between the small-property market and the government and explores why the legal enforcement campaigns of the Shenzhen government have not eliminated the small-property market. This part also expands the network of institutional innovators by incorporating the different levels and agencies of local government. Section 2.4 concludes the discussion.

2.1 Development amid Legal Ambiguity

Shenzhen is located in southern China's Guangdong province, on the northern border of Hong Kong. It was the first Special Economic Zone to experiment with a market economy in China after 1978, and it has grown from an agricultural county of about 300,000 people in 1979 to the fourth biggest city in China. From 1979 to 2010, the annual growth rate of its gross domestic product (GDP) was 25.3 percent.[1]

Originally, it consisted of hundreds of villages and an urbanized town of about three square kilometers. In a rapid urbanization process, many villages disappeared or lost much of their land due to land requisition by the local government; the remaining 320 villages are now surrounded by the urbanized areas of the city and, thus, are called intracity villages (*chengzhongcun* in Chinese). Most of the illegal buildings are located within the intracity villages.

The need for economic development in Shenzhen did not wait for definitive legal authorization from the Chinese central government for rural land development and transactions. In the 1980s, attracting foreign investment was the Shenzhen government's top priority, and it encouraged every unit under its jurisdiction, including villages, to seek foreign investment. Each village in Shenzhen had one or more so-called industrial zones, in which they built factories and received investments from Hong Kong and other parts of China. Most were called joint ventures, meaning that villagers built factories for investors, who brought equipment, money, and technology. Notwithstanding the then effective constitutional prohibition on alienation of land, the Shenzhen government encouraged investment in villages and made rules regarding the capitalization of rural land, including guidelines on land leasing rates.[2]

Once investment flooded in, factories were built and villages became commercial centers. Millions of migrant workers were drawn to the area to work in the factories. In the 1980s, the local government was in charge of supplying housing, but it was unable to build enough houses to keep up with the demand of even its own employees. Until the mid-1980s, many government agencies were located in iron-sheet houses, i.e., movable and temporary buildings made of iron sheets.[3] Migrant workers, the main force behind Shenzhen's economic development, were wholly excluded from the Shenzhen government's housing supply, because they

[1] 深圳市统计局、国家统计局深圳调查队："深圳统计年鉴（2011）"，中国统计出版社[STATISTICS BUREAU OF SHENZHEN CITY & SHENZHEN SURVEY OFF. OF THE STATE STATISTICS BUREAU, 2011 SHENZHEN STATISTICAL Y.B. 4 (2011)].

[2] 李丁财：""三来一补"在宝安农村的实践"，海天出版社1999年版[DINGCAI LI, THE PRACTICES OF SANLAI YIBU, IN BAO'AN, SHENZHEN (1999)].

[3] 张仲林：《特区早期的生活》，《深圳文史》2009年第11期[Zhang Zhonglin (2009). *Life in the Early Period of the SEZ, 11 Shenzhen Humanities And Hist.* 11].

were not legal residents of the city.[4] The huge demand for houses made rural land development and transfer very profitable.

Without legal authorization, rural land development and transactions were still illegal. But this illegality did not stop farmers from developing their land to house the millions of migrant workers and the middle- to low-income populations flooding into Shenzhen.[5] "Planting houses" replaced "planting crops" as the main livelihood of the indigenous villagers. In the 1980s and 1990s, rural houses grew taller and taller: from two floors in the early 1980s, intended mainly for self-use, to four or five floors in the early 1990s and eight to ten floors by the end of the 1990s.[6]

2.2 A Network of Institutional Innovators

A network of institutional innovators provides a mechanism for potential buyers to collect and verify the information necessary for a real estate transaction. Modern technologies of transportation and communication have greatly reduced the cost of collecting and verifying such information.

An ordinary buyer or seller has only to reach out to any participant in this network in order to obtain access to the protection provided by the network. One needs to know only the village affiliation and personal identity of his trade partner, which can be certified by a seal from the corresponding village co-op, a real estate broker located in the village, and a notarization from a lawyer invited by the corresponding village co-op. He does not have to know his partner personally. In the absence of a legal recording system, village co-ops and other participants in the network keep information on small-property houses. However, this network is motivated by profit-making, and it is not closed but is open to all. The legitimacy of the network's participants, in particular that of the village co-ops and the mechanisms they have developed to provide and verify information, makes the network credible to outsiders. Each small network is a part of the bigger and actually boundless network of

[4] Migrants are largely excluded from the mainstream housing distribution system, as the linkage between household registration and urban housing is largely intact. *See, e.g.*, Wu Weiping (2002). *Migrant housing in urban China: Choices and constraints, 38 Urb. Aff. Rev.* 90.

[5] *See* Chapter 3, Section 3.2 for an explanation.

[6] 杜安娜："深圳现抢建违法建筑热潮 最快一夜建一栋楼"，"广州日报" 2009年11月24日[Du Anna, *Illegal Building Rush in Shenzhen*, GUANGZHOU DAILY, Nov. 24, 2009], http://news.qq.com/a/20091124/000211.htm (last visited February 20, 2012).

which millions of potential buyers of small-property houses are members. Transactions abound within this network.

2.2.1 *Village Co-ops*

In Shenzhen, each village has a shareholding co-op, which is the core of a village community. On the one hand, it is a social and economic organization and is responsible for the wealth-maximization of its shareholders, who are members of the same village community. Village co-ops divide the village land into two categories: collective development land and residential land. Residential land is divided into equal-area plots (usually 100–120 square meters) and distributed to villagers for free or bought by village members at nominal prices. In general, each household is provided with one plot. Village co-ops are responsible for the daily management of collective development land and issue dividends to villagers at the end of each year. Income from collective development land is also used for road construction, the drinking water and sewer systems, the electricity system, and for maintaining sanitation and other public services within the village.

On the other hand, village co-ops function like governments by providing public services and maintaining social order within their villages; these are services that the Shenzhen government needs, acknowledges, and respects. Members of village co-ops are insiders in village communities, which are characterized by intracommunity familiarity. This gives the co-ops complete access to local property arrangements, access that is not available to even the external government branches. Moreover, co-ops are much less constrained by formal law than government branches and agencies. This is exactly why co-ops can function as catalysts and coordinators of a network of institutional innovators.

Motivated by economic incentives, village co-ops are willing to provide information and support for small-property transactions. Further, their reputation as *de facto* village governments makes them credible intermediaries and sellers to outside buyers.

Village co-ops often keep records on the construction and transaction history of buildings within a village. The records may be maps of named plots, minutes of meetings of the village co-op boards, or receipts signed by the director of the board of the village co-ops. Both villagers and outsiders acknowledge the authority of the village co-ops regarding the property rights of the illegal buildings. Sales contracts of small property are usually carefully designed as a form of cooperative house building. Using the term "cooperative house building" does not legalize the illegal sales, but it does present the relationship between village co-ops and outside buyers as a kind of cooperative joint enterprise rather than a simple transaction. Moreover, the official seals of village co-ops are often on the sales contract and serve as an endorsement of the transaction. A village co-op seals all the contracts for houses sold by it. Some village co-ops even issue certificates of honorable villager membership to buyers.[7] This is a way to strengthen the confidence of buyers – only village members can legally acquire a plot of land from the village, but an honorable villager membership means that the village treats outsiders' rights to the bought house the same as they treat villagers' rights to their houses. In other situations, such as the development of houses by individual villagers or outside investors, village co-ops charge fees for their sealing of sales contracts. In 2011, a seal from a village co-op usually cost a buyer about 6,000 RMB. With the endorsement of village co-ops, some real estate developers even issue certificates to buyers. The certificates look very similar to the official ones and assign a number to each property.

2.2.2 *Land Developers*

The expertise of land developers is in high demand in this process. Villagers and village co-ops have land in hand, but they may not know how to build modern business units or residential condominiums. Small land developers, who are often capable builders but cannot afford to bid on government land in the public auction market, are happy to participate in the rural land market. They can either form joint ventures with village co-ops or buy land directly from them. Their familiarity with officials of government agencies overseeing construction-related administration further benefits any necessary collaboration.

2.2.3 *Shenzhen Rural Commercial Bank (SRCB)*

The Shenzhen Rural Commercial Bank (SRCB) is a government-owned but profit-driven local bank. It developed from the Shenzhen Rural Credit Co-op and has one branch in each village. Indigenous villagers are its main clients and call the SRCB their own bank. The

[7] *See* 耿诺："荣誉村民"成小产权房新噱头"，"北京日报"2011年6月13日[Geng Nuo, *Honorable Villager-Ship: A New Stunt of Small-Property Houses*, BEIJING DAILY (June 13, 2011)], http://house.focus.cn/news/2011-06-13/1337355.html (last visited February 20, 2012).

managers and employees of the SRCB are mostly local villagers, recruited from the villages where its branches are located. Though open to all people in Shenzhen, the SRCB offices often reserve a VIP room for local villagers. The mutual familiarity and trust between SRCB employees and local villagers greatly reduces the need for formality. One villager told me that if she were to lose her account book, she could get a new one without presenting any official documents to the bank. As this villager said, "They know who I am. I deposit and withdraw cash from them several times a week. I lost my account book and then they should give me a new one. What documents do they need?"[8] The SRCB has played a crucial role in financing village economic development by providing loans to villagers to build industrial parks and other economic facilities. When rural real estate development became the main business for Shenzhen villagers, the SRCB gradually got involved in it just as it would in any other businesses of villagers. With a pledge from village co-ops, the SRCB provides mortgages to ordinary buyers. A buyer usually has to pay half of the price as a down payment and can pay the remaining amount as installments over half a year, five years, or even ten years.

2.2.4 Real Estate Brokers

A real estate broker's office is a common sight in a neighborhood of small-property houses. As in the formal market, in the small-property market, a real estate broker will provide all the information regarding apartments and negotiate a deal. After signing a contract, the buyer will pay the agreed price, after which the buyer will receive the keys and the contract. If he wants to rent the apartment out or resell it, the same real estate broker can help him for a fee. Buyers are mostly middle- to low-income people in the city who often cannot afford an apartment on the formal market. Real estate brokers may be invited by village co-ops to set up offices in the villages; or, village co-ops may actually set up their own real estate brokerage and management companies and employ qualified real estate brokers.

Real estate brokers promote the sales of small-property houses in many ways. Throughout the intracity villages, advertisements for the

[8] Interview with a villager in Longhua New District of Shenzhen city (March 2, 2012).

renting and selling of small-property houses are everywhere – on front doors, walls, and electricity poles, and along roads all around the city. Posters for small-property houses are quite standard, usually indicating the number of floors and buildings, the developer (usually emphasizing that the property was developed by a village co-op), the location, the provision of public utilities, the price, the area, the forms of contracts and certificates, the payment methods (installments and related terms), and the relevant contact information (cellphone, QQ[9] group number, website, etc.). The most effective way to advertise is to build a website, start a blog, or set up a QQ group, through which potential buyers can view all the small-property apartments available, ask questions, and communicate with other potential buyers. I have joined five such QQ groups and still have conversations with real estate brokers, potential buyers, and owners of small-property apartments from time to time.

2.2.5 Lawyers

Lawyer notarization (*lv shi jian zheng*), the process by which a lawyer certifies that a transaction has been made according to both parties' real will and is consistent with the principle of freedom of contracts, is part of almost all transactions. The lawyer keeps copies of all the transaction documents on file, which are then available for review. If a buyer wants to sell a bought house, he has to surrender all the related documents to the lawyer, who creates another file of documents for the new buyer. In one law firm, the earliest records could be traced back to 2003.[10] The lawyer is generally silent regarding the illegality of the transaction, and because of lawyers' special identity, the parties involved may have the impression that the transaction is legal. As a result, the Lawyers' Association of Guangdong, the province to which Shenzhen belongs, has forbidden its members to notarize transactions of small-property houses. However, this prohibition is only effective for big law firms.

[9] QQ was the most popular online chat program in China.
[10] 李杰 ："深圳开发商自己给小产权房发证"，"经济半小时" 2009年6月13日[Li, Jie., *Shenzhen Land Developers Issue Certificates of Small-Property Houses*, CCTV ECON. HALF AN HOUR (June 13, 2009)], http://finance.sina.com.cn/china/dfjj/20090613/22346345587.shtml (last visited July 3, 2014).

Many small law firms still provide this service. Notarization of small-property transactions is a lucrative business for them: a seller of apartments, either village co-ops or land developers, will invite a lawyer to make all notarizations for a residential complex, which often includes several hundred apartments.

Thus, government-certified professionals, including lawyers, land developers, and real estate brokers, and government-recognized institutions, including village co-ops and the SRCB, have developed a network to support and facilitate small-property transactions. This network is centered on the most credible participant, the village co-ops. As one government official remarked, "Village co-ops function like land developers, Bureau of Urban Planning, Bureau of Land, Bureau of Construction in building small-property houses and can do whatever the above players can do. They also work with banks to issue mortgages to buyers, and as the Registration Center for Real Estate Transfer to record and endorse the transactions."[11]

Figure 2.1 is an illustration of this network:

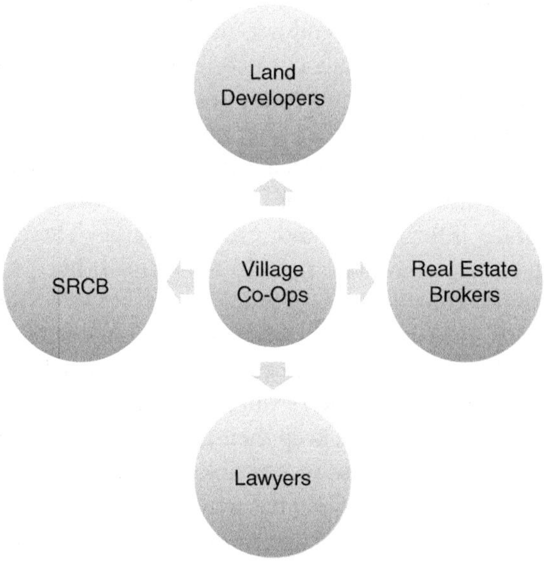

Figure 2.1 A network of institutional innovators

[11] Interview with a government official in Bao'An District of Shenzhen city (April 5, 2012).

This network also minimizes the risk of contract breach. Any transaction carries the risk of contract breach. It is important to make sure that sanctions are imposed on the party that violates the contract. In the modern state, the government is said to monopolize the force of violent sanction. But in reality, private sanction, including violent sanction, is everywhere. The advantage of public sanction lies in the state's ability to locate the party against which the sanction will be taken and to ensure the effectiveness of the sanction. Risks can be too high to control in contracts that rely on private sanction. It is important to minimize the risks in order to make transactions feasible. To make private sanction an effective deterrent, a party has to ensure that it can locate the person to be sanctioned and that it has the resources to implement the sanction. In a society of high mobility and rapid change, these conditions are not easy to satisfy. However, the network of institutional innovators has greatly facilitated the provision and verification of the information necessary for the deterrence of contract breach in small-property transactions.

In transaction contracts, sellers' addresses are written clearly and are easy to verify. It might be difficult for an outsider to know the transaction history of the small property he plans to buy. But this does not matter if the village co-op is willing to endorse the contract, as this serves as an implicit promise that the village co-op will be responsible in the case of any conflicts regarding the rights to the real estate. Lawyers are outsiders but also professionals, and they are paid for notarizing a contract. Lawyers' services are often localized, and their professional reputations are at stake in these transactions. Lawyers are thus incentivized to provide accurate information and prevent fraud. Therefore, while a village co-op's seal, a lawyer's notarization, and other privately made documents do not constitute a way to legalize illegal sales, they do offer a way to guarantee the information regarding transactions.

Moreover, village co-ops, as the economic and social engines of this network, have the credibility and resources to reassure outside buyers that participants in the network will keep their promises. Village co-ops are not impartial governments and are responsible only for the interests of their members. However, as Avner Greif has written on the community responsibility system in the context of premodern Europe, partial courts of a community are economically motivated to provide impartial justice.[12]

[12] *See* Avner Greif (2004) Impersonal exchange without impartial law: The community responsibility system, 5 5 *Chi. J. Int'l L.* 109.

Village co-ops persist longer than any of its individual members, and they have an interest in long-term economic performance. In the context of legal uncertainty, they endeavor to strengthen outsiders' confidence in transactions in order to make money from the small-property business. Rumors may be spread very quickly among groups of potential buyers through online chat rooms, blogs, and even local newspapers, and co-ops do not want to incur any extra trouble by cheating on outside buyers. As for other participants in this network, they not only have their professional qualifications and reputations at stake; they also are constrained by their continuing business relationships with village co-ops. They are therefore invested in the ongoing prosperity of the small-property market.

2.3 Development against Law

As discussed previously, after the 1988 amendments to the Chinese Constitution and LAL, legal reform for rural land development and transactions stalled.[13] In 1999, one year after the 1998 LAL revision, the Shenzhen government initiated its campaign against rural land development and transaction, calling the rural buildings "historical illegal buildings" (*lishi yiliu weifa jianzhu*). In 2004, the Shenzhen city government even established a small leading team headed by the mayor to deal with illegal rural land development. In 2009, the Shenzhen government created a new Department of Land Use Monitoring (DLUM) and established branches in all fifty-seven subdistricts of Shenzhen.[14]

However, the small-property market and the network supporting it had become so enmeshed with the economic development and social stability of Shenzhen that any serious legal enforcement of the revised measures was impossible. As a senior official of land administration of Shenzhen acknowledged, "[I]t is a war against the people that cannot be won."[15]

13 *See* Chapter 1 for more details.

14 深圳规划土地监察："我市查处违法建筑政策梳理"，2012年3月12日[*Review of the Municipal Policies of Illegal Buildings*, SHENZHEN LAND USE MONITORING (March 12, 2012)], www.szpls.gov.cn/whkj/xxdy/201203/t20120312_71655.html (last visited December 9, 2009). *See also* Section 4.2.1 of Chapter 4 for more details.

15 Interview with a government official in Futian District of Shenzhen city (March 1, 2012).

From 1999 to 2010, the number of illegal buildings grew from 221,600 to 356,852.[16]

2.3.1 *Too "Big" to Fail*

Small-property buildings are spread across the most prosperous as well as the remotest areas of Shenzhen. The more prosperous the location, the more concentrated and the taller the illegal buildings are. These illegal buildings have increased both in number and in size with the economic development and urbanization of Shenzhen, and they are too interconnected with the normal functioning of the city to fail.

First, the buildings provide shelter to the more than eight million migrant workers in Shenzhen. Shenzhen depends heavily on cheap labor from inland provinces, yet over the past three decades of development, the Shenzhen government has provided no public housing for migrant workers. Without the illegal buildings, these laborers would have few places live.

Second, these illegal buildings are concentrated in 320 intracity villages of Shenzhen, over which the city administration has never exercised effective management. In most villages, roads and basic public services such as electricity and water are maintained and provided by the villages themselves. The intracity villages maintain their own order and operation, which substantially reduces the great pressure on the city administration from rapid urbanization. The intracity villages of the illegal buildings are too important to the city to be demolished.

Third, these illegal buildings are the main livelihood of Shenzhen's indigenous people. Over 300,000 indigenous people, as the contributors and beneficiaries of Shenzhen's transformation from a small agricultural county to the most urbanized city in China, have accumulated vast economic and political resources in the past three decades. Several villages claim to be the first village under heaven or the first village of South China, and other villages are among the wealthiest in China. All the reform era's supreme leaders – Deng Xiaoping, Jiang Zemin, and Hu Jintao – have visited Shenzhen's villages. Several village heads are members of the National People's Congress or the Provincial People's Congress; many village heads are members of the City or the District

[16] 深圳市查处违法建筑领导小组办公室："深圳市农村城市化历史遗留违法建筑信息普查申报数据统计报告"（2010年）[SHENZHEN CITY GOV., INVESTIGATION REPORT ON ILLEGAL BUILDINGS IN SHENZHEN 26 (2010)] (on file with the author).

People's Congress. The strong interests of such a powerful constituency cannot be easily disregarded.

2.3.2 Competing Government Interests

2.3.2.1 Competition between Different Levels of the Local Government

The scale and functions of illegal buildings have different implications for different levels and different departments of the local government. The local government of Shenzhen is divided into three levels: the city, the district, and the subdistrict (street) level. The city and district governments of Shenzhen are responsible for economic development in Shenzhen and have stronger motivation than the subdistrict governments to eliminate small property.

First, the city and district governments prefer big investors to small ones, not to mention that they prefer these big investors to street vendors or restaurants that serve middle- to low-income populations. The Shenzhen city government's primary worry is that no land will be available to big investors if land is used for illegal rural land development.[17] Cheap and sometimes free land is the key incentive that the city government has at its disposal. For example, in an effort to prevent Huawei, one of the biggest suppliers of telecommunication facilities in the world, from moving to another city, the Shenzhen city government developed a town of 21.9 square kilometers and gave it to Huawei for free as its new

[17] Chinese local governments might also worry about the challenge to their monopoly over primary land supply brought by the small-property market. However, it is not the primary concern of the Shenzhen city government, which, although the inventor of land finance in China, has relied least on land sales revenue among all Chinese cities. In 2013, land sales revenue of Shenzhen city government amounted to 44 billion RMB; in 2009 the number was 12.6 billion, 15.5 billion in 2010, 19.3 billion in 2011 and 11.5 billion in 2012. For comparison, in 2013, land sales revenue in Beijing was 182.2 billion, 204.4 billion in Shanghai and 76.2 billion in Guangzhou. The reason is that the Shenzhen city government does not have much land left to sell after three decades of development. Facing such pressure, the Shenzhen city government has reformed its economic structure to increase enterprise taxes rather than land sales revenue. *See* "土地财政提前转型 深圳财政收入首超千亿"， "每日经济新闻"2014年8月22日[*Land Finance Was Transformed in Advance; Shenzhen Government Revenue Exceeded A Hundred Billion For the First Time*, DAILY ECONOMIC NEWS (Aug. 22, 2014)], http://house.southcn.com/fcgd/content/2014-08/22/content_107136529.htm; "深圳卖地占财政收入不足10% 被称土地财政中异类"，"第一财经日报" 2014年1月2日[*Land Sales Revenue Is Less than the Total Revenue of Shenzhen—An Exceptional Case*, FIRST FIN. NEWS, January 2, 2014, http://money.163.com/14/0102/02/9HI46OC900253B0H.html].

headquarters in 2010.[18] Big companies like Huawei are viewed as the engines of economic development in Shenzhen. The subdistrict governments, on the other hand, face millions of ordinary people in the city and are directly involved in the daily management of the city. Their daily work is centered on the housing and monitoring of millions of migrant workers and on overseeing the livelihoods of over 300,000 indigenous villagers. They understand how crucial small property is to the normal operation of the city.

Second, there are more local employees at the subdistrict level than at the city and district levels, where highly-educated graduates of elite colleges, and well-connected politicians from other cities or higher-level governments, dominate. Thus, subdistrict governments are generally reluctant to punish and deter small-property transactions. Actually, some subdistrict governments neighbor small property buildings or are even located in small-property buildings.

How do the differences between the various levels of local government influence legal enforcement? There is only one city government and there are only eight district governments, but there are fifty-seven subdistrict governments. These subdistrict governments have the closest connection with the 320 villages and the best information about people and buildings within them; they also have the most sympathy for and interest in small property. They are on the side of the villages rather than of the upper-level governments. They are inclined to help villages avoid monitoring and punishment by the upper-level governments. It is no wonder, then, that in 2004, the Shenzhen city government set up a discipline team to supervise government officials and ensure that they fulfill their responsibilities in dealing with illegal rural land development. However, as it turns out, discipline campaigns are unable to overcome such strong vested interests.

2.3.2.2 Competition between Different Agencies of the Local Government

Competing interests exist not only between different levels of the local government, but also between different agencies of the local government. There are government agencies responsible for the enforcement of land law, mainly the Commission of Urban Planning, Land and Resources and the Bureau of Land Use Monitoring, and government agencies responsible for the economic development and social stability of the city. The latter accept

[18] 陈新焱等："联盟的博弈：华为"被造城"，"南方周末" 2010年8月8日[Chen Xinyan et al., *Making a Town for Huawei*, SOUTHERN WKLY. (Aug. 8, 2010)], www.infzm.com/content/49064 (last visited September 3, 2013).

the status quo and exercise their powers based on the reality of widespread small-property constructions. For example, the Bureau of Business Administration grants business licenses to enterprises (restaurants, factories, shops, etc.) located in small-property buildings, on the condition that village co-ops certify that the buildings are rented or owned by the enterprises; meanwhile, the City Office of Housing Renting (MOHR), which was set up by the Party Committee on Political and Legal Affairs, an organ in charge of public security and social stability, registers and numbers all small-property buildings in its system. This system serves as a basis for taxation and for the management of population migration, and it has been created with the help and support of village co-ops. As a MOHR official said: "[W]e knew these buildings were illegal; our registration has nothing to do with illegality; we just want to maintain social stability by closely monitoring the migrant population, most of which live in these buildings."[19]

Of course, government agencies responsible for the enforcement of land laws have the final say on the legality of small property. They do, from time to time, take action against small property. Participants in the small-property market have two ways of dealing with this situation. One is to invite government agencies to participate in the market, and the other is to pay for government officials' collusion. Often, villagers intentionally involve government employees in the business. A CCTV[20] undercover report revealed that about forty employees of a district government agency of land administration in Shenzhen had bought illegal apartments.[21] In reflecting on its failure to stop rural real estate development, the Shenzhen city government has acknowledged corruption as an important factor. Villagers told me that payments made to government officials are part of their investment and that payments are estimated by the number of floors in a building. For example, in one village that I investigated, the price officials charge to turn a blind eye is 6,000 RMB per floor. According to *China Securities Daily*, about one-third of the profits of the informal housing market fall into the hands of government officials in charge of enforcing land and housing laws.[22]

[19] Interview with a government official in Futian District of Shenzhen city (July 1, 2012).

[20] CCTV is the abbreviation for Chinese Central Television, the official television broadcaster of the Chinese central government.

[21] Geng, *supra* note 7.

[22] 杜雅文、万晶： "百亿游资豪赌小产权房转正"，"中国证券报" 2009年8月21日[Du, Yawen, & Jing Wan, *Billions of Hot Money Bet on the Legalization of Small-Property Houses*, CHINA SEC. DAILY (August 21, 2009)], http://biz.xinmin.cn/rehouse/2009/08/21/2410786_6.html (last visited February 15, 2013).

2.3.3 *An Expanded Network*

Thus, different levels and different departments of the government are involved in the network of small-property institutions. Some disregard the illegality of small-property buildings and incorporate them into their official systems in order to effectively address issues such as the monitoring of population migration and the physical site requirements for business operation. Some try to enforce the land law and fight against small property. But without the support of other levels and agencies of local government, the effect of legal enforcement is limited. Further, bribery becomes a weapon for market participants, who use it to reduce the risk of legal action being taken against them.

Again, village co-ops play a crucial role. They cooperate with the government and grant access to it to promote the integration of small property into the official systems. They sidestep the government and resist legal enforcement with bribery when necessary.

Taking the government into consideration, the network of small-property institutions should be expanded as shown in Figure 2.2:

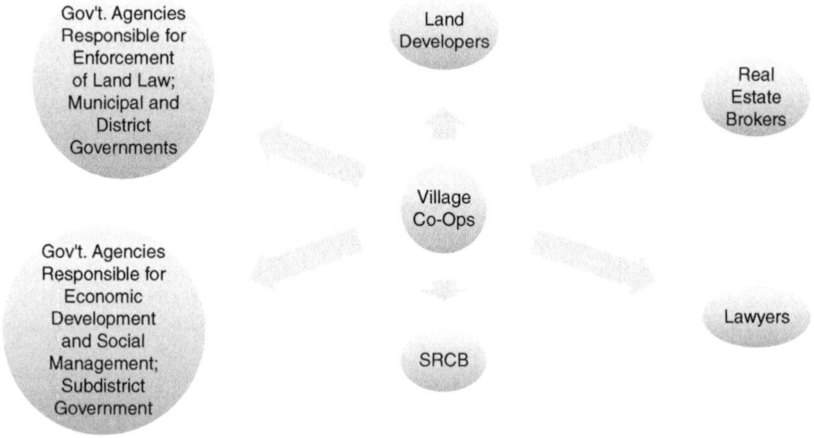

Figure 2.2 An expanded network of institutional innovators

This expanded network further reduces the risk of government demolition of small-property buildings and increases the credibility of small-property transactions by including local government agencies and branches. It provides a stronger core for the bigger, boundless network through which millions of people engage in small-property transactions.

2.4 Conclusion

A famous saying suggests how people in Shenzhen treat law: go around the red light; hurry up at the yellow light; speed past the green light (*jian le hong deng rao zhe zou, jian le huang deng qiang zhe zou, jian le lv deng kuai kuai zou*). The legal definition and protection of property rights are the green traffic lights that facilitate market transactions. However, green lights are not always available, and a well-functioning property law regime, though beneficial to the development of a market economy, may be far on the horizon for transitional countries such as China. In all the theories discussing the evolution of property rights since Demsetz, government is either absent or taken for granted as a maker and enforcer of law. Thus, in theory, all that developing countries need to do is to pass the proper laws.[23] Yet this view of the government ignores the struggle between the old (traditional or socialist) system and the reform effort. The government of a transitional country may, itself, be an uncertain factor in the development of a market economy. It is unclear whether such a government can make laws that challenge the past, and whether laws can be enforced in the event that they are made. Top-down legal reform tends to be ineffective and is frequently hindered by bureaucracy and interest groups.

Given the constraints above, hurrying up at the yellow light and going around the red light may be more feasible options. The traffic lights of China's post-Communist transition have sometimes shifted in reverse order, as red lights on rural land development and transaction have shifted to yellow. Often, it has been unclear whether rural land reform should be on the agenda. During this period, people in Shenzhen have not waited for a green light; instead they have hurried up at the yellow light – millions of transactions have occurred amid legal ambiguity and

[23] *See* Harold Demsetz (1967). Toward a theory of property rights, 57 *Am. Econ. Rev. Papers & Proc.* 347; Daniel Fitzpatrick (2006). Evolution and chaos in property rights systems: The third world tragedy of contested access, 115 *Yale L. J.* 996; Thomas Merill (2002). Introduction: The Demsetz thesis and the evolution of property rights, 31 *J. Legal Stud.* 331.

relaxed enforcement of the legal prohibition on rural land development and transaction.

The key issue, of course, is the process by which this has happened. De Soto holds that transactions in the absence of legal titles are limited to people of the same group, because the only insurance available to extra-legal businesses is that provided by their neighbors and the local mafias. As a result, property arrangements are intracommunity in character, highly reliant on local information and networks, and dispersed among hundreds of communities. To the outsider, the chain of title is blurry at best.[24] On the one hand, the small-property market testifies to de Soto's argument that local communities and various intermediaries play a crucial role in the extralegal property system; on the other hand, however, it challenges de Soto and the conventional view that transactions are limited to people within the same community. It proves that community organizations and market intermediaries can develop a network that supports large-scale, impersonal market transactions.

The Chinese government has been characterized as an authority that is fragmented at both the horizontal level (i.e., between different government agencies) and the vertical level (between different levels of the government).[25] However, this theory does not take into account other institutional players: legally certified associations such as village co-cops, and professionals such as lawyers and real estate brokers, all of which have some authority. How do these fragmented authorities work in China? How do they build the institutional foundations for a modern market economy in China? The answer is that these fragmented authorities are networked together to provide institutional support for market transactions. The theory of fragmented authority emphasizes competition and conflict between different authorities, but in the case of small property, fragmented authorities have worked together. Rather than being managed by a centralized authority that protects property rights and enforces contracts, the small-property market involves a network of credible institutional innovators, with village co-ops serving as the central coordinators. This network supports the growth of the

[24] Hernando de soto, *The Mystery of Capital: Why Capitalism Triumphs in the West and Everywhere Else* 162 (2000).

[25] *See, e.g.*, Kenneth G. Lieberthal, *The 'Fragmented Authoritarianism' Model and Its Limitations*, in BUREAUCRACY, POLITICS, AND DECISION MAKING IN POST-MAO CHINA (Kenneth Lieberthal & David M. Lampton eds., 1992).

small-property market and reduces the risks of contract breach and legal enforcement.

Can a market operate without legal titles? Yes – the small-property market in Shenzhen proves that it can. While I have not measured the efficiency of this market statistically, the gradual commodification of rural land is undoubtedly an improvement over the de-commodification of land under the Communist regime. Scholars often devalue informal property rights and view them as a barrier to market transition. For example, de Soto does "not believe the appearance of small enclaves of prosperous economic sectors in the midst of large undeveloped or informal sectors marks the dawn of an uneven but nevertheless inevitable transition to capitalist systems."[26] This case study demonstrates that, contrary to de Soto's claim, a robust and impersonal market can develop in the absence of legally enforceable rights. Set against the backdrop and in the context of China's transition, this paper presents a feasible plan for building a market economy in transitional countries, where property laws are often less than ideal. The emergence of the small-property market – like the emergence in China of the Household Responsibility System in the 1980s and of private enterprises in the 1990s, both of which were initially illegal and therefore informal – is a further step toward building a modern market economy in China

[26] De Soto, *supra* note 24, at 75.

3

Small Property, Big Market

A Focal Point Explanation

The formation and operation of the small-property market is mysterious: how did this market form despite the legal prohibition? How does this market operate without legal titles? I kept asking various persons in the field the following questions: Since it is illegal to transfer rural real estate, how dare you buy/sell it? Aren't you worried that the government might demolish your illegal buildings? Aren't you worried that the contract might be voided by the other party? According to the conventional view, informal transactions are either limited to people who have continuing business relations[1] or those who are supported by systematic institutions.[2] However, in Shenzhen there existed no centralized institution to enforce contracts of small-property transactions. A common response I received is that: "I did it when other people were doing the same thing. A lot of people are doing the same thing, why should I worry?"

This common response indicates a situation of coordination, in which one would take some action only if others are expected to also act correspondingly. The underlying question is how to coordinate people's behaviors in the absence of a centralized law – a question that has been addressed by both economists and legal scholars. Nobel Laureate Thomas Schelling first observed that, in situations requiring coordination, anything that makes salient one behavioral means of coordinating tends to produce self-fulfilling expectations that then lead to the occurrence of

[1] *See, e.g.*, Robert D. Cooter and Janet T. Landa (1984) Personal vs. impersonal trade: The size of trading groups and the law of contracts, 4 *Int'l Rev. L. & Econ.* 15; Janet T. Landa (1981) A theory of the ethnically homogeneous middleman group: An institutional alternative to contract law, 10 *J. Legal Stud.* 349; Stewart Macaulay (1963) Non-contractual relations in business: A preliminary study, 28 *Am. Soc. Rev.* 55.

[2] *See, e.g.*, Lisa Bernstein (2001) Private commercial law in the cotton industry: Creating cooperation through rules, norms, and institutions, 99 *Mich. L. Rev.* 1724; Lisa Bernstein (1996) Merchant law in a merchant court: Rethinking the code's search for immanent business norms, 144 *U. Pa. L. Rev.* 1765; Lisa Bernstein (1992) Opting out of the legal system: Extralegal contractual relations in the diamond industry, 21 *J. Legal Stud.* 115.

that result. Schelling calls the salient solution the "focal point."[3] Weingast models the policing of rights as a coordination problem among citizens, and suggests that self-enforcing limits on the state could result from a focal solution constructed in a constitution or a galvanizing event such as a major riot, or by a charismatic leader.[4] Sugden explains that self-enforcing conventions about coordination, reciprocity, and property rights that resolve rival claimants disputes arise from focal point equilibria.[5] Myerson argues that Schelling's focal point is among the most important ideas in social theory and that one can understand the foundations of political institutions in terms of focal equilibrium selection in a more fundamental game.[6] Dixit considers multiple settings in which coordination can be achieved by extralegal conventions, including focal point settings.[7] Several legal scholars argue that law can serve as a focal institution to help parties deliberately select an equilibrium from multiple possible self-enforcing coordination equilibria.[8] Both McAdams and Myerson observe that a rule recognizing possession as the basis of property rights can avoid wasteful contests over property by coordinating rival claimants' strategies: the concept of "rightful" ownership is expected to be applied and thus the "rightful" owner will rationally claim and the other will rationally recede.[9] Most recently, Hadfield and Weingast develop an account of legal order that relies on "a common logic," rather than a third-party centralized enforcement mechanism, to coordinate people's behaviors.[10]

However, the above insights have rarely figured in the study of market institutions. A significant exception is Avner Greif's analysis of the

[3] Thomas C. Schelling (1960). *The Strategy of Conflict.*

[4] *See* Barry R. Weingast (1997). The political foundations of democracy and the rule of law, 91 *Am. Pol. Sci. Rev.* 245.

[5] *See* Robert Sugden (2nd edn. 2005). *The Economics of Rights, Cooperation and Welfare.*

[6] *See* Roger B. Myerson (2004). Justice, institutions, and multiple equilibria, 5 *Chi. J. Intl L.* 91.

[7] Avinash K. Dixit (2004) *Lawlessness and Economics: Alternative Modes of Governance.*

[8] *See, e.g.*, Richard McAdams (2000) A focal point theory of expressive law, 86 *Va. L. Rev.* 1649; Richard H. McAdams and Janice Nadler (2005) Testing the focal point theory of legal compliance: The effect of third-party expression in an experimental hawk/dove game, 2 *J. Empirical Legal Stud.* 87; Robert D. Cooter (1998) Expressive law and economics, 27 *J. Legal Stud.* 585.

[9] For a critique of viewing property as hawk-dove games, *see* Carol M. Rose (2013) Psychologies of property (and why property is not a hawk-dove game), in *The Philosophical Foundations of Property Law* (J. E. Penner and H. E. Smith, eds., 2013).

[10] *See* Gillian K. Hadfield and Barry R. Weingast (2012) What is law? A coordination model of the characteristics of legal order, 4 *J. Legal Analysis* 471.

community responsibility system that supported impersonal exchanges in the context of premodern Europe.[11] Set against the backdrop and context of China's market transition, this chapter hopes to enrich our understanding of market institutions by applying the updated insights from coordination games and focal points to an examination of a contemporary example of a market without formal property rights.[12] It also contributes a significant real world example to the theories of coordination games and focal points, most of which are based on laboratory experiments.

This chapter is organized as follows. Section 3.1 introduces the focal point theory and applies it to the Shenzhen case. Section 3.2 models the formation of the small-property market as an assurance game among social entrepreneurs in Shenzhen, models the demolition risk as a hawk-dove game between the Shenzhen government and farmers, and models contract risk as a hawk-dove game between a buyer and a seller. Section 3.3 summarizes the broad implications of the focal point theory and coordination game models to law and development.

3.1 Focal Point

3.1.1 Theory

As Schelling says,

> most situations – perhaps every situation for people who are practiced at this kind of game – provide some clue for coordinating behavior, some focal point for each person's expectation of what the other expects him to expect to be expected to do. Finding the key, or rather finding a key – any key that is mutually recognized as the key becomes the key – may depend on imagination more than on logic, it may depend on analogy, precedent, accidental arrangement, symmetry, aesthetic or geometric configuration, casuistic reasoning, and who the parties are and what they know about each other.[13]

[11] Avner Greif (2004) Impersonal exchange without impartial law: The community responsibility system, 5 *Chi. J. Int'l L.* 109.

[12] For research that integrates game theories and sociological materials, *see* Peter T. Leeson (2009) The laws of lawlessness, 38 *J. Legal Stud.* 471; Avner Greif (1994) beliefs and the organization of society: A historical and theoretical reflection on collectivist and individual societies, 102 *J. Pol. Econ.* 912. Both studies examine historical materials rather than contemporary cases.

[13] Schelling, *supra* note 3, at 57.

In his classic *The Strategy of Conflict*, Schelling began his analysis with the study of tacit bargaining – bargaining in which communication is incomplete or impossible. Specifically, Schelling began with the special, simplified case in which two or more parties have identical interests and face the problem not of reconciling interests, but only of coordinating their actions for their mutual benefit.[14] In the Grand Central example, the sample population began in New Haven, Connecticut, so Grand Central Station was their first stop in New York City. This makes Grand Central a more salient choice of where to meet than other famous places in New York City, such as the Empire State building.[15] People were thus able to meet each other at the same place in the absence of prior arrangements. Schelling then proceeds to consider tacit bargaining of divergent interests. The outcome of his experiments suggests that among all the available options, one particular option usually seems to be the focal point for coordinated choice, and the party to whom it is a relatively unfavorable choice quite often accepts it simply because he knows that the other participants will expect him to.[16] In the end Schelling investigated explicit bargaining in which communication was possible and there was no apparent need for intuitive rapport.[17] There was abundant evidence that the influence of the focal point was powerfully present even in explicit bargaining.

The essential idea of the focal point is that "the intrinsic magnetism of particular outcomes, especially those that enjoy prominence, uniqueness, simplicity, precedent, or some rationale makes them qualitatively differentiable from the continuum of possible alternatives."[18] These particular outcomes are what Schelling calls focal points. Schelling presents the focal point theory as generally applicable to situations involving coordination, such as the formation of interest groups, spontaneous revolt, and bargaining.[19] In recent decades, a number of researchers have observed high coordination rates in games with a focal point and symmetric payoffs; though the influence of focal points can become weaker with the increasing divergence of interests.[20] Though most laboratory experiments are limited to the study of focal points in tacit bargaining

[14] *Id.* at 54–58. [15] *See also* McAdams, *supra* note 8.
[16] Schelling, *supra* note 3, at 60. [17] *Id.* at 67. [18] *Id.* at 70. [19] *Id.* at 70–74.
[20] *See, e.g.*, Nicholas Bardsley et al. (2010) Explaining focal points: Cognitive Hierarchy Theory versus Team Reasoning, 120 *ECON. J.* 40; Vincent P. Crawford, Uri Gneezy and Yuval Rottenstreich (2008) The power of focal points is limited: Even minute payoff asymmetry may yield large coordination failures, 98 *Am. Econ. Rev.* 1443; Judith Mehta, Chris Starmer and Robert Sugden (1994) The nature of salience: An experimental investigation, 84 *Am. Econ. Rev.* 658.

situations, a recent study by Anders Poulsen and Robert Sugden, two of the foremost researchers of focal points, have proved that focal points also play an important role in explicit bargaining situations.[21]

3.1.2 Focal Point in Shenzhen

In the context of Shenzhen, three elements made private rural land development and transfer a more *focal* choice than the legal prohibition. First, the Shenzhen government's urban land use reform successfully challenged the old Constitution and sent out a signal to people in Shenzhen that land-use rights can be sold for money. Second, Shenzhen was designated to pilot market-oriented reforms and by doing so "blaze a bloody trail," i.e., break the old rules, which encouraged people in Shenzhen to innovate new institutions. Third, the Shenzhen farmers saw how the Shenzhen government made money from land requisitioning and saw no justification for depriving themselves of the same profit opportunities. Overall, Shenzhen people strongly believed that farmers should have the right to develop and transfer rural land.

When the Shenzhen SEZ was founded in 1980, the biggest barrier to becoming an attractive destination for foreign investment was a lack of financing for urban infrastructure. The central government could provide very limited support to the Shenzhen government's infrastructure construction projects.[22] A Hong Kong lawyer provided Shenzhen government with the solution: "Isn't the land money? Even your ancestor Marx admitted that land was wealth."[23] The Shenzhen government leaders got the message. They knew that land could generate the money they urgently needed for urban construction, but two barriers existed: (i) land was inalienable in the orthodox ideology of a country that had abolished private ownership of land; (ii) the Constitution stated very clearly at that time that commercial land alienation was illegal.[24]

[21] Anders Poulsen and Robert Sugden, *Understanding Focal Points in Bargaining Situations: An Experimental Investigation*, ESRC END OF AWARD REP. *2010*, RES-000-22-3322 (2010); Anders Poulsen & Robert Sugden, *Understanding Focal Points in Bargaining Situations: An Experimental Investigation, ESRC Impact Rep. 2011*, RES-000-22-3322 (2011).

[22] 冯杰："深圳土地管理二十年"，"深圳特区报" 2006年6月22日 [Jie Feng, *Two Decades of Shenzhen Land Administration*, SHENZHEN SEZ DAILY (June 22, 2006)], www.szpl.gov.cn/xxgk/gzdt/zwdt/200908/t20090825_46190.html. (last visited August 3, 2014).

[23] *Id.* [24] *Id.*

But Shenzhen is the city of reform. As Deng Xiaoping said, "The central government has no money, but can give you policies. You should try by yourself. Blaze a bloody trail (of reform)!"[25] "To attract foreign investment, it would adopt different administration and policies, mainly market-oriented":[26] These words represented the main support the Shenzhen government received from the central government. Under such a reform spirit, the Shenzhen government decided to challenge the old Constitution. Shenzhen started with what was explicitly allowed by the central government: the charging of land-use fees to foreign investors in the SEZ.[27] The "land-use fees" filled a pressing financing gap, but they were far from enough. Public land ownership and the inalienability of land still remained the norm across the country; the Shenzhen practice of charging land-use fees to foreign investors who did not believe in Marxist ideology was viewed as a trivial exception.

As the need for money became more acute, the Shenzhen government eventually broke with the old norm of land inalienability. Bearing in mind the illegality of land alienation, it proceeded in a measured and strategic fashion. In September 1987, for the first time, the Shenzhen government sold a 50-year right to use a plot of land of 8,500 square meters to a Chinese company for the price of RMB 5,250,000.[28] In October 1987, the Shenzhen government invited celebrated theorists from all over the country to attend a conference on urban land administration reform. The question posed to them was whether land could be a commodity. Delegates of the Shenzhen government spurred debate by asking: "We have collected a lot of money from alienating land. Isn't land a commodity?"[29] The highlight came on December 1, 1987, when the Shenzhen government held the first public auction of land. The Shenzhen government was fully aware that the auction would be in public conflict with the Constitution. As a result, it invited a member of the CCP political bureau, a deputy head of the State Bureau of

[25] 冷溶、汪作玲主编："邓小平年谱：1975–1997"，中央文献出版社2004年版 [LENG, RONG AND WANG ZUOLING, ANNALS OF DENG XIAOPING (2004).]

[26] *Id.* at 33.

[27] *See* "广东省经济特区条例"（第五届全国人大常委会1980年8月26日颁布）[Guangdong Regulation of Special Economic Zones in Guangdong Province (promulgated by the Standing Comm. of the Fifth Nat'l People's Cong., Aug. 26, 1980), art. 12]; "中外合资经营企业法" (1979年7月1日第五届全国人民代表大会第二次会议通过)[Law of the People's Republic of China on Chinese-Foreign Equity Joint Ventures] (promulgated by the Standing Comm. of the Nat'l People's Cong., July 1, 1979, art. 5].

[28] Feng, *supra* note 22. [29] *Id.*

Land Administration (SBLA), seventeen mayors from the country, twenty-eight Hong Kong entrepreneurs and economists, and more than sixty journalists to observe the auction. It was a public attack on the old norm. The auctioned plot of land was eventually won by the government's own land company after forty-four other companies submitted bids.[30]

Five months later, the National People's Congress ("NPC") passed a constitutional amendment stating that land-use rights can be transferred *according to law*. At the end of 1988, the Standing Committee of the NPC made a corresponding revision to the LAL to allow the transfer of land-use rights. The State Council made a law according to which *urban* land use rights can be transferred in 1990; however, a corresponding legal authorization for rural land use rights has never materialized.[31]

Though unconstitutional, the first public auction of land use rights in Shenzhen became a landmark event in the city's history and was widely praised as one of Shenzhen's most important contributions to China's economic reform. During my interviews, SEZ citizens of various backgrounds, including government officials, indigenous farmers, and real estate developers were eager to share this story, proudly declaring that their people facilitated the constitutional amendment through the first public auction and that Shenzhen was the city of reform.

The urban real estate industry began to prosper after the establishment of a legal system that permitted and facilitated the transfer of urban land use rights. As a result of the first public auction of land use rights, Shenzhen became the birthplace of China's modern real estate industry. Among the top ten national real estate companies, four are based in Shenzhen. The real estate industry contributed greatly to both government revenue and GDP growth in Shenzhen. Even in 2010, the year when real estate industry tax revenues were at their lowest in two decades, the real estate industry still accounted for 4.82 percent of GDP growth in Shenzhen and 11.1 percent of tax revenues. In 1999, real estate industry tax revenues reached their highest levels of 14.49 percent.[32]

[30] *Id.* [31] *See* Chapter 1 for more details.

[32] This group of statistics was provided in 2011 by Wang Fan, the then Director of the Urban Planning, Land and Resources Commission of Shenzhen City. *See* 王芃：去年深圳房地产企业税收贡献率达到11.1%, 网易房产2011年7月11日 [Wang Fan, *Real Estate Enterprises Contributed 11.1% of Shenzhen's Revenue Last Year*, WANG YI REAL ESTATE, July 11, 2011], http://sz.house.163.com/11/0711/23/78NG7MB400074KDB.html (last visited October 25, 2014).

Overall, from 1988 to 2010, the Shenzhen government made at least 170 billion RMB from the direct sales of land.[33]

Participants in the small-property market are well aware of the astronomical profits the Shenzhen government has earned from land sales and development. Ordinary Shenzhen citizens, in particular farmers, have seen how the Shenzhen government seizes their land through requisition, paying them a low price but selling the land at prices many times higher. They mock the legal prohibition on rural land development and transfer with an old Chinese saying: "The magistrates are free to burn down houses, while the common people are forbidden even to light lamps."

3.2 Coordination Games and the Market

The role of a focal point is to enable coordination. Therefore, it is necessary to determine at the outset whether a coordination problem exists before applying the focal point theory. The problem of coordination is "where two or more individuals can reach some mutually desired outcome – or avoid some mutually undesired outcome – only by combining their actions in a certain way, but where more than one possible combination will suffice. The presence of multiple ways to combine actions requires that individuals coordinate on the same combination."[34]

Coordination games have multiple equilibria,[35] and, therefore, the payoffs alone do not determine the behavioral outcome.[36] Instead, the final outcome depends on the specific social settings and individual participants involved, leaving room for less concrete variables, such as history and politics, to impact oversimplified economic models. Moreover, coordination games often require the participants to make choices between the conflicting preferences of different individuals, since it is

[33] 30年18件大事：深圳地产精华录 [18 Key Events in 30 Years: A Brief of Shenzhen Real Estate], http://sz.focus.cn/news/2010-08-23/1026041_5.html (last visited February 15, 2013).

[34] Richard McAdams (2008). Beyond the Prisoner's Dilemma: Coordination, Game Theory, and Law, 82 S. *Cal. L. Rev.* 209, 219.

[35] An equilibrium refers to a "Nash equilibrium," which is the central solution concept in game theory. It is based on the principle that the combination of strategies that players are likely to choose is one in which no player could do better by choosing a different strategy, given the strategies the other players choose. A pair of strategies will form a Nash equilibrium if each strategy is one that cannot be improved upon given the other player's strategy. We establish whether a particular strategy combination forms a Nash equilibrium by asking if either player has an incentive to deviate from it. Douglas G. Baird, Robert H. Gertner and Randal C. Picker (1998). *Game Theory and the Law* 310.

[36] McAdams, *supra* note 34, at 212.

often impossible to find a solution that makes everyone better off. As a result of the above factors, coordination game models are closer to reality than the prisoners' dilemma model, which has long dominated the application of game theory in legal studies.[37]

Classic coordination games include the Assurance, or Stag Hunt, Game and the Hawk-Dove Game. The name "Stag Hunt" comes from Rousseau's illustration of the choice between hunting stag and hunting hare, where one succeeds in hunting stag only if the other hunter also hunts stag. Sharing a stag with the other hunter is the best outcome, but hunting hare is safer because one can succeed without the other hunter.[38] The formation of the small-property market in Shenzhen is a revolt against the formal law that can be likened to hunting stag in the Stag Hunt Game, since people need to coordinate amongst themselves in order to "hunt."

The Hawk-Dove Game is used to describe a situation between two players who desire the same thing that they cannot both enjoy.[39] This game is also well known as the Chicken Game, in which teenagers drive their cars directly at each other. The one who swerves first loses face, but the failure of either to swerve is catastrophic.[40] There are two strategies for players in these Hawk-Dove Games. The dove strategy is submissive – doves are not prepared to fight in support of their claims. If their opponents show any inclination toward fighting, doves immediately concede.[41] In contrast, the hawk strategy is to try to win the whole of the resource by fighting. If a hawk meets a dove, the hawk lays claim to the whole of the resource. By signaling his readiness to fight, the hawk causes the dove to back down, allowing the hawk to take the resource without having to fight for it. However, if a hawk meets another hawk, they fight it out, often with severe consequences for both parties.[42] These types of Hawk-Dove Games are present in the operation of the small-property market, particularly in the tensions between the Shenzhen government and the farmers in determining whether to demolish the illegal buildings and the tensions between contract parties deciding whether to void a legally ineffective contract. In these examples,

[37] *Id.*
[38] Jean-Jacques Rousseau (1755). *A Discourse on Inequality* 111 (Maurice Cranston trans., 1984), cited in McAdams, *supra* note 34, at 219.
[39] Robert Sudgen (2005). *The Economics Of Rights, Cooperation And Welfare* 61.
[40] McAdams, *supra* note 34, at 224. [41] Sudgen, *supra* note 39, at 62. [42] *Id.*

neither party wants to "swerve" first, nor do they want to directly clash with each other.

In the following sections, I will apply the Assurance and Hawk-Dove Game models to analyze the formation and operation of the small-property market in Shenzhen.

3.2.1 An Assurance Game of Market Formation

3.2.1.1 An Assurance Game of Social Entrepreneurs

The formation of the small-property market can be viewed as a change in social norms from an acceptance of the inalienability of real estate in the communist era to an adoption of the idea of the alienability of real estate in the post-communist era. Many scholars have emphasized the role of social entrepreneurs in the evolution of social norms like these. They claim that when an exogenous change creates new cost-benefit conditions that favor a switch to a new norm, social entrepreneurs tend to serve as catalysts for the switch.[43] Scholars refer to this category of social entrepreneurs as "norm entrepreneurs." It is often true that there exist entrepreneurial people more likely to initiate changes in society. However, it would be an oversimplification to assume that whenever there is an exogenous change, entrepreneurs will always succeed in accordingly changing the norm. As North would agree, inefficient institutions often persist.[44] There is always room for improvement, but improvement often does not occur.

If room for improvement always exists and potential social entrepreneurs are always present, why do social entrepreneurs initiate change at certain times and in certain places? The answer is often because these social entrepreneurs must bide their time. Therefore, the term "exogenous change" must be further qualified. Exogenous change is not simply a change resulting in new cost-benefit conditions, like the rise of the fur

[43] *See, e.g.*, Eric A. Posner (2002). *Law and Social Norms*; Emanuela Carbonara, Francesco Parisi and Georg von Wangenheim (2008). Lawmakers as norm entrepreneurs, 4 *Rev. L. & Econ.* 779; Robert C. Ellickson (2001). The market for social norms, 3 *Am. L. & Econ. Rev.* 1; Richard McAdams (2001). Signaling discount rates law, norms, and economic methodology, 110 *Yale L.J.* 625 (reviewing Eric A. Posner, Law and Social Norms (2002)); Eric Posner (1998). Symbols, signals, and social norms in politics and the law, 27 *J. Legal Stud.* 765; Cass R. Sunstein (1996). On the expressive function of law, 144 *U. Pa. L. Rev.* 2021.

[44] Douglass C. North (1990). *Institutions, Institutional Change, and Economic Performance* 7.

Table 3.1 *An assurance game of market formation*

		Player 2	
		Strategy A	Strategy B
Player 1	Strategy A	a, a	−c, 0
	Strategy B	0, −c	0, 0

trade with Europeans among North American Indian tribes, for instance.[45] Instead, an exogenous change, for the purposes of this article, also requires a change in society's broader understanding, such as a new focal point to shed light on a new choice.

A potential social entrepreneur would step forward only when he perceives that a change is not only what he expects, but also what other entrepreneurs expect and what the majority of society will come to expect. Even then, a potential social entrepreneur would only act in situations where he has a significant chance of successfully making the change by moving first. In other words, change agents want an assurance that other people expect the change to occur. A focal point can help people's expectations converge to bring about such change. To simplify the discussion, we can imagine an Assurance Game in which two farmers, acting as potential social entrepreneurs, must decide separately whether to initiate a change (Table 3.1):

- *Strategy A: To challenge the legal prohibition on rural land development and transfer*
- *Strategy B: Not to challenge the legal prohibition on rural land development and transfer.*
- a, c>0. a, c, and 0 are numbers used to describe payoffs to the two farmers. Each values the right to rural land development and transfer at the amount of a. Punishment by the government would cause a loss of c to a single challenger.

This game is an Assurance Game. If a potential social entrepreneur expects the other not to challenge the prohibition, he will not challenge the prohibition either, even if he prefers the change. This occurs because the potential social entrepreneur does not want to bear the punishment

[45] *See* Harold Demsetz (1967). Toward a theory of property rights, 57 *Am. Econ. Rev. Papers & Proc.* 347.

for challenging the law on his own, which comes at a loss of c for the single social entrepreneur who challenges the prohibition. The status quo is maintained if neither potential social entrepreneur challenges the prohibition, resulting in a gain of 0 for both parties. However, if a potential social entrepreneur expects the other party to challenge the prohibition, he will challenge the prohibition as well. When this occurs, the norm change will succeed and both will gain a from the change. As a result, the parties prefer that they both use strategies that bring about the change (A, A) rather than both using strategies that result in non-change (B, B). However, the optimal result may not occur because A is a riskier strategy than B. Choosing to challenge the prohibition might result in either a large profit or a loss, while choosing not to challenge the prohibition guarantees that there will be no loss. For this reason, both social entrepreneurs might choose not to challenge the prohibition despite the fact that each regards non-change as worse than change. Thus, the players face a problem of coordination – each needs to assure the other that he is going to play the riskier strategy and challenge the legal prohibition to induce the other to do the same.

A focal point can resolve this coordination problem. In making a decision, each player considers what choice the other would make. If both expect the other to choose strategy A, the result will be optimal for both parties. That is to say, to initiate a change, not only does a new profit opportunity need to exist, but the new opportunity should also be made salient as a focal point so that a potential change agent could reasonably expect others to share his expectation for change.

3.2.1.2 Application to the Shenzhen Case

Without a doubt, rural land development and transfer represented a lucrative new profit opportunity in Shenzhen, the first SEZ to pilot reform.[46] However, even though the Shenzhen government allowed villages to rent their land to investors to build factories, rural land development and transfer was still legally prohibited at that time. It was clear that breaking this legal prohibition would be a very profitable change. My interviews with village heads, government officials, and other participants shed light on how this change occurred.

A Hong Kong investor, after running his business in a village for several years, wanted to buy a plot to build his own house. Considering

[46] *See* Chapter 2, Section 2.1 for more details.

that his business required him to live in the village for more than 200 days a year, and he may have had a second family there, this need seemed very reasonable. Also, as a Hong Kong entrepreneur, he might have had a stronger sense of private property and a more acute sense of the changes occurring in Shenzhen and in China. The focal point created in the urban land-use reform in Shenzhen must have been clear to this entrepreneur: (1) land could be sold for money, a fact readily apparent to the Chinese central and local governments, especially the Shenzhen government; (2) old laws could be broken and revised in the reform era. The Hong Kong investor was very conscious of these factors in his decision to buy land from villages. He expected others to see the same trends that he did. The Hong Kong investor contacted the village co-op head to make his request. The village co-op head, who had done everything in his power to attract and satisfy outside investors, had made profits for the co-op from the early capitalization of rural land through joint ventures with outside investors. He was aware of the government reform of the urban land-use system and expected rural land-use reform to be the next step. As a result, the village co-op head approved this request and sold a plot to the Hong Kong investor, even though it was illegal to do so.

Social entrepreneurs included not only Hong Kong investors, but also other major players in the rural industrialization of Shenzhen. Government agencies responsible for investment approval and land administration, such as the Bureau of Land Administration ("BLA") and the Bureau of Investment Promotion ("BIP"), observed these types of situations and studied the legal and policy issues. These bureaus likely determined that the focal point of rural land development and transfer was so powerful that it would become a widespread trend. The old government housing allocation system had not been able to keep up with the explosive population increases. Directors of the bureaus were troubled by the problem of how to house their employees, and my interviews reveal that casual conversations with village leaders and other players often led to suggestions that village land could be used for employee housing.

In another example taken from these interviews, a land developer, who had leveled the hilly land in Shenzhen to build roads and other infrastructure for a village, asked the village for payment. Over a dinner conversation, the village head told the developer that the village had no money to pay him, but offered two hills in the village instead. The village head told the developer that if he leveled them, the land developer could have the land. While the land developer preferred a cash payment, he had little choice. Moreover, he was well aware of the emerging focal point through his contacts with village co-op heads, government officials, and Hong Kong investors in his land development businesses. As a result, he accepted this offer and built a luxury villa neighborhood in Shenzhen on the land he received as payment.

These types of land transactions encouraged other parties to buy and sell rural land. These parties included a village head who had managed all the transactions with Hong Kong investors and government agencies and wanted to develop and transfer some of the excess land he was allocated; an official in the BIP, who did not receive an apartment from the bureau but had money to spend on personal housing; other government employees who were eager to resolve their housing shortage after learning of this trend from friends in the BIP or BLA; and a migrant worker who made enough money to afford such housing.[47] Government employees participated so widely in rural land development and transfer that the Shenzhen government had to take special measures to address this situation in the 1980s.[48]

After this cluster of social entrepreneurs made the first move, their friends and relatives followed.[49] The social entrepreneurs were all influential people in their social networks and, thus, had much more weight in influencing the changing of norms.[50] Further transactions encouraged

47 Interview with a retired government official, in Nanshan District of Shenzhen City (March 13, 2012).

48 The Shenzhen government's declarations prohibiting its employees from participating in rural land development and transfer were often seen in the first pages of the Shenzhen SEZ Daily in the 1980s, a testament to the prevalence of the practice. The general rhetoric was that the government would build houses for its employees and that all government officers should stop building private houses on rural land by a fixed date. Punishments would be imposed on violators. The number of such declarations demonstrated, paradoxically, the limited enforcement and effect of the government's efforts. *See, e.g.*, "违章建私房、陈煌被撤职", "深圳特区报"1981年9月8日第1版 [*Building Houses Illegally, Chen Huang Being Fired from His Office*, SHENZHEN SEZ DAILY 1 (Sept. 8, 1981)]; "要制止任意乱建私房", "深圳特区报" 1982年12月27日第2版[*We Must Stop Building Private Houses Illegally*, SHENZHEN SEZ DAILY 2 (Dec. 27, 1982)]; "我市清理违章建私房取得成效", "深圳特区报"1984年2月20日第1版[*Our City Made Success in Stopping Private House Construction*, SHENZHEN SEZ DAILY, Feb. 20, 1984, at 1]; "市政府办公厅宣布继续违章乱建私房一律没收", "深圳特区报" 1985年4月3日第1版[*The Office of the City Government Declared that All Illegal Buildings would be Confiscated*, SHENZHEN SEZ DAILY 1 (April 3,1985)].

49 *See* Randal C. Picker (1997). Simple games in a complex world: A generative approach to the adoption of norms, 64 *U. CHI. L. REV.* 1225.

50 *See* Timur Kuran (1989). Sparks and prairie fires: A theory of unanticipated political revolution, 61 *PUB. CHOICE* 41.

more transactions, and this continued until the formation of a small-property market in Shenzhen, during which the focal point of rural land development and transfer overcame the legal prohibition and ultimately served to coordinate people's behaviors.

3.2.2 *Two Hawk-Dove Games of Market Operation*

3.2.2.1 A Hawk-Dove Game of the Demolition Risk

In 1999, one year after the 1998 LAL revision, the Shenzhen government initiated its campaign against rural land development and transfer, calling the rural buildings "*lishi yiliu weifa jianzhu*," or "historical illegal buildings." In 2004, the Shenzhen government established *lingdao xiaozu*, a group headed by the mayor and made up of directors of relevant government departments to deal with illegal rural land development and transfer. Later in 2009, the Shenzhen government established the Department of Land Use Monitoring ("DLUM"), which had branches in all fifty-seven sub-districts of Shenzhen.[51] Demolition of illegal buildings was often reported in the local newspapers. Still, the small-property market remained active and robust. Based on interviews with local farmers, buyers of the small-property houses, and government officials directly in charge of demolishing illegal buildings, I found that demolition cases were, in reality, rare and symbolic – for instance, the government seldom demolished finished buildings.

The focal point of rural land development and transfer plays an important role in the interactions between the Shenzhen government and farmers with regards to rural land development and transfer. The Shenzhen government hopes its threats are an effective signal to people to stop developing and transacting rural land. In turn, Shenzhen farmers hope the government will yield to the prevalent practice. Whether Shenzhen farmers would continue to develop and transfer rural land and whether the Shenzhen government would demolish the buildings if they did depends on each party's respective expectations. Their interactions can be explained by a Hawk-Dove Game, a general way of modeling any

[51] 深圳规划土地监察："我市查处违法建筑政策梳理"，2012年3月12日[Shenzhen Land Use Monitoring, *Review of the City Policies of Illegal Buildings*, (Mar. 12, 2012)], www.szpls.gov.cn/whkj/xxdy/201203/t20120312_71655.html (last visited December 9, 2009). For a comprehensive examination of the Shenzhen government's policies regarding small-property buildings, *see* Chapter 4.

Table 3.2 *A hawk-dove game of demolition*

		Player 2: Farmers	
		H_2	D_2
Player 1: Shenzhen Government	H_1	$-a, -d$	$b, 0$
	D_1	$0, c$	$(1-p)b, pc$

situation where an individual chooses between an aggressive or submissive strategy, as shown in Table 3.2:

- *Strategy H_1: Shenzhen government plays hawk and demolishes small-property buildings.*
- *Strategy D_1: Shenzhen government plays dove and does not demolish small-property buildings.*
- *Strategy H_2: Shenzhen farmers play hawk and fight against the Shenzhen government's demolition efforts.*
- *Strategy D_2: Shenzhen farmers play dove and accept the demolition of their small-property buildings without any resistance.*
- *a, b, c, d >0; a, b, c, d, and 0 are numbers used to describe the payoffs to the Shenzhen government and farmers. p is the probability of the government not enforcing the law.*

The starting point of this game is that small-property buildings have been built, resulting in the separation of legal rights and *de facto* control. Maintaining legal control over the land is valued at b for the government, while maintaining *de facto* control over the land is valued at c for the farmers. Assuming the probability for the farmers to maintain *de facto* control over the land without suffering legal enforcement from the government is p, the probability for the government to maintain legal control over the land would be $1-p$. Therefore the payoffs for the government and the farmers under the status quo would be $(1-p)b$ and pc. Under this *status quo*, the government was not ready to demolish the small-property buildings at the risk of conflict with the farmers, while the farmers were not ready to resist the demolition. The Shenzhen government and the farmers might wait for a change of situation that would give one party an advantage over the other, or they might negotiate with each other to share the benefits of developing and transferring rural land. This would not be a stable situation until the parties reached a deal and each party believed that the other would honor the deal.[52]

[52] A solution is provided in Chapter 4.

If the Shenzhen government played hawk to enforce the legal prohibition and the farmers were not prepared to fight the demolition efforts, the small-property buildings would be demolished. As a result, farmers would lose their *de facto* control, and their payoff would be 0; the government would gain its legal control over the land and its payoff is b.

On the other hand, if the farmers were willing to protect their buildings against government demolition and the Shenzhen government was not prepared for conflict with the farmers, small-property buildings would not be demolished. This would result in the ineffectiveness of the government's land use control, and the government's payoff would be 0. The farmers' payoff would be c, the *de facto* control over the land getting rid of the risk of legal enforcement.

If the government decided to demolish the small-property buildings at any cost, while the farmers were also ready to protect their buildings, the parties would have a conflict. At some point during the conflict, a winner would emerge and take control, while the loser would accept defeat. However, under this set of circumstances, both the winner and the loser would suffer some harm in the fighting.[53] Conflicts between both parties would cause loss in the amount of a to the government and a loss in the amount of d to the farmers.

If the Shenzhen government had played hawk to enforce the old law, it would incur a huge loss resulting from a direct clash with farmers. This loss would encompass social instability, which would discourage foreign investment, as well as fierce resistance from farmers when attempting to requisition their undeveloped and unsold land. In a country where local governments tend to seize villagers' land arbitrarily,[54] it is at first puzzling that the Shenzhen government has not been able to deter illegal rural land development and transfer. However, upon closer scrutiny, it is clear that the enforcement costs for the Shenzhen government against the small-property market are unusually high. Shenzhen farmers have both the political and social resources to inflict large costs to the local government, since they have much stronger political and social connections than farmers in other areas of China. Shenzhen farmers have become the wealthiest farmers in China by making money from the land over which they have maintained control, with the accompanying political influence. The Chinese government,

[53] Sudgen, *supra* note 39, at 62–63.

[54] Josh Chin, *China's Blood-Stained Property Map*, Wall St. J., (Oct. 29, 2010), http://blogs.wsj.com/chinarealtime/2010/10/29/chinas-blood-stained-property-map.

both at the central and at the local level, has also held prosperous Shenzhen villages as the shining example of China's successful economic reform. All the former supreme leaders of China in the reform era, Deng Xiaoping, Jiang Zemin, and Hu Jintao, visited villages in Shenzhen. For instance, in 1984, during his first southern tour after designating Shenzhen as the first SEZ, Deng visited the village of Yumin and viewed the farmers' two-story houses as an indication of the success of his "reform and opening-up" policy.[55] In another symbolic example, hundreds of houses built by local farmers stand at the entrance of the village of Nanling, behind a huge portrait of the former Chinese President Hu Jintao, who visited the village twice. In addition, several village heads are members of the NPC or the Provincial People's Congress.

What's more, many Shenzhen farmers have family overseas, who fled to Hong Kong before 1980 and became residents there. These *huaqiao,* or overseas Chinese, have access to overseas newspapers and other public media and thus can inflict great reputational cost to the Shenzhen government and even the Chinese central government. The influence of overseas Chinese was amply demonstrated by a situation in Wukan, a village two hundred kilometers from Shenzhen, at the end of 2011. The government of Guangdong province, to which Shenzhen belongs, gave in to key demands of protesting villagers after a nearly two-week standoff with police. The government agreed in a rare compromise to release detainees and return some land to farmers.[56] During the villagers' confrontation with the government, their overseas families and friends, mostly located in Hong Kong, gave timely support by donating food and other supplies and, most importantly, by mobilizing wide overseas media attention, without which Wukan would have been just another voiceless village of several thousand landless farmers.

Shenzhen is an icon of China's market economy. Since 1978, the Chinese government has tried to maintain a policy of "reform and opening-up" to attract investment and support from overseas Chinese. If legal enforcement were to result in confrontation with local villagers,

[55] 梁灵光："陪同小平同志首次南巡"，"广东党史"1997年第2期[LIANG LINGGUANG, ACCOMPANYING COMRADE XIAOPING'S FIRST SOUTHERN TOUR, GUANGDONG PARTY HISTORY, NO. 2 (1997), at 6].

[56] *See, e.g.,* Andrews Jacobs, Residents Vote in Chinese Village at Center of Protest, *N.Y. Times*, (February 2, 2012), www.nytimes.com/2012/02/02/world/asia/residents-vote-in-chinese-village-at-center-of-protest.html; Michael Wines; A Village in Revolt Could Be a Harbinger for China, *N.Y. Times*, (December 26, 2011), www.nytimes.com/2011/12/26/world/asia/in-china-the-wukan-revolt-could-be-a-harbinger.html.

the Shenzhen government would not dare take forceful action, since the government cannot afford to acquire a reputation for repression. In the past three decades, the Shenzhen government has requisitioned a large amount of rural land from villagers, but has managed to avoid bloodshed by paying the villagers compensation higher than the market value. It is widely reported that a village redevelopment plan initiated by the government in 2009 created multiple village millionaires.[57] In addition, for the farmers, a direct conflict with the government would result in the loss of their small-property buildings, additional fines, and criminal prosecution if they were to use violence against the government. As a result, both parties prefer to avoid (H_1, H_2).

We can further analyze this situation by noting that both the Shenzhen government and the farmers would choose to play hawk if the other party chose to play dove and would choose to play dove if the other party chose to play hawk. The equilibrium would be either (H_1, D_2) or (D_1, H_2). However, the political and economic changes in Shenzhen made rural land development and transfer the focal point. The Shenzhen government has tried to change ordinary people's expectations through selective enforcement to signal that laws will continue to be strictly enforced. But even these selective cases, rather than signaling strict legal enforcement, often merely serve to show the Shenzhen government the power of the social resources a rural land user can mobilize to defend his "rights" of development and transaction. The key is the prevalence of the focal point of rural land development and transfer. Even government employees who enforced the laws did not agree with the legal prohibition, and they often discounted the effect of legal enforcement. For example, a government enforcement officer reported often told farmers, "The leader of the Shenzhen government required me to enforce the laws. So don't do these things in the daytime. But I have no obligation to watch you 24 hours. [It is] just a campaign, which will cease soon." Since rural land development and transfer served as a focal point, the equilibrium became (D_1, H_2), and the legal prohibition was not enforced. Demolition cases were rare and symbolic in Shenzhen, and the small-property market continued to expand despite the threat of demolition from the Shenzhen government.

57 南方都市报编著："岗厦涅槃" [SOUTHERN METROPOLIS DAILY ED. *The Rebirth of Gangxia* (2009)].

3.2.2.2 A Hawk-Dove Game of the Contract Risk

In addition to the risk of government demolition, we can also model transaction risks using a Hawk-Dove Game. Because the small-property houses have no legal titles, none of the transactions are recognized or protected by the government. A seller could refuse to surrender possession of the illegal buildings to the buyer or could revoke the contract at any time. Yet, buyers from all over the country still buy small-property apartments. Surprisingly, on the small-property market, several formal documents are widely used, which use professional legal terms and constitute a form of "legal magic." In the following part, I analyze the legal implications of the formal documents and apply a Hawk-Dove Game model to explain why the legally-void contracts are still obeyed, taking into consideration the social meaning of these formal documents in the bargaining between contract parties as well as the specific circumstances.

The Legal Magic Compared to other informal transactions, such as drug or organ transactions, which are more removed from formal laws, the involvement of government-recognized village co-ops and lawyers confers an aura of legality on illegal rural real estate transactions. This phenomenon is a form of "legal magic." For instance, a seal from a village co-op company costs a buyer 6,000 RMB, while a testimony from a lawyer costs 500 RMB. In some cases, privately-made real estate certificates and certificates of honorable villager-ship are also used. The question is whether these documents have any legal effect beyond casting an aura of legality on the transaction.

Contract of Cooperative House-Construction Cooperative house-construction is a mechanism where a group of individuals pool their money and construct a multi-apartment building together. In the end, each person receives an apartment. In the 1980s and 1990s, the centralized system of housing allocation could not supply enough houses to people, and cooperative house-building was encouraged as a way to provide housing. Employees of a government agency or a company could form a co-op. The government agency or the company would collect money from its employees, apply for a plot from the government, build houses, and allocate one unit to each contributor. There has been a revival of the idea of cooperative house-construction in recent years, since houses on the formal market are too expensive, and the practice is viewed as a cheaper way to own houses by avoiding payments to big real estate companies. Cooperative house-construction is not prohibited, and is theoretically feasible.

However, it is well-established within the legal profession that the cooperative development of rural land is still considered to be a way of developing and transferring rural land, which directly defies the LAL. Therefore, it does not seem that the term "cooperative house-construction" officially camouflages the illegality of rural house sales, which would help explain why most transactions adopt contracts of cooperative house-building. Since contracts of cooperative house-building cannot make small-property house transactions legitimate in the eyes of the law, this raises the question of what function these kinds of contracts serve.

Village Co-Op Seal, Lawyer Testimony, Private Real Estate Certificate, etc. Village co-ops manage the land within the villages and issue dividends to their villager shareholders. The co-op company, which serves as the core of a village community, also builds roads and other public facilities within the village. A village co-op seal on the sales contract is an endorsement of the contract and is widely used in small-property transactions. Village co-ops are often one party to small-property transactions, and they sign and seal the contracts. In other situations, such as houses developed by individual villagers or outside investors, the village co-op charges to affix its seal on the sales contract. However, from a legal perspective, the village co-op seal means nothing because the development and transfer of rural land are prohibited and cannot be legalized by a village co-op's endorsement.

Lawyer testimony is also nearly always part of such transactions. A lawyer testifies that the transaction is made according to both parties' real intentions and is consistent with the principle of freedom of contract. As there is no centralized system for keeping small-property records, the lawyer typically keeps a copy of all transaction documents on file, to be available for reference. If a buyer wants to sell the purchased house, he must surrender all the documents to the lawyer, who would then make another file for the new buyer. In one law firm, the earliest record can be traced back to 2003.[58] The lawyer testimony says nothing about the illegality of the transaction, which might give the parties the impression of the transaction's legality due to the lawyer's perceived authority. As a result, the Lawyers' Association of Guangdong, the province to which

[58] Interview with a law firm partner, in Futian District of Shenzhen City (April 5, 2012).

Shenzhen belongs, has forbidden its members to provide testimony for transactions of rural houses. In reality, this prohibition is only effective on large law firms, and many small law firms continue to provide this service. In some other cases, privately made certificates play a role in securing the transactions. For instance, some real estate developers issue certificates to buyers. These certificates look very similar to official certificates, even including unique numbers for each apartment.

If neither village co-op seals, nor lawyer testimony, nor privately-made real estate certificates can make these illegal sales contracts legal, why are they so popular and why are buyers willing to pay for them? What is the magic of these legal constructs? The answer comes from outside the law.

The Game In this contract game, the issue is the effectiveness of the contract. Both parties could claim that a contract is legally void if that result benefits him. In recent decades in China, the prices of small-property houses have increased several-fold, due to increasing housing demand and rocketing prices on the legal housing market. Thus, sellers often have incentives to go to court to void the contract. The courts would refuse to enforce the contract, and the seller would have the right to return the buyer's money and get his house back. In Beijing, one rural house transaction case caught nationwide media attention when a seller wanted her house back for the increased value after the transaction.[59] According to a judge in Bao'An district court of Shenzhen city, as of the time of interview (May 15, 2013), similar disputes were still relatively few in number, but were on the rise.[60] The courts in Shenzhen declined to adjudicate most of the cases involving small-property transactions. According to a senior judge in the Shenzhen city intermediate court, Shenzhen courts declined to accept such cases because they involved a policy matter for which the Shenzhen city government was actively exploring solutions.[61] In Table 3.3, I apply a Hawk-Dove Game model

[59] 王秋实："宋庄画家村小产权房续：艺术家索要48万房屋差价"，"京华时报" 2008年1月4日[Qiushi Wang, Small-Property Houses in the Painters' Village Continued: The Painter Asked for 480,000 for Difference in Prices, JINGHUA DAILY, (Jan. 4, 2008)], www.chinanews.com/estate/tswq/news/2008/01-04/1123147.shtml. See also Chapter 6, section 6.2.2 for more details.

[60] Transcript of Xia Linfei's Interview with a judge, in Bao'An district court of Shenzhen city (May 15, 2013).

[61] Interview with a judge, in Shenzhen intermediate court (July 2, 2012). Chapter six utilizes more recently data revealing two approaches of the Shenzhen court: one is declining to accept such cases; the other is confirming the illegality of small-property contracts while intentionally leaving the consequence of illegality unelaborated.

Table 3.3 *A hawk-dove game of contract effect*

		Player 2: Buyer	
		H_2	D_2
Player 1: Seller	H_1	−b, −c	a, 0
	D_1	0, a	a/2, a/2

to analyze the parties' choices of whether to void a contract. The purpose is to explain why both parties typically honor contracts detailing small-property transactions in most of the situations in Shenzhen.

- *H_1: Void the contract after the value of the house has increased.*
- *D_1: Do not void the contract, despite the fact that the value of the house has increased.*
- *H_2: Insist on the binding effect of the contract after the value of the house has increased.*
- *D_2: Do not insist on the binding effect of the contract after the value of the house has increased.*
- *$a, b, c>0$; $b>c$. a, b, c and 0 are numbers used to describe the payoffs to both players. Conflicts would cause losses to both parties at the amount of b and c, respectively. If one is a hawk while the other is a dove, the dove retreats leaving the increased value for the hawk.*

The starting point of this game is that the value of small-property houses has multiplied since the occurrence of the contract, but it is unclear which party will receive the increased value, which is in the amount of a. Both parties can choose whether to play an aggressive hawk strategy or a submissive dove strategy. If the seller insists on voiding the contract to get the increased value, while the buyer is not ready to fight, the seller will receive a payoff in the amount of a. In contrast, if the seller immediately concedes defeat when the buyer shows any inclination to fight, the seller's payoff would be 0, while the buyer would receive the increased value in the amount of a.

The most desirable outcome for each party comes from playing hawk against the other party's dove. If the seller expects the buyer to yield to his request to void the contract, he will play hawk and gain a, the increased value of the real estate, if the buyer does yield to the seller's request. If the buyer expects the seller to yield to his insistence on the binding effect of the contract, he will play hawk and gain a if the seller does agree to the effectiveness of the contract. The buyer would keep all the increased value of the real estate. Another alternative is that the buyer and the seller could both play dove and share the increased value of the real estate. Neither party will gain if they play dove against the other's hawk. Therefore, both parties prefer an outcome where they play hawk against the other party's dove. However, the worst outcome would be that the seller plays hawk, insisting that the contract is void, against the buyer's hawk, insisting on the binding effect of the contract. The cost of these disputes would be high for both parties.

The Cost of Hawk-Hawk If the seller insists on voiding the contract, the buyer might resort to private sanctions, since the Shenzhen courts are likely to decline to hear such cases. Some might wonder how serious these private sanctions could be, considering that sellers are usually local villagers or land developers, while buyers are often members of the migrant population, who can only afford an apartment on the informal market. It is true that local villagers and land developers are both wealthier and more powerful than the newcomers who can only afford the small-property apartments. However, that does not mean that sellers are more likely to win in a hawk-hawk situation. Sellers view the dispute as just one apartment in a building of hundreds, and they have made money from the transaction with the buyer. The seller could gain more by revoking the contract, but the marginal gain from this move is relatively low. For buyers, the price is higher, as the apartment is their home and is a substantial investment of their money. While buyers are not typically wealthy or powerful, they do possess "weapons of the weak."[62] As one buyer told me, "[A]s far as the seller wanted to stay in Shenzhen, he would not dare void the contract. I know where he lived and who his family is."[63] To make private sanction an effective deterrence, a party has to make sure that he can locate the person he wants to sanction. The legally void documents play an important role here. In contracts of cooperative house-construction, sellers' addresses are written clearly and are easy to verify. It might be difficult for an outsider to know the history of the transactions involving the real estate in question, but this does not matter as far as the village co-op is willing to endorse the contract, which would be an implicit promise that the village co-op will be responsible if there are any conflicts regarding rights to the real estate. Lawyers are outsiders, but they are also professionals paid for their testimony. Regardless of the contents of the testimony, the bottom-line

62 *See* James Scott (1985). *Weapons of the Weak: Everyday Forms of Peasant Resistance.*
63 Interview with a buyer, in Bao'An District of Shenzhen City (November 14, 2011).

is that a lawyer may not participate in contract fraud. Moreover, lawyers' services are often localized and are not easily relocated. Therefore, the village co-op's seal, lawyer testimony, and other privately made documents are not a way to legalize the informal sales, but they do serve as a way to reveal information regarding the transactions and local parties.

In addition, buyers within the same buildings find it easy to unite to take action against the seller. Disputes with buyers would also expose the sellers' business to public attention, which would damage his reputation and might make his business an easy target for the local government's selective legal enforcement. As a last resort, the buyer might report the dispute to the local government. In such a case, the seller can no longer ensure that the Shenzhen government will continue to turn a blind eye to his illegal business.[64] In W village in Shenzhen, villagers found their co-op's share of profits from a small-property project was significantly lower than it used to be, and they blocked the entrance to the sold small-property building to ask for more money from the developer. In response, buyers, most of whom were from outside of Shenzhen, hung out a banner saying, "Who stole my house? I want to go home! Give back my home!"[65] The conflict turned to a "mass incident," and in the end, the village co-op leaders were forced to assure buyers that the apartments

64 The illegality of the small-property business includes two complementary parts: illegal land development and illegal transfer. As discussed in Section 3.2.2.1, through the years, the Shenzhen city government has taken measures to demolish small-property buildings, which are called illegal buildings by the government. *See also* Chapter 4. In the illegal transfer of real estate, including both land and apartments, sellers and buyers are not usually subject to punishment. However, the risk of legal punishment does exist, although it rarely occurs. For example, a local villager was prosecuted for "illegal transfer of land use rights," a crime defined in Article 228 of the Chinese Criminal Law as illegal transfer of land use rights "with the purpose of making profits and in violation of land administration laws." *See* Chapter 5 for more details. A red-head document issued by the Yantian district government of Shenzhen city instructs the Yantian Division of the Shenzhen Bureau of Public Security to "assist other government departments in dealing with illegal buildings, strike hardly violent resistance to legal enforcement, and investigate and punish suspect criminal activities including illegal fundraising (*jizi*), illegal investment and sales of small-property apartments, and illegal printing and alteration of real estate certificates." 深圳市盐田区人民政府："关于印发盐田区查处违法建筑销售行为专项整治工作方案的通知"（深盐府办[2009]58号）[Shenzhen Yantian District People's Government, *Notice on the Issue of Work Plan on Investigating and Punishing Sales of Illegal Buildings*, No. 58, 2009].

65 陈小瑛："深圳小产权房冲突祸起集体土地贱卖 危局待解"，"华夏时报" 2013年4月20日 [Xiaoying Chen, *A Crisis to Be Resolved: Conflicts of Shenzhen Small-Property Houses Were Caused by Cheap Sales of Collective Land*, HUAXIA DAILY (April 20, 2013)], http://finance.sina.com.cn/china/dfjj/20130420/001615212277.shtml.

were theirs because they had paid for them and that they should not worry that their apartments would be taken away."[66]

In cases involving an individual buyer, the more powerful sellers might still need to use coercive measures, typically violence, to regain possession of the contested real estate, which would trigger criminal punishment from the government. For example, a group of villagers were prosecuted and sentenced to prison for kidnapping and beating a buyer of their small-property real estate.[67]

In short, the hawk-hawk scenario is costly even more so to the sellers, so in the chart above, b>c.

The Focal Point and the Choice of the Equilibrium There are two equilibria in the Hawk-Dove Game between buyers and sellers: (1) the seller plays hawk, while the buyer plays dove and (2) the seller plays dove, while the buyer plays hawk. Given these possibilities, what matters in determining the outcome is what each party expects the other to do. In short, there is room for a focal point to influence both parties' expectations. As previously discussed, rural land development and transfer are widely recognized in Shenzhen. The various documents involved in the transactions, such as contracts, lawyer testimony, and the village co-op's seal, serve as evidence and a reminder of this fact. Thus, the seller would expect the buyer to insist on the binding effect of the contract, even though the contract is not legally enforceable.

The buyers, fully aware of this focal point, would expect the seller not to void the contract, and they would choose to fight if the seller tried to void the contract. The buyer is also confident that he would be able to mobilize other members of the community who share this focal point to fight with the seller under the worst-case scenario.[68] Buyers often bond with each other to form a powerful community, which can effectively sanction sellers who breach their promises. These communities are so powerful because colleagues, relatives, and friends often buy apartments

66 *See* Chapter 5. 67 *Id.*

68 Consider the medieval Iceland case: For several hundred years, Iceland had functioning courts with no formal or informal enforcement powers. During this time, courts issued rulings to resolve disputes and proclaimed appropriate penalties, but there was no executive arm – police or sheriffs – to execute these judgments. Nonetheless, there was private enforcement of court decrees, carried out by the kin of the judicial winner. The explanation, according to McAdams, is that, "Each party expects the one declared by the court as being 'in the right' to play the Hawk strategy – enforcing the remedy with violence, if necessary." McAdams, *supra* note 8, at 1682.

in the same building. During my interviews, buyers of small-property houses repeatedly insisted that they were not worried about the risks of not having legal titles because many of their friends lived in the same building. The sellers themselves may inadvertently facilitate such communities. For instance, sellers of small-property houses may require a former customer's recommendation to permit an outsider to buy an apartment. While this may reduce the seller's uncertainty in bringing in an unknown buyer, this requirement also increases the solidarity of the buyer community, making them more powerful in enforcing their contracts against the sellers. In a survey conducted by the Shenzhen government, when asked whether they considered the risks of not having legal titles when they bought small-property houses, a common response was that buyers did not worry because so many others have bought small-property houses. As a result, an equilibrium occurs where the seller plays dove and the buyer plays hawk.

3.3 Conclusion

This chapter challenges the conventional view of the necessity of formal property rights in a market economy by providing a concrete example from first-hand fieldwork in which an impersonal market has developed in the absence of legal titles. Second, this chapter provides a new perspective on law and economic development by introducing and applying research on coordination games and focal points to this real-life situation.[69] Finally, it contributes a significant and contemporary case study from the real world to theories of coordination games and focal points, which have, to date, mostly relied on laboratory experiments.

For a long time, property rights in developing countries remained a mystery, since we did not fully understand the dynamics between property rights and market transition, and we did not have a proper theoretical approach to explain why many titling programs sponsored by the World Bank and other international aid organizations did not work.[70]

[69] Professor Daniel Fitzpatrick adopts a similar approach to explain property rights in developing countries in a working paper uploaded to the NYU website in October 2014. *See* Daniel Fitzpatrick, *Getting to Coase: Equilibrium and the Institution of Property* (Working Paper) (www.law.nyu.edu/sites/default/files/upload_documents/Daniel%20Fitzpatrick%20-%20Global%20Fellows%20Forum.pdf).

[70] *See, e.g.*, Daniel W. Bromley (2009). Formalising property relations in the developing world: The wrong prescription for the wrong malady, 26 *Land Use Pol'y* 20; David

One reason for this is the failure to fully incorporate the historical, political, and other contextual factors that not only structure the interactions of relevant parties but also influence their expectations, into our analysis of their incentives. Therefore our strategies to change their incentives are often misguided. Modeling the formation and operation of a market as coordination games presents a framework that incorporates contextual factors into the interactive analysis of relative incentives. In coordination games, the focal point theory explains one way that contextual factors influence relevant parties' expectations of each other. This chapter argues that the incorporation of these theories provides a more powerful and nuanced explanation of property rights in developing countries.

This chapter's analysis has substantial explanatory force in the so-called "China problem," or why China has enjoyed several decades of rapid economic growth with a weak legal system.[71] Nobel Laureate Ronald Coase and Ning Wang co-authored a book to address the question of how China became capitalist in 2012.[72] Joseph Stiglitz and David Kennedy co-edited a book titled *Law and Economics with Chinese Characteristics* to understand the China mystery in 2013.[73] Two opposing terms are used by *The Economist* magazine in recent years to depict "capitalism with Chinese characteristics:" "bamboo capitalism," i.e., capitalism grown bottom-up from China; and state capitalism, i.e., the state's visible hand as the driver of China's economic success.[74]

Undoubtedly, many of China's crucial economic reforms were initiated by entrepreneurs from the bottom up. Examples include the invention of the household responsibility system (HRS) in Xiaogang Village of An'hui province, which replaced the inefficient collective farms in

Kennedy (2011). Some caution about property rights as a recipe for economic development, 1 *Acct. Econ. & L.* 1; Geoffrey Payne, Alain Durand-Lasserve and Carole Rakodi (2009). The limits of land titling and home ownership, 21 *Env't & Urbanization* 443.

71 *See, e.g.*, Donald C. Clarke (2003). Economic development and the rights hypothesis: The China problem, 51 *Am. J. Comp. L.* 89; Victor Nee and Sonja Opper (2012) *Capitalism from Below: Markets and Institutional Change in China*; Frank K. Upham (2009). From Demsetz to Deng: Speculations on the implications of Chinese growth for law and development theory, 41 *N.Y.U J. Int'l L. & Pol.* 551.

72 Ronald Coase AND Ning Wang, *How China Became Capitalist* (2012).

73 *Law and Economics with Chinese Characteristics: Institutions for Promoting Development in the Twenty-First Century* (David Kennedy & Joseph Stiglitz eds., 2013).

74 *China's Economy: Bamboo Capitalism*, ECONOMIST (March 10, 2011), www.economist.com/node/18332610; *China's State Capitalism: Not Just Tilting at Windmills*, ECONOMIST (October 4, 2012), www.economist.com/node/21564235.

China in the 1980s;[75] the emergence of the township and village enterprises (TVEs), which was the engine for economic growth in China in the 1980s;[76] and the flourishing of private enterprises (PEs), which have provided many job opportunities for China.[77] There is one character these reforms share: All of them have developed in the absence of a legal mandate.

However, it would be unfair to ignore the Chinese government's contributions to these economic reforms. Entrepreneurs are everywhere and in every age – why did the HRS, TVEs and PEs fail to emerge in Mao's era, but rather emerged in the reform era? Thus a pure bottom-up explanation cannot resolve the so-called China problem. A plausible speculation from this study is that the focal point of economic development created by the Chinese government in 1978 and further strengthened in the following years provides the missing link. As in the Old Testament, God said, "[L]et there be light; and there was light." Deng Xiaoping made market reform a focal point for coordinating people's expectations in the absence of a corresponding legal regime.

This chapter also has broad implications for research on law and economic development. Scholars have referred to exchanges of untitled real property in their studies of Vietnam property reform,[78] squatters in Hong Kong,[79] and informal housing in Peru,[80] the Brazilian Amazon,[81] and the US frontier.[82] Systematic case studies of informal real estate

[75] *See, e.g.,* Justin Lin (1988). The household responsibility system in China's agricultural reform: A theoretical and empirical study, 36 *Econ. Dev. Cult. Changes* S199.

[76] *See, e.g.,* Louis Putterman (1997). On the past and future of China's township and village-owned enterprises, 25 *World Dev.* 1639.

[77] *See, e.g., China's Third Economic Transformation: The Rise of the Private Economy* (Ross Garnaut and Ligang Song eds., 2004).

[78] Annette M. Kim, (2004). A market without the 'right' property rights - Ho Chi Minh City, Vietnam's newly-emerged private real estate market. 12 *Econ. Transition* 275.

[79] *See* Alan Smart (1986). Invisible real estate: investigations into the squatter property market, 10 *Int'l J. Urb. & Regional Res.* 29; Alan Smart (2001). Unruly places: Urban governance and the persistence of illegality in Hong Kong's urban squatter areas, 103 *Am. Anthropologist* 30.

[80] *See* Hernando de Soto (1989). *The Other Path.*

[81] *See* Lee J. Alston, Gary D. Libecap and Bernardo Mueller (1999). *Titles, Conflict, and Land Use: The Development of Property Rights and Land Reform on the Brazilian Amazon Frontier.*

[82] *See* Terry L. Anderson and P. J. Hill (1978). An American experiment in anarcho-capitalism: The not so wild, wild west, 3 *J. Libertarian Stud.* 9.

markets around the world would greatly enrich our understandings of law and economic development. Structuring these informal property markets as coordination games and delving into historical and political backgrounds to understand the contextual factors that shaped bargaining would deepen our understanding of how to build modern market economies in developing countries.

4

Small Property, Adverse Possession, and Optional Law

"How to deal with these illegal buildings?" I frequently was asked in my interviews with government officials in Shenzhen. To demolish them has proved to be a mission impossible; to legalize them would encourage more illegal buildings. This binary choice seems difficult. The complication is that the small-property problem is a multiple period, multi-person game rather than a one-period, two-party game. In a pure one-period, two-party game, compromise is often a better strategy than conflict between both parties. In the real world, the government does not want to compromise with an individual owner due to concerns about the consequences in the future: It would encourage other owners to develop their land illegally, and even this particular owner to develop this particular plot illegally again in the future.

This logic also explains why most countries do not allow adverse possession against the government. However, adverse possession against the government does *de facto* exist all over the world and a simple "law enforcement" strategy does not work.[1] Adverse possession is a useful framework for thinking about the small-property problem. Traditionally, our thinking about adverse possession is who should have the title – the adverse possessor or the original owner? This is also consistent with our understanding of the structure of legal entitlements before Calabresi and Melamed published their landmark piece "Property Rule, Liability Rule, and Inalienability: One View of the Cathedral" in 1972, in which they developed a framework ("cathedral") of legal entitlements and in particular introduced the concept of liability rules.[2] In 1985, Thomas Merrill suggested protecting an original owner's property in adverse possession

[1] *See, e.g.*, Justus Reid Weiner, *The Global Epidemic of Illegal Building and Demolitions: Implications for Jerusalem*, JERUSALEM CENTER PUB. AFF., May 15, 2003, www.jcpa.org/jl/vp498.htm.

[2] Guido Calabresi and A. Douglas Melamed (1972). Property rules, liability rules, and inalienability: One view of the cathedral, 85 *Harvard L. Rev.* 1089.

with liability rules.[3] Since then, the cathedral of legal entitlements has been further refurbished and expanded. In particular, Ian Ayres and his coauthors have reconceptualized liability rules with option theory: there are both "call option" liability rules and "put option" liability rules.[4] This chapter frames the Chinese small-property problem as adverse possession against the government in light of this expanded cathedral of legal entitlements. My argument is that the allocation of initial options matters at least as much as the allocation of initial entitlements and that options should be granted to parties that have the best information to make decisions. In the small-property case, these are the individual owners of small-property houses.

Section 4.1 frames the case as an adverse possession question, applies Ayres' structure of legal entitlements to analyze adverse possession, and introduces his best-chooser principle to resolve the small-property problem. Section 4.2 discusses Shenzhen government's policies in addressing small-property houses, categorizes them into six rules of legal entitlements, and compares their effects. Section 4.3 concludes and considers the role of options in resolving the tension between informal property rights and formal property law in developing countries.

4.1 Framing the Question: Adverse Possession in Ayres' Cathedral

4.1.1 The Concept: From Possession of Things to Possession of Rights

Adverse possession is a method by which someone, without the owner's permission, acquires a new root of title to property already owned. The adverse possessor acquires title in this fashion by possessing the property until the statute of limitations for the relevant action by the title owner to recover possession has run out.[5] American law often requires that possession must be exclusive, open and notorious, actual, continuous, and adverse under a claim of right.[6]

[3] Thomas W. Merrill (1985). Property Rules, Liability Rules and Adverse Possession, 79 *Nw. U. L. Rev.* 1122.

[4] Ian Ayres (2005). *Optional Law: The Structure of Legal Entitlements*; Ian Ayres (1997). Protecting Property with Puts, 32 *Val. U. L. Rev.* 793; Ian Ayres and J. M. Balkin (1996). Legal Entitlements as Auctions: Property Rules, Liability Rules, and Beyond, 106 *Yale L.J.* 703; Ian Ayres and Eric Talley (1995). Solomonic Bargaining: Dividing a Legal Entitlement to Facilitate Coasean Trade, 104 *Yale L.J.* 1027.

[5] Henry E. Smith and Thomas W. Merrill (2010). *The Oxford Introductions to U.S. Law: Property* 34.

[6] *Id.* at 35.

The concept of adverse possession can be extended beyond the possession of things. For example, the revival of research on adverse possession in the 1980s was attributed partly to a decision of the California Supreme Court, *Warsaw v. Chicago Metallic Ceilings, Inc.*, which was about prescriptive easement.[7] Prescription is "the effect of lapse of time in creating or extinguishing property interests."[8] It is based on the theory that if "one makes non-permissive use of another's land, and the landowner fails to prevent such use, such acquiescence is conclusive evidence that the user is rightful."[9] A prescriptive easement is created "by such use of land, for the period of prescription, as would be privileged if an easement existed, provided its use is (1) adverse, and (2) for the period of prescription, continuous and uninterrupted."[10]

Merrill calls prescriptive easement a first cousin of adverse possession.[11] Prescriptive easement and adverse possession are different in that the former involves nonpossessory use of property, which ripens into an easement, and the latter possession of property, which ripens into a fee simple. Though the nonpossessory nature of an easement generally means that the continuity and exclusivity elements must be interpreted differently, the same legal requirements apply to both adverse possession and prescriptive easements. Scholars often do not distinguish too sharply between the rules of legal entitlements under adverse possession and prescriptive easement. Probably due to the more significant position of adverse possession in property law, the discussions of "the effect of lapse of time in creating or extinguishing property interests" are discussed more often under the framework of adverse possession.

In essence, village collectives own rural land, but cannot develop or sell it to other entities or individuals for nonagricultural uses or real estate development. Only the state can convert rural land to urban land and sell it to real estate developers. In such a case, villagers are entitled to compensation equal to the agricultural value of the land. Therefore, the right to develop, a crucial stick of property rights, has been detached from collective ownership of rural land and added onto state property rights.[12] Individual villagers and village collectives have the legal rights to possess their village land, but no legal rights to develop the land. Thus, small property rights are the result of adverse possession of the

[7] Merrill, *supra* note 3.
[8] William G. Ackerman and Shane T. Johnson (1996). Outlaws of the past: A Western perspective on prescription and adverse possession, 31 *Land & Water L. Rev.* 79.
[9] *Id.* [10] *Id.* at 86–87. [11] Merrill, *supra* note 3, at 1124, footnote 11.
[12] *See* Chapter 1 for more details about state monopoly on rural-urban land conversion.

government's rights to develop rural land. It is not exactly a prescriptive easement as defined in either American law or Chinese law. However, it is prescription, that is, prescriptive acquisition of incorporeal interests.[13] If we could discuss prescriptive easement under the framework of adverse possession, it is also proper to discuss the small-property case under the same framework. Both cases have to deal with the tension between the *de facto* possession and the *de jure* rights and to resolve whether *de facto* possession could lead to *de jure* rights with the lapse of time.

4.1.2 Property Rule, Liability Rule and Adverse Possession

As Calabresi and Melamed write, the first issue that must be faced by any legal system is one we call the problem of "entitlement."[14] Whenever a state is presented with the conflicting interests of two or more people, or two or more groups of people, it must decide which side to favor. Moreover, the state must decide not only which side wins but also the kind of protection to grant. Calabresi and Melamed define three types of entitlements: entitlements protected by property rules, entitlements protected by liability rules, and inalienable entitlements.[15] An entitlement is protected by a property rule to the extent that someone who wishes to remove the entitlement from its holder must buy it from him in a voluntary transaction in which the seller agrees upon the value of the entitlement.[16] Property rules protect entitlements by deterring nonconsensual takings. Whenever someone may destroy the initial entitlement if he is willing to pay an objectively determined value for it, the entitlement is protected by a liability rule. Liability rules protect entitlements by compensating the entitlement holder if such takings do occur.[17]

Applied to adverse possession disputes, the state can choose among four different rules (Table 4.1).

- Rule 1: the state prohibits adverse possession – OO has the title, which cannot be taken nonconsensually.
- Rule 2: OO has the title, but AP can take it by paying compensation.
- Rule 3: the state grants title to AP without requirements of compensation to OO.
- Rule 4: the state grants title to AP, but OO can take the title back by compensating AP.

13 Ackerman and Johnson, *supra* note 8, at 87–88.
14 Calabresi and Melamed, *supra* note 2, at 1090–1092. 15 *Id.* 16 *Id.*
17 Ayres, Optional Law, *supra* note 4, at 5.

Table 4.1 *Calabresi and Melamed's Two-by-Two Box applied to adverse possession*[18]

	Method of protection	
Initial Entitlement	Property Rule	Liability Rule
Original Owner ("OO")	Rule 1	Rule 2
Adverse Possessor ("AP")	Rule 3	Rule 4

The Calabresi and Melamed categorization has dominated the discussions of legal entitlements – scholars have discussed different aspects of these rules, tried to expand their contents, and even invented new rules. Among many others, Ayres significantly expanded the content of liability rules by introducing option theory into this field.[19] Options are defined by identifying who has the option, whether the option is to buy (a call) or to sell (a put), and the price of exercising the option.[20] A call option is an option to buy. The option holder can force a sale at the exercise price even if the seller does not want to sell. According to Ayres, traditional liability rules give potential takers a call option to take. A liability rule gives at least one party an option to take an entitlement nonconsensually and pay the entitlement owner some exercise price. Once the traditional liability rules were reconceived as granting a potential taker a call option, it became almost inevitable to think about put-option rules. A put option is an option to sell. While call options give the option holder the choice of whether to pay a non-negotiated amount, put options give the option holder the choice of whether to be paid a non-negotiated amount. Call options when exercised give rise to "forced sales"; put options give rise to "forced purchases."

Applied to adverse possession disputes again, the possibility of put options suggests two additional rules:

- Rule 5: the state grants title to AP, but also gives AP the option of waiving his title in return for compensation from OO.
- Rule 6: OO not only can keep his title, but also has the option to give up his title and receive compensation from AP.

Incorporating the possibility of "put option" rules, the structure of legal entitlements in adverse possession is as follows (Table 4.2):

[18] For a similar table, *see Id.* at14. [19] *Id.* at 5–15. [20] *Id.*

Table 4.2 *Ayres' Two-by-Three Box applied to adverse possession*[21]

Method of protection			
Initial entitlement	Property rule	Liability rule call option	Liability rule put option
OO	Rule 1	Rule 2	Rule 6
AP	Rule 3	Rule 4	Rule 5

Table 4.3 *Ayres' Table of Claims applied to adverse possession*[22]

	OO's claim	AP's claim
Rule 1	Asset	0
Rule 2	Asset − Call	Call
Rule 3	0	Asset
Rule 4	Call	Asset − Call
Rule 5	−Put	Asset + Put
Rule 6	Asset + Put	−Put

According to the distribution of asset and options, the structure of legal entitlements in adverse possession can be depicted by Table 4.3. In Rules 2 and 4, one party's title is subject to the other party's call option. In Rules 5 and 6, one party not only has the title, but also a put option.

4.1.3 *The Best-Chooser Principle*

How to allocate legal entitlements efficiently? Ayres' optional law theory tells us that: "Liability rules delegate allocational authority – allocational options – to privately informed disputants. The delegation effect gives us strong reasons to believe that liability rules do a better job than property rules in harnessing the private information of disputants."[23]

[21] For similar tables, *see* Ayres, Optional Law, *supra* note 4, at 16; Chang Yun-chien, *Optional Law in Property: A Theoretical Critique*, N.Y.U. J.L & Liberty, at 2, http://papers.ssrn.com/sol3/papers.cfm?abstract_id=2351651.

[22] Ayres, Optional Law, *supra* note 4, at 17. [23] *Id.* at 183.

In the small-property case, the government knows its own needs and valuation of the right to develop; individual small-property owners have the information of their illegal real estate. The government has double roles in this case: one as a disputant and potential entitlement holder; the other as a policymaker, which can decide who decides, and does not have to decide the final allocation of entitlements. Thus the policymaker in this case has complete information about one disputant – the government, but has not enough information about numerous small-property houses and their owners' valuation of them, which is more speculative than that of the government.

As Ayres writes in the American law context: "When the court is choosing between a litigant whose value is commonly known and another litigant whose value is not, the litigant with the known value is never the efficient chooser because he has no private information to bring to the allocative table."[24]

In this case, the government's information is known to itself as a policymaker; what it does not have in making a policy is the information of numerous individuals. Thus, the government is not the efficient chooser in this case. Small-property owners should be the efficient choosers because they can bring their private information to the allocative table.

Krier and Schwab have argued that less-numerous parties are more efficient choosers than more-numerous parties because of the collective-action problem.[25] As Ayres has correctly pointed out, Krier and Schwab focus too narrowly on numerosity as the exclusive determinant of which side will be the more efficient chooser.[26] As discussed previously, information is still a crucial element in deciding which party is the more efficient chooser. Moreover, the cost of overcoming the collective-action problem of numerous parties also varies according to the specific institutional and social contexts. As Ostrom,[27] Ellickson,[28] and many others have proved both theoretically and empirically, the problem of collective action can be overcome if the numerous parties constitute a close-knit

[24] *Id.* at 45.

[25] *See* James E. Krier and Stewart J. Schwab (1995). Property rules and liability rules: The cathedral in another light, 70 *N.Y.U. L. Rev.* 440.

[26] Ayres, Optional Law, *supra* note 4, at 31.

[27] Elinor Ostrom, GOVERNING THE COMMONS: THE EVOLUTION OF INSTITUTIONS FOR COLLECTIVE ACTION (1990).

[28] Robert C. Ellickson (1993). Property in land, 102 *Yale L.J.* 1315.

community or has a well-functioning decision-making mechanism, as shown in the *Caiwuwei* case in the following section.

Ayres makes another point: "The litigant with the more speculative valuation will tend to be the more efficient chooser because he has greater informational advantage."[29] This also applies to the small-property case. Individual valuation is more speculative to the market than government's valuation of land development. The number of individuals amplifies the government's information disadvantage. It is impossible for the government to have precise information about each individual's valuation of his or her particular small-property houses; or even to set an average valuation.

The third point is about the problem of multiple takings. As recognized by Ayres, liability rules might induce disputing parties to engage in a protracted series of destructive takings of the same entitlement from one another, and multiple takers to threaten taking.[30] Epstein argues that Ayres' optional theory only applies to two parties playing a one-period game, and that traditional property rules work better when many parties play the game over many periods.[31] Epstein correctly points out that "in all real world settings, the legal rules must work over many periods and must be resistant not only to the machinations of the two parties to the original dispute, but also to third parties who might come in."[32] Epstein supports his critique with a real world case – whether the government is entitled to decree without paying compensation that owners are not allowed to develop their land if that development will interfere with the survival of endangered species.[33] In this specific case, Epstein argues:

> The rule which denies the owner compensation could induce him to destroy valuable habitat lest his lands be frozen by government action. A decision to allow the government to designate land as habitat makes renegotiation of property rights impossible. The owner who buys back the rights faces the risk that a second designation will result in another loss of these rights to the government.[34]

[29] Ayres, Optional Law, *supra* note 4, at 44. [30] *Id.* at 125.

[31] Richard Epstein (1997). Protecting property with legal remedies: A common sense reply to Professor Ayres, 32 *Val. U. L. Rev.* 833, 844-845.

[32] *Id.*

[33] *See* Richard A. Epstein (1996). Babbitt v. Sweet Home Chapters of Oregon: The law and economics of habitat preservation, 32 *Sup. Ct. Econ. Rev.* 1.

[34] Epstein, *supra* note 31, at 844–845.

Small-property development and its legalization is a multi-period and multi-party game. There is a concern similar to Epstein's, but in the opposite direction: The Shenzhen government is worried that legalizing the existing illegal buildings would encourage further illegal development of rural land, not only on the land of existing small-property buildings, but also on land on which small-property buildings have not been built. Over time, small-property buildings have grown from two floors to four floors, to six floors, and to over eight floors or higher today; the number of illegal buildings and the land area they cover also have exploded.[35]

Epstein's worry about the abuse of government power should be left to the political process, as it is in most land use regulation practices.[36] We should consider not only the possibility of multiple takings, but also which party is more capable of multiple takings in specific case settings. In the situation of land use regulation, such as in my small-property case and in Epstein's habitat preservation case, it is one government dealing with numerous individuals, who not only have the information advantage, but also the advantage of overall control through their daily possession and operation of a specific plot against the government. These individuals are more capable of using the land according to their will, even when the law prohibits a particular land use, than the government's law-enforcement capability.

In Shenzhen, the reality has proved that individuals are much more capable than the government in deciding the use of a particular plot when the widespread illegality makes legal enforcement infeasible.[37] The huge number of small-property houses makes the situation even more difficult to deal with. Granting legal titles to the existing small-property houses would not only encourage individuals who have not used their land illegally to do so, it also would encourage further illegal use of the land by individuals granted the legal titles. It is exactly a multi-period, multi-party game as depicted by Epstein. However, we need to investigate the real-world specifics to decide which party is more capable of multiple takings of a specific plot. It turns out that in cases of one government versus numerous individuals, it is often the individuals that are more capable of multiple takings. As in Epstein's habitat preservation situation, the party that is more capable of multiple takings is the more efficient chooser.

[35] *See* Chapter 2.
[36] *Land Use Controls: Cases and Materials* 46 (Robert Ellickson and Vicki Been eds., 2005).
[37] *See* Chapter 2 and Section 4.2.1 of this chapter.

In summary, the best chooser should be the party that has private information unknown to the policymaker, with the more speculative valuation, and is more capable of multiple takings. As shown in the following section, it is the numerous owners of small-property houses in my case.

4.2 Structuring Legal Entitlements for Small Property

As early as in 1982, the Shenzhen government tried to make a feasible plan to deal with the illegal rural houses.[38] In recent years, the Shenzhen government has tried five of the six rules under Ayres' optional law framework, the efficiency of which thus could be tested in this case. I analyze and discuss the results of these Shenzhen government's efforts. The only missing rule in the Shenzhen government's policies, Rule 5, is actually applicable to a certain group of cases. I discuss the theoretical application of Rule 5 to these cases. It is worth pointing out that the rules below are used to structure the *de jure* entitlements, rather than *de facto* arrangements.

4.2.1 Rule 1

Content: *Only the government is entitled to develop rural land; adverse development of rural land is prohibited and deterred through legal enforcement.*

The Shenzhen government's initial response to the illegal development of rural land was to enforce the legal prohibition on rural land development and to demolish the illegal buildings, which turned out to be a huge task. From the 1980s to the mid-1990s, the Shenzhen government promulgated a series of regulations to deal with the illegal development of rural land. However, compared to the widespread illegal development of rural land, the government's enforcement power seemed to be limited. When daily legal enforcement did not work, the Shenzhen government tried campaign-style legal enforcement, which means concentrating government resources in a fixed period to demolish illegal

38 "关于严禁在特区内乱建和私建房屋的规定"（深府[1982]1号，1982年3月29日）[Shenzhen City Government. *Stipulations on Strictly Prohibiting Private and Non-Planning Housing Building within the Special Economic Zone*, SZ GOV'T., March 29, 1982.]

buildings and to punish people who violated the legal prohibition with a hope of deterring further violations. This was not successful and the number of illegal buildings continued to increase as time went by. As land available for development became less and less, the Shenzhen government's tolerance of illegal rural land development became lower and lower.

In 1999, the Standing Committee of the People's Congress of Shenzhen made a decision to monitor and punish illegal rural land development.[39] It made a comprehensive plan to deter illegal rural land development, including:

- The Department of Planning and Land should strictly monitor and punish illegal rural land development;
- The Department of Housing Renting should not issue permits to illegal buildings and should seriously punish the renting of illegal housing;
- The Department of Business Administration should not issue licenses to businesses located in illegal buildings and should suspend the licenses of businesses operating in illegal buildings;
- The Department of Construction Administration should not issue permits to illegal rural land development and should punish construction companies that participate in illegal rural land development;
- The Department of Public Security should punish and deter activities held in illegal buildings;
- The Departments of Electricity, Water, and Gas should not supply electricity, water, or gas to buildings without legal approval documents.

In 2004, the Shenzhen government established a small leadership team headed by the mayor and consisting of the heads of relevant government departments, and a discipline team to supervise government officials to ensure that they fulfill their responsibilities in dealing with illegal rural land development. In 2009, the Shenzhen government established a new Department of Land Use Monitoring ("DLUM"), which has branches in all fifty-seven sub-districts of Shenzhen.[40]

39 "深圳市人民代表大会常务委员会关于坚决查处违法建筑的决定"（1999年2月26日第二届人民代表大会常务委员会第三十次会议通过）[Shenzhen People's Congress Standing Comm., Decision on Monitoring and Punishing Illegal Buildings, February 26, 1999.]

40 深圳规划土地监察："我市查处违法建筑政策梳理"，2012年3月12日[*Review of the Municipal Policies of Illegal Buildings*, SHENZHEN LAND USE MONITORING, March 12,

According to a senior government official of Shenzhen, each street-level unit of the DLUM has to spend six to ten million RMB each year to monitor illegal rural land development and demolish illegal buildings. A typical demolition of illegal buildings involves dozens of government employees, including construction workers who are responsible for demolition and policemen who maintain order during the demolition.[41] The huge expense of demolition has become unaffordable to the government. In March 2013, the local People's Congress published a draft of Regulation of Land Use Monitoring, which required the owners of illegal building to pay the demolition fees. In order to do that, the DLUM could take the owners' properties, such as automobiles, legal real estate, and bank savings as lien.[42]

The crackdown was ineffective. Even the small leadership team, the specialized legal enforcement organ, and the supporting legal measures have not deterred illegal rural land development. From 1999 to 2010, the number of illegal buildings has grown from 221,600 to 348,400.[43]

These legal enforcement measures not only triggered widespread corruption, but also increased social conflicts. In my interviews with journalists, rural land investors, and retired government officials, it was widely acknowledged that many government employees bought apartments and even villas developed on the rural land. Villagers intentionally get government employees involved in the business. Selling part of their real estate to government employees is a strategy used in many cases of rural real estate development. Generally, a village head would approach a government official and tell him that their village has a plot or dozens of apartments for sale, and he can pay whatever price he likes. A Chinese Central TV (hereinafter "CCTV") report also testified to this fact. In a CCTV reporter's undercover investigation of a rural building of

2012, www.szpls.gov.cn/whkj/xxdy/201203/t20120312_71655.html (last visited December 9, 2009).

[41] 付可："深圳拆除私房遭抵制多名警察受伤"，"南方都市报"2007年1月23日[Fu Ke, *Many Polices Got Hurt in Demolition of Private Houses*, SOUTHERN METROPOLITAN DAILY, Jan. 23, 2007.] http://news.sina.com.cn/c/l/2007-01-23/115112115150.shtml (last visited December 9, 2009).

[42] 彭琰："特区规划土地监察条例征求意见 强拆费用或由违建人出"，"深圳商报"2013年3月12日[Peng Yan, *New Regulations Require Owners of Illegal Buildings to Pay for the Demolition Expenses*, SHENZHEN COMMERCIAL DAILY, March 12, 2013.], www.ceosz.cn/SzNews/SzYw/SzNews_20130312093619_166233_2.html (last visited May 6, 2014).

[43] SHENZHEN CITY GOVERNMENT, INVESTIGATION REPORT ON ILLEGAL BUILDINGS IN SHENZHEN 26, (2010) (on file with the author).

residential apartments, the reporter was told by both villagers and house brokers that about forty employees of the district government agency of land administration had bought apartments in the building.[44]

At each level of government (street/sub-district, district, and city), there is a division responsible for the enforcement of land laws and the demolition of the illegal buildings. There are many publicly reported cases of corruption in this division of the government.[45] In reflecting upon its failure to stop rural real estate development, the Shenzhen city government also acknowledged corruption as an important reason. In a reported case, an accounting note prepared by a land developer revealed that the cost of development included a land use fee of 15.3 million and "other fees" of 5 million paid to government officials.[46] According to China Securities Daily, about one-third of the profits of the informal housing market fall into the hands of government officials in charge of enforcing land and housing laws.[47]

In cases where "other fees" are not paid or where the legal prohibition has to be enforced due to political pressure from the city level, social conflicts might occur. Under this risk, each demolition is a battle between the government and villagers, which frequently results in bloody conflicts. Here is a real typical case from Shenzhen:

> Hundreds of fully equipped legal enforcement officials assembled in a village to demolish illegal rural buildings. Several miles away, the traffic police blocked the road to stop "irrelevant parties" entering the village. Nevertheless, when the big machines began to demolish the illegal buildings, desperate villagers climbed onto the roof of the buildings and threw stones at the legal enforcement officers. The conflict resulted in five policemen and more villagers hurt.[48]

On the villagers' side, the legal enforcement did bring uncertainty to their *de facto* property and brought great loss to them from each successful

[44] 李杰 ："深圳开发商自己给小产权房发证"，"经济半小时"2009年6月13日[Li Jie, *Shenzhen Land Developers Issue Certificates of Small-Property Houses*, CCTV ECON., June 13, 2009.], http://finance.sina.com.cn/china/dfjj/20090613/22346345587.shtml (last visited August 3, 2014).

[45] 杜雅文、万晶："百亿游资豪赌小产权房转正"，"中国证券报" 2009年8月21日[Du Yawen, & Jing Wan, *Billions of Hot Money Bet on the Legalization of Small-Property Houses*, CHINA SECURITIES DAILY, Aug. 21, 2009], http://biz.xinmin.cn/rehouse/2009/08/21/2410786_6.html (last visited February 15, 2013).

[46] 陈小瑛： "查违费：小产权房的买路钱"， "华夏时报" 2013年05月10日[Chen Xiaoying, *Chawei Fee: Toll for Illegal Buildings*, HUAXIA DAILY, May 10, 2013.], http://house.hexun.com/2013-05-10/154000572_1.html (last visited September 15, 2013).

[47] Du and Wan, *supra* note 45.

[48] Fu, *supra* note 41.

demolition of illegal buildings. In 2012, the Shenzhen government took 7,093 legal enforcement actions and demolished illegal buildings totaling 1.39 million square meters.[49] In a case the Shenzhen government flags as a model of legal enforcement, a mall for automobile sales was demolished without any violence. Twenty-three car companies had salerooms in this mall, which employed more than 1,900 employees. The annual sales revenue of the mall was more than six billion RMB. Unfortunately, the building was illegal and was demolished. The government demolished it with a wide mobilization of government resources, including one working team for each automobile saleroom.[50] Obviously, this method of legal enforcement cannot be widely reproduced. Additionally, the possessors of the illegal mall incurred huge economic losses from the demolition, not to say other costs that might be caused by the demoralized possessors[51] or the bribes they paid to evade the legal enforcement.

Finally, organized violence emerged in this illegal world to reduce demolition and social conflicts. For example, in 2012 the Shenzhen City Court adjudicated the case of the so-called biggest mafia in the history of Shenzhen.[52] In this case, the main business of the gang was illegal rural land development. It exercised huge influence in the governance of many villages within a sub-district of Shenzhen through bribing government officials of the sub-district government and violence against villagers. This is definitely neither the best nor the most efficient order.

4.2.2 Rule 3

Content: *The government grants legal titles to adversely developed buildings without demanding compensation.*

In the United States, an adverse possessor can acquire title by possessing the property until the statute of limitations for the title owner to recover possession has run. Chinese law does not recognize the rights

49 周昌和 、刘庚怀："查处违法用地违法建筑服务城市科学发展"，"南方都市报" 2013年6月28日[Zhou Chang & Liu Genghuai, *Punishing Illegal Land Use to Serve Scientific City Development*, SOUTHERN METROPOLITAN DAILY, June 28, 2013]., http://sz.house.sina.com.cn/news/2013-06-28/08263288834.shtml (last visited May 6, 2014).

50 *Id.*

51 *See* Robert C. Ellickson (1986). Adverse possession and perpetuities law: Two dents in the libertarian model of property rights, 64 *Wash. U. L. Q.* 723.

52 *See* Chapter 5.

of adverse possession.[53] But that does not mean there is no adverse possession in reality. Actually, the tension between *de facto* possession and the *de jure* rights is particularly acute in the rapidly changing China, as we can see from the small-property case in Shenzhen. Shenzhen government officials do think very seriously about granting titles to adverse possessors. But they worry that such a measure would encourage further adverse possession. This worry has proved to be well founded.

Rule 3 means the AP gets title without paying for it after satisfying several conditions. The Shenzhen government tried such a policy in dealing with small-property real estate. In 1993, in the first regulation that recognized illegal rural land development as a serious problem, the Shenzhen government made a policy that houses built before 1986 could be registered without paying any fines.[54] For houses built after 1986, the Shenzhen government cannot afford to grant all of them legal titles. Instead the Shenzhen government said that it recognized indigenous villagers' rights to have their own residential houses. This meant the legal entitlement to a house on an 80-square-meters plot, with a total floor area of 240 square meters in 1986 (SZ Govt. [1982] 185)[55] and to a house on a 120-square-meters plot, with a total floor area of 480 square meters in 2001.[56]

Meanwhile, to respond to some villagers' claim that they did not have a chance to build their own houses because of the Shenzhen government's harsh deterrent of illegal rural land development, the Shenzhen

[53] In the legislative process of the Property Law, many Chinese scholars suggested incorporating acquisitive prescription into the law, which is very similar to adverse possession. In the end, acquisitive prescription was not included in the Property Law, in opposition to the consensus among Chinese mainstream scholars. *See* Yun-chien Chang (2012). Property law with Chinese characteristics: An economic and comparative analysis, 1 *Brigham-Kanner Prop. Rts. Conf. J.* 345.

[54] "关于处理深圳经济特区房地产权属遗留问题的若干规定"（深府[1993]426号，1993年11月9日）[Shenzhen City Government, STIPULATIONS ON PROPERTY RIGHTS OF HISTORICAL REAL ESTATE PROBLEM, (No. 426, November 9, 1993)]

[55] According to a standard set up in a 1982 regulation. *See* "深圳经济特区农村社员建房用地的暂行规定"（深府[1982]185号，1982年9月17日）[Shenzhen City Government, TEMPORAL REGULATIONS ON RURAL COLLECTIVE MEMBERS' USE OF LAND FOR HOUSING CONSTRUCTION 185 (Sept. 17, 1982)]

[56] 深圳经济特区处理历史遗留违法私房若干规定（2001年10月17日深圳市第三届人民代表大会常务委员会第十一次会议通过，市人大常委会公告第33号）[Shenzhen People's Congress Standing Comm., STIPULATIONS ON HISTORICAL ILLEGAL RESIDENTIAL BUILDINGS 33 (October 17, 2001)]

government promulgated a policy in 2006 to issue permits to villagers to build a house if they have not already built one.[57]

This free-titling policy greatly encouraged illegal rural land development. First, villagers devoted substantial resources to obtaining a permit to build a house, regardless of whether they had already built one. Getting a permit sometimes depended on how a "household" was defined. One household could be divided into two households just to get the benefits from the "one household, one house" policy. Many resources were spent on lobbying and bribing government officials with authority to issue such permits. Once villagers obtained such permits, almost no villager built property of only 480 square meters. Rather, 1000 square meters (eight to ten floors) was the average.[58] Some villagers even made fake permits to post at the construction sites. It was difficult to distinguish between the fake permits and the real ones. Thus, this policy has significantly increased the monitoring cost of the government. Not only did it take more time to identify construction projects with fake permits, but it also was costly to deter the construction of the extra floors beyond the legal four (480 square meters). Moreover, with a hope of getting legal titles, villagers devoted time and money to building houses, which they would not have done without this policy. To strengthen their claim of rights under this policy, they also tended to build houses very rapidly – the rate was one floor per two days at the cost of safety and quality. Construction workers built twenty-four hours a day without adequate safety precautions, and some were hurt or even killed in accidents.[59]

Second, many people viewed this and other policies that provide mechanisms for villagers to legalize their illegal real estate as a signal that the government was unable to enforce harsh demolition rules and would have to grant legal titles to all the illegal buildings. Villagers

[57] 深圳市政府："深圳市原村民非商品住宅建设暂行办法"（深府[2006]105号，2006年6月19日）[SHENZHEN CITY GOVERNMENT, TEMPORAL STIPULATIONS ON INDIGENOUS VILLAGERS' CONSTRUCTION OF NON-BUSINESS RESIDENTIAL HOUSES 105 (June 19, 2006)]

[58] *See* 谢孝国、欧阳四平、 余胜容："深圳市建筑4成违规 利益集团游说市长"，"羊城晚报"2010年2月23日[Xie Xiaoguo et al., *Interest Groups Lobby the Mayor of Shenzhen for Illegal Buildings*, YANG CHENG EVENING NEWSPAPER, Feb. 24, 2010.], http://news.163.com/10/0223/14/607CRQ0G0001124J.html (last visited July 26, 2014).

[59] *See* 申文峰："部分社区大肆违法"抢建新村"公开出售"，"深圳晚报"2009年11月1日[Shen Wenfeng, *Some Communities Rush to Build Houses Illegally for Sale*, SHENZHEN EVENING NEWSPAPER, Nov. 1, 2009.], http://news.dayoo.com/shenzhen/200911/01/73553_100291041_4.htm (last visited September 15, 2013).

responded with more illegal rural land development to secure their claims of rights in the possible situation of free-titling-for-all. This was the main reason that each time the Shenzhen government initiated a campaign to deal with illegal buildings, there was a burst of illegal rural land development.[60] As time passed, the government was more likely to recognize the historical illegal buildings and to seek to deter future illegal rural land development. For villagers, this gave them an incentive to develop adversely as much and as quickly as possible for fear of losing the chance in the future and in anticipation of receiving legal titles for their developments.

In Shenzhen, the free-titling policy has been limited to the "one household, one house" policy and several other very limited situations. In addition to encouraging illegal rural land development, the Shenzhen government gained very little revenue from this policy.

4.2.3 Rule 6

Content: *The government not only has a monopoly of rural land development, but also has the option of giving up its monopoly and receiving compensation from the adverse developers.*

If neither property rule works out, one should consider liability rules. Liability rules under the Calabresi and Melamed framework are actually call-option liability rules. Surprisingly, the liability rule that the Shenzhen government has used most was a put-option liability rule: Rule 6, according to which the government not only can keep its title, but also has an option to transfer its title to villagers, without the villagers' consent, in exchange for compensation.[61] This might be simply because the government was accustomed to a top-down approach and control.

[60] Interview Transcript II: 637, 648 (2012).

[61] Chang argues that the Ayresian Rule 6 is not a put as it is premised on the condition that a dispute has happened. He further argues that the contract/*in personam* nature of options makes it incompatible with the *in rem* nature of property rights. Whether property rights are *in personam* or *in rem* rights is an open question. A short response is that whenever we examine a property dispute, it is a relationship between certain parties, and thus *in personam* relations. Property rights are defined to avoid and resolve disputes. Both property rules and liability rules are rules of protecting a legal entitlement, that is, rules that define available remedies whenever a violation of a legal entitlement happens, and not rules that grant extra *in rem* rights to an entitlement holder. Thus, a put-option liability rule is not supposed to grant a property holder rights

Early in 1988, the Shenzhen government promulgated a policy of allowing villagers to keep their illegal houses after paying fines, which were calculated according to the area of the illegally developed real estate: each household has the right to develop 80 square meters, but beyond that, the more they developed, the higher the fines they had to pay.[62] In 1993, an owner of an illegal building could get a legal title after paying RMB 100 per square meter if the building was for industrial use and RMB 500 if for commercial use. Even non-villagers who bought the illegal houses could get legal titles after paying some amount of money.[63]

In 2001, recognizing the reality that almost half of the houses in the city were illegal, the standing committee of the Shenzhen People's Congress promulgated a detailed decree to legalize most of the illegal buildings. Except for those in serious conflict with the city planning system, such as blocking a main road, the Shenzhen government required all owners of illegal buildings to pay fines and land-use fees and apply for legal titles. The standards of fines and fees were again set according to owners' identities and the total areas of the buildings. Owners of illegal buildings were required to apply for legal titles from the government within one year of the decree's promulgation, giving the Shenzhen government information on illegal buildings within its jurisdiction.[64]

This did not work out well. It was not until 2010 that the Shenzhen government obtained the first detailed report on illegal buildings, which acknowledged that the 2001 legalization plan had not been well received despite the government's major efforts. From 2002 to 2010, among the 221,600 illegal buildings built before 1999, only 57,400 were granted legal

to force a random person to purchase his property. In this sense, I do not see put-option liability rules as fundamentally different from property rules or call-option liability rules. Also regarding Chang's critique that a real-world example of Rule 5 "is hard to come by," Section 4.2.6 of this chapter argues that Rule 5 could provide a better solution than direct condemnation to *Jingui* villagers who have been unable to make use of their illegal buildings due to the environmental regulation in Shenzhen. *See* Yun-chien Chang, Optional Law in Property: A Theoretical Critique, N.Y.U. J.L. & LIBERTY, Retrieved from http://ssrn.com/abstract=2351651.

62 "深圳市人民政府关于处理违法违章占用土地及土地登记有关问题决定" （深府[1988]253号）[Shenzhen City Government, STIPULATIONS ON ILLEGAL LAND DEVELOPMENT AND LAND REGISTRATION 253 (1988).]

63 Shenzhen City Government, *supra* note 54.

64 深圳经济特区处理历史遗留生产经营性违法建筑若干规定（2001年10月17日深圳市第三届人民代表大会常务委员会第十一次会议通过，市人大常委会公告第34号）[Shenzhen People's Congress Standing Committee, STIPULATIONS ON HISTORICAL ILLEGAL PRODUCTION AND COMMERCIAL BUILDINGS 34 (October 17, 2001]; Shenzhen People's Congress Standing Committee [2001] 33, *supra* note 56.

titles. In addition, by 2010, the total number of illegal buildings had increased to 348,400 and kept growing day-by-day.[65] There were owners of illegal buildings who applied for legalization but who declined to pay the fines and fees at the end. There were also cases in which the local government sent legal certificates to owners of illegal buildings but the latter rejected to accept the delivery.[66] These owners preferred to stay illegal because they did not want to pay the prices or did not see any substantial benefit from getting their illegal buildings legalized. The government, despite its intention to force all owners to buy legal titles, did not have effective measures to deal with such situations.

In 2009, the government thought it might have set the prices too high and made the procedures too complicated. The People's Congress of Shenzhen promulgated another decision to legalize the increasing number of illegal buildings with more willingness to compromise.[67] Article I of the decision says that the government should respect history (*zunzhong lishi*), an indication of its respect for the rights of owners of the illegal buildings. This time the government tried to set lower prices and to make the procedures more convenient. This decision also required that a detailed plan should be made within one year. However, such a plan, which adopted both Rule 1 and Rule 6 to deal with small-property houses, was not promulgated until December 30, 2013.[68] The Shenzhen government has decided to test this plan in several selected intracity villages before fully implementing it, which would encourage villages not selected to develop further their land illegally.

This plan will not resolve the conundrum with which the Shenzhen government has been confronted. The information cost is too high for the government to enforce the put-option liability rule. It has to accumulate all the information on all illegal building within its jurisdiction, which is actually impossible. First, physical information might be the

[65] Shenzhen City Government, *supra* note 43, at 28–29.

[66] Interview with a city government official, at Longhua New District of Shenzhen City (March 5, 2012).

[67] "深圳市人民代表大会常务委员会关于农村城市化历史遗留违法建筑的处理决定"（2009年5月21日深圳市第四届人民代表大会常务委员会第二十八次会议通过） [SHENZHEN PEOPLE'S CONGRESS STANDING COMMITTEE, DECISION ON DEALING WITH HISTORICAL ILLEGAL BUILDINGS IN RURAL URBANIZATION 101(May 21, 2009).]

[68] 深圳市人民政府："<深圳市人民代表大会常务委员会关于农村城市化历史遗留违法建筑的处理决定>试点实施办法" （深圳市人民政府令第261号，2013年12月30日）[SHENZHEN CITY GOVERNMENT, EXPERIMENTAL IMPLEMENTATION OF THE DECISION ON DEALING WITH HISTORICAL ILLEGAL BUILDINGS IN RURAL URBANIZATION 261 (December 30, 2013).]

easier part: the location, height and floor areas are not difficult to collect; however, the history, quality, and other invisible characteristics of the illegal buildings are actually very costly to collect. What's more complicated are the social and economic relations of the illegal buildings: Who owns them? Who should get the legal title? What is worse, even with all the qualities of a building fixed and its owner identified, it is hard to know how much the owner values it. The cost of strategic bargaining could be prohibitively high, in particular when the government exercised its put option and thus had no opportunity to know the owner's evaluation. The complicated titling procedure makes the situation worse. For owners of illegal buildings, the complicated procedures imposed high information costs to them and fostered distrust of the government, both of which might prevent them from even thinking about whether the fees and fines charged by the government are reasonable or not. Several government officials told me that the fees and fines for a particular group of villagers were actually not high at all. Villagers in this particular group told me that they did not understand the government policies and that their friends had told them that the government would charge a lot of money for granting titles to their buildings. The amounts of both sides differed by a hundredfold.

In summary, there might be a price that both the government and adverse possessors would accept for legalization of the illegal buildings. But the government's put option is too costly to exercise. To make sure that the price was set right, the government had to design complicated rules, which in turn caused great information costs to villagers.

4.2.4 Rule 2

Content: *The right to develop rural land belongs to the government, but adverse developers can get legal titles to their adversely developed buildings by paying compensation.*

The most successful and promising solution has been the application of Rule 2. The government has the title, but adverse possessors can take it by paying compensation. This rule gradually emerged in numerous village redevelopment projects of Shenzhen. Originally, in redeveloping the intracity villages where the illegal rural land development was prevalent, the Shenzhen government insisted that only legally developed land could be redeveloped and only legally built houses could be compensated, which turned out to be infeasible. It is clear to the government, the villagers, and other market participants that village redevelopment would bring them substantial profits. Slowly, the government relaxed the requirements of legality. Whether the demolished buildings were legal or illegal fell to the wayside when one could build a modern neighborhood or a luxurious commercial center at the same location. In the end, the government set its standard: If a redevelopment project can supply 20 percent of its land to the government for free and develop another 12 percent of land for public roads and other public facilities, the government would approve the project without considering whether the old buildings were illegal or legal.[69]

It is essentially a call-option liability rule. The government has the title, but the village can pay the fixed price, that is, 32 percent of its land, to the government for legal rights to develop the remaining land. It is an option villagers can choose if they find it profitable. (They can choose not to exercise the option if they find it unprofitable.) The government needs to do very little. Villagers know best the value of their land. The cost of getting such information is much lower for them than for the government. This rule differs from the government's put-option liability rule in several aspects: First, this decentralized approach leaves the decision to villagers, who are more attuned to opportunities in the market, in addition to their better knowledge of the real estate under their control. Second, titling becomes a continuous process under this rule. Thus, villagers can decide whether to exercise their call option based on real market opportunities, rather than a theoretical prediction that legal titles would increase the value of their real estate. This flexibility in timing can even counteract the negative effects of the government's potential bad pricing – the price of exercising the call option might be too high for villagers this year, but with new market opportunities and increasing prices of real estate, the villagers might exercise their options anytime in the future. Villagers do not have this advantage when the government exercises its put option. The government could also choose the timing of exercising its put option, but without knowing the villagers' information, it is more difficult to choose the right time than it is for villagers, who have both their own information and the government's. Thus, Rule 2 leaves the decision to the party with better information.

[69] 北京大学国家发展研究院： "深圳市土地产权制度改革与二次开发利用机制创新研究报告" [NATIONAL SCHOOL OF DEVELOPMENT, REPORT ON LAND REFORM IN SHENZHEN 33 (2013)], (on file with the author).

Reality has proved that Rule 2 is the most effective one. In 2011, among the newly developed 3.8 million square meters of houses on the formal market of Shenzhen, 1.5 million square meters came from village redevelopment. Compared with the reluctant responses to other legalization plans, villagers have very actively applied for village redevelopment. From 2009 to 2012, there have been 342 such projects, involving 30 square kilometers of the illegally developed land.[70] In the following, I would like to present an example.

Caiwuwei is a village in the central area of Shenzhen. Villagers developed its land illegally, relying on rent from the illegal buildings for their livelihood. Life was quite good for them because of the strong rental market. Many middle to low income people, including factory workers, restaurant waitresses, and even white-collar company employees, rented apartments in this village because of the convenient location and the lower rents and living expenses in the village. Most villagers did not see any necessity of applying for legal titles to their buildings from the government, which, in turn, did not want the instability risk from demolishing this village where thousands of people lived.

But everybody saw the wide gap between the rental price of small-property apartments within the village and legal apartments outside of the village, which were only one or two blocks away. There was huge capital embedded in this village. After the government set the standards of village redevelopment, village leaders began to think about the possibility of awakening this sleeping capital. Land developers also came to tell villagers how much money they could make from the proposed redevelopment.

The project demolished illegal buildings of about 150,000 square meters and built a 100-floor skyscraper on the plot of 45,000 square meters. The total area of saleable floors of the building was 480,000 square meters, one-third of which were used to compensate the owners of the illegal buildings. (A few villagers chose compensation in cash, which turned out to be a big mistake.) Owners of the illegal buildings received the same amount of housing space as compensation after the village redevelopment. However, the value of this real estate was about ten times higher, making many villagers millionaires or even billionaires. The government got revenue of RMB 200 million and well-built public roads, parks, and schools in the neighborhood. The land developer, which spent over six billion RMB

[70] *Id.* at 33.

redeveloping this village, got about 300,000 square meters of commercial real estate worth at least 15 billion RMB.[71]

Not all village redevelopment can bring such a dramatic change. However, the advantage of Rule 2 is that it greatly reduces the information costs required to make it possible. Moreover, since the option is at the hands of villagers, it cannot make the situation worse – *status quo* is the baseline.

4.2.5 *Rule 4*

Content: *The government grants legal titles to the adversely developed buildings, but has an option to take these buildings so long as it compensates their owners.*

Another option that the government tried was to requisition illegal buildings with compensation to the owners. In the past five years, the Chinese central government has required local governments to build some amount of public housing for low-income population. The Shenzhen government did not have enough land to build public housing required by the central government. At the same time, most low-income people in Shenzhen lived in small-property houses. The Shenzhen government found that rather than developing extra houses, requisitioning small-property houses might be a better solution.

Zhongmin Garden was a small-property building built by villagers and outside land developers in violation of the governmental prohibition of rural land development. The total floor area was 74,352 square meters. The Shenzhen government requisitioned it at the price of RMB 3,642 per square meter, which was about one-third of the average price of legal buildings in the surrounding area. The Shenzhen government made a comprehensive examination of the quality of the building and found that it was safe. The reason was that it was designed by qualified construction designers and built by qualified construction companies, as most small-property high-rises were. The price was a bit higher than the construction cost and thus the developer and villagers could still make a small profit.[72]

This single case was successful. However, it is unclear how widely it could be replicated. As the number of cases increases, the costs to the government of finding proper buildings and requisitioning them would increase rapidly. Setting a proper price is also a key issue, the failure of

[71] *Id.* at 72–74. [72] Interview Transcript II 11-2(2012).

which would be more disastrous than Rule 6. There would be social conflicts if the government insisted on requisitioning the illegal houses with too little compensation. The costs of information and bargaining to set the proper price could be high. Moreover, the Shenzhen government could not afford to purchase more than 400 million square meters of illegal buildings and might not even need so much public housing at all. At the end, the purpose of "requisitioning small-property buildings for public housing" is dubious. If small-property buildings were good for public housing and indeed served as homes to the low-income population through the small-property market, why should the government intervene?

4.2.6 *Rule 5*

> Content: *The government not only grants legal titles to adversely developed buildings, but also gives their owners an option of selling their buildings in return for compensation from the government.*

Under Rule 5, villagers would not only have the legal title, but also an option to waive their titles in return for government compensation. The Shenzhen government has not taken such a rule in dealing with the illegal rural land development in its history, but this rule could be very helpful in dealing with a special category of illegal buildings in Shenzhen.

Jingui Village is located close to the water sources of the city. It is about 13 square kilometers and has about 1,200 villagers. In 2004, the Shenzhen government delineated ecological control lines and the whole village is within these control lines. There were 408 illegal buildings with total floor area of 125,000 square meters and total land area of 64,700 square meters. The Shenzhen government could not afford to demolish these buildings because they were shelters and factories on which villagers relied for living. On the other hand, the villagers could not make full use of these illegal buildings or even make necessary maintenance and repairs due to environmental regulations. These illegal buildings were in quite poor states. In contrast to villagers in other parts of Shenzhen who have become rich from illegal rural land development, Jingui villagers are poor.[73] Jingui village is not alone. In 2006, the total land area of illegal

[73] Interview Transcript II 418–21(2012)

buildings within the ecology control lines was 31.76 square kilometers, about 500 times that of Jingui village.[74]

Some have proposed ecological compensation to involved villagers. Similar to the discussions on regulatory compensation in the United States, the proposed ecological compensation would be a huge financial burden on the government. Moreover, the value of these buildings and land has not dropped to zero. Not all of them can be used for industry or commerce. It would be hard to decide on the standards of compensation. Instead, Rule 5 is a good choice here. The Shenzhen government should not only grant legal titles to the villagers' illegal buildings; it also should give them an option to sell those buildings to the government at a fixed price. With all values in consideration (efficiency, aesthetics, quietness, and so forth.), villagers should have the freedom to choose whether to sell their buildings to the government or not. As distributional fairness is a main concern behind this rule, the government does not have to set prices high, and should set them at reasonable levels to help villagers maintain an average standard of living.

4.3 An Optional Law Approach to Informal Property Rights

The tension between legal entitlements and *de facto* possession is prevalent in developing countries.[75] How to revive dead capital has been a hot topic in developmental economics in the past decades.[76] Scholars have argued about whether to formalize the informal property rights but we do not understand well how to incorporate the informal property rights into the formal legal system. In de Soto's words, how to "root the law in the social contracts?" The conflicts between formal law and informal property rights are essentially those between *de facto* possessors and *de jure* owners. Adverse possession provides a feasible mechanism to integrate informal property claims to the formal system, and avoids the shock of a top-down centralized rearrangement of property rights.

[74] 刘芳："深圳生态控制线的利益博弈"，"中国青年报" 2010年10月25日[Liu Fang, *Bargaining about the Ecological Lines in Shenzhen*, CHINA YOUTH DAILY, Oct. 25, 2010.], http://zqb.cyol.com/content/2010-10/25/content_3432311.htm (last visited September 15, 2013).

[75] *See, e.g.*, Daniel Fitzpatrick (2006). Evolution and chaos in property rights systems: The third world tragedy of contested access, 115 *Yale L.J.* 996; Michael Trebilcock and Paul-Erik Veel (2008). Property rights and development: The contingent case for formalization, 30 *U. Pa. J. Int'l L.* 397.

[76] *See, e.g.*, Hernando de Soto (1989). *The Other Path*; Hernando de Soto (2000). *The Mystery of Capital: Why Capitalism Triumphs in the West and Fails Everywhere Else.*

More importantly, by applying Ayres' framework of legal entitlements to the particular area of adverse possession, this case study shows that there are actually more choices for structuring the legal entitlements than simply deciding whether to grant a title to the original owner or the possessor.[77] The essential idea is that the government should decide who decides, rather than deciding the final allocation of resources. Options, rather than titles, should be granted to individual adverse possessors as they are more numerous and more capable of multiple takings than one government, and have both private information unknown to the government and a more speculative valuation of the land than the government.

This case study is also further evidence for the relevance of Ayres' optional law theory to real-world policymaking. It does not investigate the property/liability rule debate comprehensively, but it does provide examples in which liability rules are more efficient than property rules.

[77] *See, e.g.*, Winter King (2003). Illegal settlements and the impact of titling programs, 44 *Harv. Int'l L.J.* 433; Erica Field (2003). Property rights, community public goods, and household time allocation in urban squatter communities: Evidence from Peru, 45 *Wm. & Mary L. Rev.* 837.

5

Small Property in Transition

A Tale of Two Villages

In previous chapters, I have discussed the formation of a small-property market and various government responses to such a market. Overall, the formal institutions have begun to accommodate this market and make adaptive changes, but the road ahead toward the convergence of formal property institutions and the small-property sector may be long and bumpy. This chapter investigates the different destinies of small property in the transitional period based on cases in two villages in Shenzhen.

Chinese use color to distinguish the legality of organizations and their activities: "black" means totally illegal and often involves mafia[1] activities marked by violence and crime; "white" means totally legal and official recognition. On most occasions, small property is "grey," i.e., between black and white. However, some villages successfully gain government recognition of their real estate business by making use of various government policies. Unfortunately there are also villages that have gone the opposite route, i.e., giving up any legal dialogue with the official system, and resorting to bribes most often and sometimes to violence. Both "whitening" and "blackening" exist in Shenzhen.

From a purely economic perspective, there should be no difference in the development of small property across different villages, though there might be a difference in the degrees of market development. A typical Demsetzian story would be that private land rights emerge in response to increasing demand for housing in Shenzhen.[2] But this story would raise a question as to

[1] Mafia is a vague term with no consensus definition. But generally speaking, their primary activities involve the use of violent intimidation to manipulate local economic activity, in particular illegal transactions. As Milhaupt and West argue, mafia, or organized crime, is "an entrepreneurial response to inefficiencies in the property rights and enforcement framework supplied by the state." Curtis J. Milhaupt and Mark D. West (2000). The dark side of private ordering: An institutional and empirical analysis of organized crime, 67 *U. Chi. L. Rev.* 41, 43. *See also* Letizia Paoli (2003). *Mafia Brotherhoods: Organized Crime, Italian Style* 106.

[2] Harold Demsetz (1967). Toward a theory of property rights, 57 *Am. Econ. Rev. Papers & Proc.* 347.

why some villages go white and some go black. The reasons cannot be sought solely within the market itself, but must also be sought in village governance and in the villages' engagement with fragmented and layered government policies and laws. More importantly, the three social-control systems, the market, the community, and the formal legal and policy system, are coevolving and mutually influencing. A village leader in Shenzhen has three identities: operator of the village co-op company and thus responsible for maximizing its economic performance; villagers' elected representative that should take care of villagers' interests; and implementer of government policies. How a village leader plays these three roles both influences and is influenced by the three coevolving systems.

Section 5.1 presents two possible paths for the development of small property: one is the mafia-style small-property business, in which a village co-op is captured by a mafia and maintained through violence and bribing government officials; the other is a village co-op that from time to time takes actions "in the name of law" in their bargaining for legal property rights with the government and with a hold-out couple who refused to submit their "nailhouse" (the Chinese term for such buildings because they stick out and are difficult to remove, like a stubborn nail)[3] to the village co-op for redevelopment. Section 5.2 introduces the concept of layering and fragmentation of law and discusses its challenge to law and social norms, and explores how Professor Robert Ellickson's controller-selecting norms need to consider the coevolving and mutually influencing nature of different social control systems. Based on the above critiques, I borrow a multiple-network evolution model to explain the difference. Under this multiple-network evolution model, Section 5.3 investigates the three identities of village co-ops in the triple-system of social control (market, community, and law) and explores how the three identities influence each other and the systems in which they are embedded. Section 5.4 concludes the chapter.

5.1 Two Destinies of Small Property

The emergence of a small-property market accompanied three decades of rapid urbanization in Shenzhen. Even when facing the same market

[3] Stubborn as a Nail: China Residents Who Refuse to Move, *ABC News*, http://abcnews.go.com/International/photos/stubborn-nail-china-residents-refuse-move-19827908/image-19828396. For a scholarly discussion of such a case, *see* Shitong Qiao, *Preventing Land Grabbing by Privatization: Illusion or Reality?* (May 2010, unpublished manuscript) (on file with author).

demand and the same formal institutional structure, however, villages have different destinies. Some villages, such as Caiwuwei Village discussed in Chapter 4, made their members millionaires and even billionaires. Their rights to develop their land were recognized by the city government and cashed out through village redevelopment projects. Some villages' development of rural land was strictly restrained by the city government for environmental and other kinds of considerations, such as occurred in Jingui Village, a case discussed in Chapter 4. In this case, villagers' rights to develop their land were not recognized, and these villagers remain poor. Some villages' small-property businesses were warned and fined by the government and even became a target of criminal prosecution, as in the W village case discussed in the following sections. Many other villages are still on their way to gaining government-recognized rights to develop and sell their land.[4]

Sometimes, even between villages sitting on opposite sides of a small river, completely different outcomes occurred. On one side is a village full of small-property constructions where villagers have shown no respect for the legal prohibition on rural land development and transfer and have "planted" as many houses as possible in each vacant plot.[5] On the other side is a village in which construction has been restricted by the village co-ops, which in turn have devoted time and resources to applying for legal rights to develop and sell their land from the adaptive institutional openings. These disparities are possible due to the fragmentation and layering of laws.

From a long-term perspective, with officially recognized rights, villages can get access to capital, strategic investors, business ideas and technology available to the legal real estate business, and can make much more money from their land. This bright but uncertain future involves substantial costs. Many in such "legal" villages complain that, "We're losing money every day by not developing our land – the cost of complying with law is too high!"[6]

As discussed in previous chapters, violation of the legal prohibition usually does not lead to serious penalties, though villagers pay government officials bribes regularly to reduce the risk of legal enforcement.

[4] *See* 南方都市报编著："未来没有城中村" [*Southern Metropolis Daily ed., No IntraCity Village in the Future* (2011)].

[5] *See* Chapter 2 for more details.

[6] 北京大学国家发展研究院："深圳市土地产权制度改革与二次开发利用机制创新研究报告" [NAT'L SCHOOL OF DEV., INVESTIGATION REPORT OF LAND REFORM IN SHENZHEN 18 (2013)]

But the "gray" small-property business could also go black and totally flout the law. This involves "flagrant forms of criminal activity,"[7] which often incur immediate social costs – in such cases, the government often punishes it through law-enforcement.

One must then wonder why and how some villages have stuck to the legal approach, despite the high costs of wandering "before the law." One must also wonder why and how some villages have been swamped by illegal activities such as bribery and organized crime. Later I will discuss two cases in detail to investigate the above questions.

In one case, W village and its leader were prosecuted for bribing government officials to cover up their small-property business, and the leader was also convicted for participating in a mafia, of which the main business was small property in recent years. In the other case, Z village co-op has acquired legal rights to redevelop the village land and has even resolved the hold-out problem by the majority voting of villagers' assembly and suing a nailhouse holder in court.

5.1.1 W village: The Mafia-Style Small-Property Business

W village is located in the Shajing sub-district of Bao'An district. It has an area of 6.8 square kilometers with a total population of 60,000, only 2,067 of whom are official residents of the village. Most of them share the family name Pan. It used to be one of the top four super-villages in China in the 1990s because of its wealth, which was accumulated mainly through building factories to rent to outside investors.[8] It was also the first village in Shenzhen that experimented with village co-ops, a form of collective economic organization that has been adopted by all other villages in Shenzhen. Under the village co-ops, the board is in charge of the management of collective-owned land in the village and responsible for issuing dividends to villagers each year.[9] It was also one of the earliest villages that conducted large-scale commercial residential housing development under the name of building residential housing for their own villagers, most of which were actually put onto the small-property market.

[7] *See* Kellee S. Tsai (2006). Adaptive informal institutions and endogenous institutional change in China, 59 *World Pol.* 116, 126–127.

[8] 折晓叶： "村庄的再造：一个"超级村庄"的社会变迁" [ZHE XIAOYE, THE VILLAGE REMAKING (1997) (a classic book on Chinese super villages based on the case of W village.)]

[9] *See* Section 5.3 for more details.

With the rise and growth of a mafia of local villagers, the small-property market in W village, and in the Shajing sub-district in general, became a partnership between corrupt government officials, the mafia, and village co-op leaders, resulting in criminal prosecution and a crisis of the market.

5.1.1.1 Brother Dragon and His Xinyian

Xinyian, considered "the biggest mafia in the history of Shenzhen," was created by a local villager of HS village, located in the Shajing sub-district and close to W village. Its leader, Brother Dragon ("BD") became a member of a local mafia in the 1980s, during which time various mafias fought for territory and resources. BD gradually made himself the ultimate leader and mediator of all mafias in the Shajing sub-district and united them under a single name, Xinyian, a famous Hong Kong mafia in which BD's uncle was a leader.

To be a "little brother" (*mazai*) of BD means there are rules to follow, the most important three of which include:

(1) No fighting within the mafia; territories are divided according to the boundaries of villages and crossing the boundaries to "develop business" is forbidden;
(2) Mutual support should be offered whenever it is needed; outside people must be told that "I'm Brother Dragon's man"; and
(3) BD's orders must be followed absolutely.[10]

Little brothers who violated any of the above rules were beaten. In the case of infighting, prices were clearly set: RMB 3000 for one punch; RMB 30,000 for one cut; the initiator pays.[11] However, the real threat is the loss of BD's support, in which case this "little brother's" business would be subject to others' encroachment without any remedies.[12]

Eventually, Brother Dragon controlled all of Shajing. Almost all of the garbage collection stations, gas stations, clubs, and real estate businesses were either managed or owned by his men. It is said that he was "the emperor of Shajing."

What is more surprising is BD's influence in village elections and grassroots government operations. BD intentionally chose the most

[10] 广东省深圳市中级人民法院刑事附带民事判决书（2012）深中法刑一初字第227号 [Shenzhen Intermediate Court Criminal Case First Trial No. 227, at 193 (2012)]. (hereinafter Shenzhen Court Decision).

[11] *Id.* at 198–199. [12] *Id.* at 219.

influential men (as determined by wealth or connections) in each village to be little brothers.[13] It is said that almost every elected village official had to get support from BD to different degrees and that BD could control at least one-half of the votes in each village.[14] In some cases, BD's men would be present in village elections to deter any dissidents.[15]

A party secretary of a villagers' group disclosed a case to government officials during the investigation of BD's mafia:

> Two or three years ago in our village election, one person was not obedient; the next morning when he got up, his car was smashed. It is the big brothers of Xinyian that decided our elections, even party-secretary Liu of the Shajing sub-district government did not count. I feel that is not the country of the Communist Party, but the mafia's.[16]

BD also had good connections with the Shajing sub-district government. It is rumored that even party-secretary Liu would follow BD's orders. Liu was prosecuted as a "protection umbrella" (*baohusan*) for BD's mafia: He received over 12 million RMB in total from BD for various conveniences he provided for BD's businesses. For example, in 2008, BD bought about 20,000 square meters of land from BG village. In 2009 the Shajing sub-district government planned to requisition the same plot: BD invited Liu to dinner and gave him a bag of HKD 2 million in cash afterwards. The plot has still not been requisitioned.[17]

Meanwhile, it is interesting to note that Liu confessed that he had to rely on BD to govern Shajing. Liu was not from Shajing. He had been appointed as the party secretary of the Shajing sub-district in 2003 and was introduced to BD by a subordinate, who was from Shajing and was BD's friend. Liu was told that "he can displease anybody in Shajing but not BD." It turned out Liu had to seek help from BD for official and legitimate government affairs. For example, in 2008, when a little brother of BD organized over thirty villagers to disturb the party branch election in his village, Liu had to ask BD to call this man off.[18]

Overall, BD's Xinyian functions like a government. Villagers describe BD as encompassing both the black and the white societies ("*hei bai liang dao tong chi*"). The following is an example:

> Five years ago, our company's elevator was found inconsistent with safety guidelines by the safety inspection department of the Shajing government, which required us to uninstall it within a month. At the expiration of the

[13] *Id.* at 145. [14] *Id.* at 328. [15] *Id.* [16] *Id.* at 307–308. [17] *Id.* at 31.
[18] *Id.* at 733–734, 741–745.

> one-month deadline, the safety inspection department came to uninstall it on site. Somebody in our company called one of BD's little brothers, who came in less than 15 minutes and told the safety inspection department that it was BD's business. As a result the officials gave us two-month extension to change it. From this we know that BD is well connected with the government. Moreover, whenever our employees were beaten or things in our factory were stolen, we would notify BD's men, who would come and check. Then our factory would be more peaceful for a while.... We outside investors all hope to have a good work environment and dare not irritate BD's black society.[19]

In the early 2000s, BD saw huge profits in the real estate business and found Chen, a real estate developer, to do business with him.[20] BD bought a lot of land from villages at low prices. BD had little brothers in each village of Shajing, some of whom were village co-op board members, village party branch members, or villagers' committee members. Even in villages where BD's men did not have official positions, they still had influence in the village governance due to their violence, wealth, and connections. Moreover, these deals were often opaque. Usually BD only had to deal with one or two village leaders, though legally, transactions involving village assets had to be approved by the village co-op board or at the shareholders' meeting of the village co-op.[21] For example, in 2003, BD bought an industrial plot of 30,000 square meters from SL village at 6 million RMB. The price was 200 RMB for 50-year use rights per square meters. BD sold this plot to HY village for 55.2 million RMB in 2007. The 2003 transaction was made after BD's private conversation with the village's party secretary.[22] As for the 2007 transaction, according to the director of the HY villagers' committee, "We were willing to sign the contract because it was BD's company."[23]

BD made quick profits from such resales. A more significant case occurred in 2007. On September 11, 2007, BD and Chen bought 70-year use rights of 41,549 square meters of land at a price of 30 million RMB from the SX village co-op. After a little over one month, they sold it to the Haosi village co-op at 158 million RMB on October 26, 2007.[24]

In some cases, BD and Chen also developed real estate programs with other partners. Violence was used in their pursuit of profits. At the end of 2008, Li, an outside investor, bought three floors of YFY, a

[19] *Id.* at 315. [20] *Id.* at 282. [21] *Id.* at 546. [22] *Id.* at 545 [23] *Id.*
[24] *Id.* at 34.

small-property building from Chen. The total amount agreed to was 140 million RMB. Li paid five million RMB as front money and agreed to pay the remaining amount from future sales income. Li very successfully introduced a shopping mall with the three floors; the income from selling the first 25 percent of the units alone amounted to 70 million RMB. That meant the total amount would be about 280 million RMB. Chen had not expected that the three floors could make so much money, and he asked Li to withdraw from the project. BD brought Li to Chen's office and told him: "Boss Li, YFY is not a big deal; Chen told you not to do it – you should not continue; if you withdraw, I can give you several million RMB and another project to do." BD sat for a while and then left. Chen ordered Li to stay for a whole night and forced him to sign a contract and submit relevant documents, including the project license to them, but Li kept the original contract from them, which prevented Chen from finishing the official transfer procedure. As the result, in October 2009, BD's men kidnapped Li for a whole week and forced him to sign other contracts and submit the original contract and other remaining documents to finish the official transfer procedure.[25]

It was not rare for violence to be used as the last resort to maintain BD's business. It is said that most of the fighting in Shajing in recent years was related to BD; BD's mafia members committed quite a few murders.[26] Villagers in Shajing can be horrified at the mention of BD's name. Nobody dared resist what BD planned to do. For example, BD seized some villagers' land to build a club to treat his men and clients, and the villagers dared not complain until he was arrested.[27] A village cadre told another story to the police after BD's arrest, saying "Don't like the 24-hour operation of the laundromat near your home? It was BD's business – look out your home window during the night (if you complained)!"[28]

5.1.1.2 Criminal Prosecution, the Fall of W village, and A Crisis of the Market

W village has been heavily influenced by the Xinyian Mafia. The village co-op board chairman, Pan, became a little brother of BD. As Pan's defender argued in the court, Pan had no motivation to participate in

[25] *Id.* at 383–384. Here it means the change of the owner of the company at the business administration bureau. *See* Chapter 2: though small-property houses are not recognized, businesses based in small-property constructions are legally recognized.

[26] *Id.* at 307. [27] *Id.* [28] *Id.*

BD's Xinyian mafia, since he was the party secretary and village co-op board chairman. In other words, his defender claimed, Pan would not profit economically, socially, or politically from joining a mafia.[29]

This seemingly plausible argument was contradicted by Pan's own testimony and the facts. Pan confessed, "I devoted myself to BD with all my heart. Upon BD's call, I would drop anything at hand and run to his office and call him boss. Their real intention in controlling me was to force me to sell land cheaply to them at the expense of our villagers' interests, but I cannot control my own fate and have to follow their control."[30]

Pan did keep close ties with BD and sold him village land at low prices. Pan sold a lot of land to BD and even cooperated with BD in small-property development in the name of building concentrated residential apartments for villagers, a plan that was not approved by the village co-op board and was unknown even to many ordinary villagers. Much of the land has been transferred to BD. W village is located in the central area of the Shajing subdistrict, where land is very valuable. But W village co-op has not paid dividends to villagers since 2002 due to bank debt, which amounted to over 1 billion RMB.[31] On the other hand, villagers saw village land developed into small-property buildings one plot after another without any benefits for villagers. In reality, most of the buildings were controlled by BD's companies, even some constructed under the pretense of being "unified-constructed buildings for villagers."

As powerful as BD and his mafia were, they eventually became targets of criminal prosecution. In February 2012, the Guangdong provincial government launched a campaign called "three strikes and two build-ups." The three strikes were striking the "monopolization of the market through violence," striking the "making and selling of counterfeit products," and striking "commercial bribes"; the build-ups were building up "a social reputation system," and building up "a market supervision system."[32] BD's monopoly of the small-property market in Shajing and

[29] *Id.* at 69. [30] *Id.* at 244–245.

[31] 田加钢、景剑峰："深圳"万丰神话"17年后走入窘境"，"民主与法制时报" 2006年2月12日 [Jiagang Tian & Jianfeng Jing, *The Mystery of Wanfeng Fell into Quandary after 17 Years*, DEM. & RULE OF L. NEWS, February 12, 2006], http://news.sina.com.cn/c/2006-02-12/10499078862.shtml.

[32] 新华网专题报道：广东全面部署 "三打两建" [Symposium: *Guangdong Fully Implements "Three Strikes" and "Two Build-Ups*, XINHUA NEWS GUANGDONG CHANNEL], www.gd.xinhuanet.com/zt12/sdlj/. This campaign was initiated by Wang Yang, then governor of Guangdong province and currently Vice Premier of the State Council of

his bribery of government officials became prime targets under the campaign. In early 2012, the police rooted out the Xinyian mafia; 102 mafia members were arrested, leading to over one hundred criminal prosecutions.[33]

BD was prosecuted for organized crime, murder, kidnapping, bribery, etc. Most interestingly, however, he was also prosecuted for "illegal transfer of land use rights" despite the fact that village leaders who sold the land to his company were not prosecuted for the same crime. Pan, the head of W village, was prosecuted for participating in a mafia and bribing government officials but not for "illegal transfer of land use rights."

The crime of "illegal transfer of land use rights" is set forth in Article 228 of the Chinese Criminal Code, which defines it as "with the purpose of making profits and in violation of land administration laws, transferring land use rights illegally, in a serious situation." Such "serious situations," as defined by the Chinese Supreme Court, include "making more than 500,000 RMB profits," "transferring more than five *mu* of basic agricultural land," etc. BD's crime was defined as "particularly serious." Penalties were increased according to the amount of profits made from the crimes.[34]

The court decision also cited the findings of the Shenzhen Commission of Urban Planning, Land and Resources to support its decision, which investigated BD's land transfer businesses and transferred the whole case file to the court.[35]

China. As stated, the main purpose was to improve the market environment. Before that, Bo Xilai, former Mayor of Chongqing and member of the Political Bureau, also had a campaign under his jurisdiction against organized crime. Both politicians were viewed as strong competitors for the new standing committee of the Political Bureau.

[33] 杨涛："小产权房挽救集体经济 终引发土地产权争夺战"，南方都市报2013年11月26日[Yang Tao, *Small Property Saved Collective Economy, but Led to Fighting over Land Rights at the End*], SOUTHERN METROPOLITAN DAILY, November 26, 2013], http://ndnews.oeeee.com/html/201311/26/532165.html.

[34] *See also* 全国人大常委会关于刑法第228条第342条第410条的解释（2001年8月31日第九届全国人民代表大会常务委员会第二十三次会议通过）[Interpretation of the National People's Congress Standing Committee on Articles 228, 342 and 410 of the Criminal Code (August 31, 2001) (passed in the 23rd Meeting of the Ninth Nat'l People's Cong. Standing Comm.)].

[35] 深圳市规划土地监察局："涉嫌非法转让、倒卖土地使用权犯罪案件移送书"（深规土行移字[2012]第0004号），引用于前述深圳中院判决书第543页[Shenzhen Bureau of Planning and Land Supervision, Document of Transferring Criminal Case of Illegal Transfer and Sales of Land Use Rights No. 0004 (2012), *cited in* Shenzhen Court Decision, at 543.]

First, BD's lawyer argued that BD's transfer of land use rights was not among the four situations prohibited by the Decree on Transfer of Collective-Owned Land Use Rights ("No. 100 Decree") promulgated by Guangdong province. No. 100 Decree is a product of Guangdong province's efforts to accommodate widespread rural land development and transfer within its jurisdiction, which play a crucial role in its economic development.[36] Second, BD's lawyer argued that Guangdong province has allowed the lease of rural land with multiyear terms. BD's transfer of rural land use rights actually took the form of long-term lease and thus was consistent with No. 100 Decree. Third, BD's lawyer argued that the Guangdong Higher Court also promulgated Guiding Opinions on the Transfer and Lease of Collective-Owned Non-Agricultural Land Use Rights, which further recognize the legality of transfer of rural land use rights.[37] Fourth, Guangdong is at the frontier of reform and has experimented beyond the national practice, which is why the above decree and guiding opinions have been made. In practice, small-property transactions have been prevalent and there are cases in which the local courts have recognized the effectiveness of such transactions.[38] Numerous other transactions occurred without incurring criminal punishment. For example, before BD's "illegal transfer of land use rights" of one plot of land, its owner, SX village, had sold the same plot to a public university and bought it back to sell to BD.[39] The court did not ask why the SX village or the public university was not prosecuted for the "illegal transfer of land use rights."

There were other parts of the court decision that showed the carelessness and inconsistency with which this crime of "illegal transfer of land use rights" is defined and punished. For example, among the 22,845 square meters of land BD bought from SL village, 2286.92 square meters of land has been given legally transferrable rights to the SL village co-op by the Shenzhen Commission of Urban Planning, Land, and Resources.[40] The court did not bother to distinguish this patently legal part of the transaction from the overall illegal transaction.

Altogether, it is clear that this was not a case of enforcing the current legal prohibition on the transfer of collective-owned/rural land use rights. Instead, it was a case against organized crime, which is a "flagrant form of criminality" that elicits the governments' legal enforcement. There is a

[36] *See* Section 1.4 for more details.
[37] Shenzhen Court Decision, *supra* note 11, at 551–52. [38] *Id.* [39] *Id.*
[40] *Id.* at 543.

Chinese saying that "a fire on city wall brings disaster to the fish in the moat." In this case, BD and his mafia are the city wall on fire while small-property business are the suffering fish, i.e., collateral damage. This also explains why the Shenzhen Commission of Urban Planning, Land, and Resources bothered to investigate the "crime of illegal land transfer" in this case but rarely does so in other situations.

Pan and his village are other fish that are suffering. After BD and Pan were arrested, W villagers finally felt secure enough to claim their land rights. Some villagers then blocked the entrance of a small-property building that buyers had not yet moved into and cut off the supply of electricity and water. Villagers claimed that Pan and his colleagues sold the land too cheaply and demanded a renegotiation of the contract with the real estate developer for a higher price. Their argument was that the conventional division of profits in Shajing between village co-ops and their partners in small-property development was 3:7. But in the original contract, W village got much less than that ratio. W villagers even blocked a main avenue in Shajing to protest and claimed that they would defend their land interests to the death. On the other hand, buyers, most of whom were from out of Shenzhen, also hung out a banner reading, "Who stole my house? I want to go home! Give back my home!" Thus it became a so-called mass incident.

The Shajing government dared not declare the transactions invalid. Rather, it left the renegotiation to the real estate developer and the W village co-op. It expected that the real estate developer would pay more money to the village co-op. Recalling my previous discussion on the security of small-property contracts, it is worth noting that even after the villagers' protest, the village co-op actually assured buyers several times that the apartments were theirs because they paid for them; they should not worry that they would be taken away.[41]

Nevertheless, the crackdown on the Xinyian mafia created a crisis for W village and its small-property business. It also signified that the gray small-property market could be captured by organized crime, a problem that ranks much higher on the agenda of legal enforcement. It is worth wondering why W village went from gray to black, i.e., why Pan participated in BD's mafia and why he sold land so cheaply to the mafia. As

[41] 陈小瑛："深圳小产权房冲突祸起集体土地贱卖 危局待解"，"华夏时报"2013年4月20日[Xiaoying Chen, *A Crisis to Be Resolved: Conflicts of Shenzhen Small-Property Houses Were Caused by Cheap Sales of Collective Land*, HUAXIA DAILY, April 20, 2013], http://finance.sina.com.cn/china/dfjj/20130420/001615212277.shtml.

Pan's lawyer would argue, neither seemed a rational decision. I will explore explanations for his decisions in Parts II and III.

5.1.2 Z village: In the Name of Law

Z village is located in the Nanwan subdistrict of Longgang District. It has an area of 0.85 square kilometers, with a total population of 11,270, only 424 of whom were official residents of the village in 2004.[42] All the villagers share the same family name, Deng.

As discussed previously, formal institutions have adapted to the small-property market and have left narrow openings for villages to get legal rights to develop and transfer their real estate. Despite the uncertain and costly nature of such an endeavor, quite a few villages have succeeded. The most successful example, as I introduced in another chapter, is the Caiwuwei case, in which the highest skyscraper in Shenzhen was developed from village land, and villagers got a substantial portion of the profits. Z village is a more ordinary example that has gone white. Crucial steps in this decade-long process were undertaken in the name of the law. The village made intentional use of law, sometimes even making interpretations of the law opposite to those of the Shenzhen government, in order to achieve its goals. The two key factors in getting legal rights to real estate development are the government's recognition and support, and the collective action problem of villagers. The corresponding questions are: (1) as villagers are basically free to build small-property constructions with only sporadic inference from legal enforcement, why should the Z village co-op bother to spend several years getting approval, incurring costs and lost profits in the process and (2) why did it bother to sue a nail household, when usually it is the opposite situation, i.e., the nail household seeking legal redress?

As in many other villages, including W village, as early as 1982, Z village began to build factories to rent to Hong Kong investors. Most such factories did not go through any procedure before construction and were thus small-property constructions. For example, the first outside investor, a private printing house, rented its factory from four village

[42] 深圳市樟村股份合作公司章程（2014年10月5日股东大会通过）[Shenzhen Z village Coop Charter (passed by Shareholders' Assembly on October 5, 2014.)]; 龙岗区民政局："关于村改居的通知"（龙民[2004]43号，2004年9月3日）[Approval of Replacing Villagers' Committees with Residents' Committees (Longgang Dist. Bureau of Civil Affs. Doc. [2004] 43, September 3, 2004)].

cadres, who rented land from the village collective and built factory space. One of the cadres said that they did this in response to the Shenzhen government's call for industrial development and the need to create jobs for villagers, but they did not apply for any certificate for the building from the government.[43] The factory was built in 1993, and by 2012 now it had more than 100 employees, quite a few of whom were local villagers.[44]

Z village is different from many other villages in that it is close to the Shenzhen Reservoir, a main water source for the city. In 1986 the Shenzhen city government designated part of the village as a protected area, planned to move all factories within this area elsewhere, and prohibited any further building within the area. Before the government fully enforced its prohibition, Z villagers they built several factories to create a situation in which, as the Chinese saying goes, "the rice is cooked" (i.e., what is done cannot be undone).[45]

Economic development in Z village is full of tales of making money from land. In addition to the above industrial land development, housing land development also played a significant role. For example, in 1992 Z village divided one portion of the village land into small plots and then sold them to outsiders to build residential houses.[46]

Gradually, land became the main income source for village members. In particular, since the late 1990s, villagers found that they could live a good life just by renting their houses to migrant workers. To accommodate this demand, it became a trend for individual villagers to rebuild and expand houses.[47]

But villagers' business of "planting houses" did not go much further before it was stopped. In 1999, DYJ, then thirty-two years old, returned to Z village from his job as a vice president of a large real estate company in Shenzhen to run for the directorship of the villagers' committee. He succeeded and decided to stop his fellow villagers' chaotic house building. Meanwhile, under his leadership, Z village began to apply for legal rights to redevelopment from the Shenzhen government in 2000.

[43] *See* Chapters 2 and 3 for more details.

[44] 程瑜、刘思霆、严韶："一个客家村落的都市化——深圳樟树布村改革开放30年的发展与变迁"，广东人民出版社2010年版。[Yu Cheng, Siting Liu & Shao Yan, URBANIZATION OF A HAKKA VILLAGE: THREE DECADES OF DEVELOPMENT AND CHANGE IN ZHANGSHUBU OF SHENZHEN 115 (2010)].

[45] *Id.* at 79. [46] *Id.* at 80. [47] *Id.* at 82–83.

In 2003, Longgang District government approved the redevelopment plan of Z village; the Shenzhen City Bureau of Environmental Protection also finished an environmental impact evaluation in 2004. WK, a top real estate company in China, also set up a project company to work on the Z village redevelopment; a contract between the project company and Z village co-op was signed in 2004.

According to the village redevelopment plan, 191,648 square meters of land would be redeveloped, among which 104, 870 would be used for housing development, 32,000 would be used for public green space, and 54,778 would be used for roads. The neighborhood would have more green space and better roads than before. The redevelopment would demolish 173,241 square meters of housing but would eventually add 471,915, including 15,500 square meters of public housing to be operated by the Shenzhen government, 3,200 square meters of housing for a kindergarten, and 2,500 square meters of complementary facilities.[48] Overall, the redevelopment would increase both the quantity and quality of housing in the village. As compensation, villagers would be given one or one and a half times the total floor area actually demolished.[49] Most important, the new houses would have certificates of legally alienable rights.[50]

No villagers opposed the redevelopment plan in principle, but negotiations with a few did not succeed. As in any other real estate projects, hold-out was a problem. The following is an excerpt from a negotiation transcript between DYJ, chairman of the village co-op board, and Ms. DXH and Mr. LRL, a couple who owned a small-property building of about 1000 square meters:

> DXH: Overall 55,000 per square meters, Sister wants this price, you help your sister get this (from the real estate developer).
>
> DYJ: Impossible! What's the market price? I can only do that.
>
> DXH: This is my offer. You do your best!
>
> DYJ: The market price is a bit over 10,000 and up to 20,000; how can you ask for 55,000 from them? Too far from the market price!
>
> DXH: It's impossible to do it according to the market price.

[48] 樟旧村改造合作合同（2004年12月6日）[Z Old Village Redevelopment Cooperation Contract (December 6, 2004)].

[49] Most villagers have at least two buildings: one is left by their ancestors and is usually only one floor; the other is more modern and is several floors high. The ancestor's house would be compensated at 1.5 times the total floor area; the other kind of housing would be compensated as if it were new housing after redevelopment. *Id.*

[50] *Id.*

DYJ: Bargaining has limitations. Give you an example: assuming the market price is 20,000 and you ask for 25,000, that's okay! – I wouldn't say you're over and would only say it's a bit high. Beyond that, it's absurd! . . .

LRL: You tell me whether our house is worth 50 million!

DYJ: You're joking!

LRL: Not a joke! You tell me yes or no.

DYJ: Impossible.

DXH: It's hard to say impossible. You help me (to negotiate with the developer)!

LRL: We're not threatening. We have our needs. We're talking to you because we support (your redevelopment plan.) Otherwise we wouldn't negotiate with you. We support you, but we have our needs. It's another thing whether such a need is right or not.

DYJ: It's absurd for you to ask for such a price. 25,000 would be rational. But the price you asked (55,000) is irrational.

LRL: It's not very absurd. We should have mutual understandings.

DYJ: That's beyond what I can do.

DXH: I don't even have a job. You help me (get this deal done)![51]

In such a situation, what can the village co-op and the real estate developer do to push this redevelopment plan forward? I would like to point out first that violence and threats were involved in this case: one of the nailhouses, not the one discussed above, was demolished in the early morning when the owners were not there. According to a manager of the developer, it was a mix-up by the workers.[52] A coffin had been put in front of the house before the demolition by unidentified people.[53]

This actually makes the question more perplexing: if violence and threats were the common and effective ways to get things done, why did the village co-op, the developer's partner, bother to sue the owners of the nailhouse in court, as discussed below?

On August 27, 2011, seven years after the official approval of the village redevelopment plan, the village co-op had an extraordinary shareholders' meeting that passed a resolution by 83.39 percent of the total shares to *regain the use rights to the collective-owned land within the redevelopment area and to sue the owners of nailhouses who refused to*

[51] 与邓、梁的谈话记录（2011年9月21日）[Transcript of Negotiation with DXH and LRL (Sept. 21, 2011).]

[52] 冯易："房子"被拆错"业主还被打"，"深圳晚报"2011年9月2日[Yi Fen, *House Demolished Wrongly and Owner Beaten*, SHENZHEN EVENING NEWS, September 2, 2011], http://wb.sznews.com/html/2011-09/02/content_1731660.htm.

[53] *Id.*

sign a contract with the village co-op.[54] The court accepted the case on September 23, 2011. According to the Z village co-op, by September 19, 2011, 91.32 percent of the households had signed contracts with it on 92.20 percent of total floor area to be demolished. Only nineteen households, i.e., 8.68 percent of the total, owning 7.80 percent of total floor area to be demolished, had not signed contracts.[55]

This is an unprecedented case in Shenzhen and it raises two legal questions: (1) Is the village land still collective-owned after the Shenzhen government's land nationalization in 2004 and (2) even if the village land is collective-owned, could the village collective by a majority vote reclaim use rights to residential plots that have been allocated to individual households?

In 2004, the Shenzhen government initiated a so-called land nationalization after urbanization (*chengshihua zhuandi*) campaign. The government declared that Shenzhen had finished urbanization and was the first city in China without agriculture. Accordingly, all land within its jurisdiction should be state-owned pursuant to Article 10 of the Chinese Constitution, which states that "urban land is state-owned," and Section V, Article 2 of the Implementing Decrees of Land Administration Law, which states that, "The following land is state owned: in the case that members of all village collectives are all converted to urban residents, the land originally owned by village collectives."[56]

Following its interpretation that the conversion of the status of villagers from rural to urban would convert the collective-owned land to state-owned land, the Shenzhen city government initiated a year-long campaign to replace 300,000 villagers' rural *hukou* with urban *hukou*, integrating them into the urban welfare system. The Shenzhen city government, which was the actual controller and manager of state-owned land within its jurisdiction, intended to grab the collective-owned rural land through this land nationalization.[57] Eventually, the Shenzhen city

[54] 樟村股份合作公司股东代表大会决议（2011年8月27日）[Res. of the Shenzhen Z village Coop Shareholders' Representative Assemb. (August 27, 2011).]

[55] 广东省深圳市龙岗区人民法院民事判决书（2011）深龙法民三初字第4886号 [Longgang Dist. Court Decision Civil Case First Trial No. 4886 (2011).] (hereinafter Longgang Court Decision)

[56] 中华人民共和国土地管理法实施条例（1998年12月27日国务院令第256号发布）[Implementing Decrees of Land Admin. Law, art. 2, § V (State Council No. 256, December 27, 1998).]

[57] *See* Chapter 1: Though urban land is state-owned, in reality it is the city/county governments which control and manage the land.

government did grab a lot of rural land, but not all of it as the government had planned – in reality, farmers still exercised *de facto* control over 300 square kilometers of the original rural land.[58]

This land nationalization was a serious encroachment on villagers' land rights. It was also an intentional misinterpretation of the Chinese Constitution and LAL and was designed to get around the increasingly strict approval procedure of the central government in controlling local governments' land requisitions. Although the Shenzhen government managed to get acquiescence from the central government leadership and finish the land nationalization before the Ministry of Land and Resource ("MLR") could stop it, the Chinese MLR still declared publicly that, "This practice in Shenzhen cannot serve as a precedent." ("*shenzhen zuo fa, xia bu wei li.*") To minimize the challenge of such a practice to the Chinese land administration system, the MLR even promulgated a special opinion interpreting Section V, Article 2 of the Implementing Decrees of Land Administration Law, stating that when the land of village collectives is requisitioned *according to law* and all its members have become urban residents, the little amount of remaining land can be requisitioned to become state-owned land *according to law*. This means, for example, that when all land allocated to rural households within a village have been requisitioned according to law (in particular, the central government's land use quota system), the remaining land that has not been allocated could also be requisitioned because all the rural residents have become urban residents. Thus a local government cannot nationalize rural land within a village by declaring its members to be urban residents. A certain sequence must be followed to requisition rural land: rural residents can lose their rural status only after their land is taken; it cannot be done in reverse order.[59]

Notwithstanding the above, the central government has essentially acquiesced in the official position of the Shenzhen city government: officially, all land within Shenzhen has been nationalized and no collective-owned rural land remains. The Z village co-op's resolution explicitly contradicted the Shenzhen city government's official stance that all land was state-owned. The resolution claimed that land in the village was still collective-owned and thus the village co-op had rights to

58 *See* Interview Transcript II 132–157 (2012).

59 网易专题： "小产权房"合法化"，深圳只能是特例" [Symposium: *Legalization of Small Property?: Shenzhen Is a Special Case*], http://news.163.com/special/00012Q9L/xiaochanquanfang090602.html.

regain the individual use rights to the collective-owned land. The relationship between the village co-op and individual village households is one of "land administration," as in the relationship between a land owner and land users. As the owner's rights are superior to that of users, the village co-op has the right to regain the use rights.

The second basis of the Z village co-op's argument was that this redevelopment plan had been passed by the majority vote of the village shareholders, and owners of the nailhouses, as shareholders of the village co-op, were bound by the resolution of the shareholders' meeting. This is quite an innovative argument. The nailhouse owners challenged this argument on the ground that the shareholders' meeting did not have the authority to decide this issue because their residential plots and houses were not part of the village co-op's property. They even checked the asset sheet of the village co-op and found that their property was not listed there.

Nevertheless, the local court decided that the village co-op had the authority to regain the land underneath the nailhouse and pay compensation to the owners at its objective value, which, according to an appraisal company hired by the village co-op, was only a little over one million RMB.

The court's decision consists of two parts. In the findings of fact, the court highlighted the fact that the redevelopment plan would serve the public interest at large, and had been passed by the majority votes of the village co-op shareholders, and that before the suit over 90 percent of the villagers had signed a contract with the village co-op.[60] In this factual part of the opinion, the court also reviewed the history of this nailhouse plot, which had been allocated to the owners for free due to their village membership.[61] In the part of the opinion on the interpretation of laws, the court decided that the relationship between the village co-op and individual households should be governed by the Chinese laws relating to rural residential plots, and thus their relationship was that between owners and users.[62] The court avoided explicitly stating that the land was still rural land; rather, it said that the relationship between the village co-op and its members should still be governed by the rural land law. This intentional ambiguity left room for the court to pursue what it saw as a decision made in the public interest and the interests of the local

[60] Longgang Court Decision, *supra* note 55. [61] *Id.* [62] *Id.*

government without directly conflicting with the official interpretation of the Shenzhen government. If pressed, the court could say that even if the land is nationalized, the relationship between village co-op and its members should still be governed by the rural land law as the Shenzhen government did not make special provisions about this relationship. In fact, village co-ops are officially recognized by the Shenzhen government as the dominating form of collective economic organizations, although in the changed situation, "collective economic organizations" do not have to be rural anymore.[63]

The court did not really point out the specific laws that grant the village co-op the right to regain use rights from its members. There are no such laws. Even during the Cultural Revolution, People's Commune's members had relatively secure rights to their houses and the land underneath, as residential houses were part of "living materials" (*shenghuo ziliao*).[64] The communist ideology is that "productive materials," such as water buffalo and agricultural land and facilities, should be owned and used collectively, but land underneath commune members' houses, though part of the collective ownership of rural land, was "living material" and members' rights to use it should be respected.[65] Thus there is no valid legal basis for the village co-op to regain residential plots from its members.

Nor did the court's recognition of the majority vote for the redevelopment plan have any valid legal basis. Z village co-op's practice is similar to what Heller and Hills propose as "Land Assembly Districts" ("LADs"). Here the problem facing the Z village co-op and the land developer is the same problem that LADs are designed to resolve:

> After the land assembler has purchased a part of the planned larger parcel, the assembler becomes locked into purchasing the rest of it to avoid duplicating the site-specific investment at another site. Thus, existing owners become monopoly suppliers of the assembled land. Knowing that the assembler requires each of their parcels, every owner

63 "深圳经济特区股份合作公司条例"（1994年4月29日深圳市第一届人民代表大会常务委员会第二十二次会议通过 1997年9月4日深圳市第二届人民代表大会常务委员会第十七次会议第一次修正 2010年12月24日深圳市第五届人民代表大会常务委员会第五次会议第二次修正）[Shenzhen Special Economic Zone Decree of Share Coops (passed on April 29, 1994; revised on September 4, 1997 and December 24, 2010).

64 韩俊主编："中国农村土地问题调查"，上海远东出版社2009年版[HAN JUN, ED., SURVEY ON CHINA'S RURAL LAND ISSUES 89 (2009).]

65 *Id.*

> may seek to be the last to sell, and then to hold out for all of the extra value created by the assembly. With several such holdouts, negotiations collapse because the assembler, of course, cannot pay the entire surplus to each owner.[66]

The only difference is that village co-ops have been created ex ante, rather than ex post as the LADs had, and this might cause intra-group exploitation.[67] Nevertheless, overall, this solution would be appealing to Chinese local governments as it would "defuse hostility toward eminent domain and avoid drastic limits on local governments' capacity to assemble land."[68] Actually, in Shenzhen and several other Chinese cities, the local government has encouraged intracity villages to do "redevelopment by themselves" ("*zixing gaizao*"). Village community organizations are often better than local governments at persuading their members to sell their residential plots and houses and thus reduce the probability of hold-outs as members value their connections with other members of the community.[69] This innovation created by Z village Coop would further smooth redevelopment of intracity villages by providing a legal solution to the collective action problem and would increase the village communities' bargaining power in dealing with nailhouses. Actually, in this case, the owners of the nailhouse accepted compensation of about 25 million RMB, a figure close to the offer the village co-op board chairman gave in the negotiation described above.[70]

What Z village co-op has achieved in this case is astounding. It not only challenged the official definition of land ownership in Shenzhen, but it also provided a new solution to the collective action problem in village redevelopment projects. What is more astounding is that it won the suit in a local court. Both Z village and the local court made use of the layering and fragmentation of law and made use of laws in its favor. But still the question remains as to why and how Z village achieved this.

[66] Michael Heller and Rick Hills (2008). Land assembly districts, 121 *Harv. L. Rev.* 1465, 1473.

[67] *Id.* [68] *Id.* at 1490.

[69] For theoretical discussions on the role of communities in law and economics, *see* Gideon Parchomovsky and Peter Siegelman (2004). Selling Mayberry: Communities and individuals in law and economics, 92 *Cal. L. Rev.* 75; Robert Ahdieh (2011). Beyond individualism in law and economics, 91 *B.U. L. Rev.* 43.

[70] Of course, the extra amount was paid under the table to avoid other villagers' protests.

5.2 Searching for an Explanation[71]

5.2.1 Layering and Fragmentation of Law

Many laws are involved in the above two cases, including:

(1) Clauses in the Chinese Land Administration Laws that prohibits rural land transfer and development.[72]
(2) Clauses in the Chinese Constitution and Land Administration Law on land ownership: "urban land is state-owned; rural land is collective-owned."[73]
(3) Clauses in the Chinese Criminal Law that criminalize the "illegal transfer of land use rights."[74]
(4) The Guangdong Provincial Decree (No. 100 Decree) that allows transfer of rural land use rights.[75]
(5) The Shenzhen City Decree that nationalizes collective-owned land in Shenzhen.[76]
(6) Interpretation of the LAL by the Chinese Ministry of Land and Resources that contradicts Shenzhen city's interpretation of the LAL, on which the above Shenzhen city decree is based;[77]
(7) Variously, the Shenzhen City Decrees on old village redevelopment, on historical illegal buildings, and on enforcement of the national

[71] This part provides only a preliminary explanation in the sense that it does not investigate the influence of different demographic factors of the two villages on their property arrangements. In particular, W village has much more official residents and is farther to the city center than Z village. The author plans to investigate this issue through a more comprehensive and systematic study in the future.

[72] Chinese Land Admin. Law art. 43, 63. For more details, *see* Chapter 1.

[73] Chinese Land Admin. Law art. 8; Chinese Const. art. 10.

[74] Chinese Crim. Code art. 228; 关于审理破坏土地资源刑事案件具体应用法律若干问题的解释(2000年6月16日最高人民法院审判委员会第1119次会议通过)[Chinese Supreme Court Interpretation on the Application of Laws in Criminal Cases of Damaging Land Resources (June 16, 2000)] (passed by the 1119th Meeting of the Supreme Court Judicial Committee)].

[75] 广东省集体建设用地使用权流转管理办法（广东省人民政府令第100号）[Guangdong Provincial Decree on the Transfer of Use Rights to Collective-Owned Construction Land (June 23, 2005, Guangdong Provincial People's Government No. 100 Decree)].

[76] "深圳市宝安龙岗两区城市化土地管理办法"（深府[2004]102号，2004年6月26日）[Shenzhen City Government Decree on Urbanization Land Administration in Longgang and Bao'An Districts (No. 102, June 26, 2004)].

[77] 国务院法制办公室、国土资源部关于对"中华人民共和国土地管理法实施条例"第二条第（五）项的解释意见国法函[2005]36号[Opinion on Interpretation of Implementing Decrees of Land Administration Law art. 2, § V (State Council Office of Legal Affairs and Ministry of Land and Resources, March 4, 2005).]

> prohibition on rural land development and transfer, which are mutually contradictory to each other.[78]

This case shows both the layering and fragmentation of law. "Layering" refers to variety, competition, and conflicts of laws in the vertical dimension, i.e., between laws made by different levels of authorities, such as those between the Chinese central government, provincial governments, and cities.[79] "Fragmentation" refers to the fact that even laws and policies made by the same government could conflict with each other and that reconstitution of the same law at different local settings might lead to different outcomes.[80] The application of laws is far from unified. It is thus a question of which laws would be applied to a situation. Unfortunately, there are often no clear rules defining jurisdiction, as many laws and policies are made ad hoc. Even laws that are supposed to be applied uniformly can be interpreted and applied to unforeseen situations. The use of laws in ways that deviate from their intended purpose can be called "legal conversion,"[81] which is an oft-adopted strategy by actors in a fragmented and layered institutional framework. As we have seen from the two villages, it is hard to expect these fragmented and layered laws to be applied systematically to all villages. The question is then why Z village successfully gained legal rights to develop its land despite its challenge to the local government's definition of land ownership, while W village suffered from criminal prosecution. In other words, why didn't the Shenzhen government punish Z village for challenging its definition of land ownership? Or why did W village not get legal rights to develop their land from the government? In brief, why did the two villages end up in different social control systems?

5.2.2 *The Challenge to Law and Social Norms*

The layering and fragmentation of law has not received much attention in the existing research on law and social norms, which focuses more on the evolution of social norms and how law can change social norms, but not how social norms can change law and the *co-evolution* of law and

[78] *See* Chapter 4 more details. [79] *See* Tsai, *supra* note 7, at 121.

[80] *See* Ryken Grattet and Valerie Jenness The reconstitution of law in local settings: Agency discretion, ambiguity, and a surplus of law in the policing of hate crime, 39 *Law & Soc'y Rev.* 893 (2005).

[81] *See* Tsai, *supra* note 7, at 122; Kevin J. O'Brien (1996). Rightful resistance, 49 *World Pol.* 31.

social norms. A systematic theory of the choice between law and social norms, and more broadly, between the five different "social controllers," though elaborated by Professor Ellickson in his groundbreaking book published in 1991, has not been fully explored.

According to Professor Ellickson's system of social control, there are five controllers that form the sources of rules. An actor who imposes rules and sanctions on himself is exercising first-party control. A promise-enforced contract is a system of second-party control. Third-party control differs from second-party control in that the rules are ones to which the actor may not have agreed and enforced by persons not involved in the primary interactions, including social norms, organization rules, and law.[82] In Chapter 3, I discussed how second-party control can effectively bind participants of the small-property market as their interactions mostly rely on a focal point to coordinate their behaviors. In the above mafia-style small-property business, the controlling system seems to be the mafia's organization rules; in the "in the name of law" village case, the controlling system seems to be the law.

Professor Ellickson also discusses the choice of different controllers. According to him, there are controller-selecting norms, which are defined as "informal rules through which nonhierarchical groups seek to apportion tasks among these various sources of social control."[83] As Ellickson writes:

> The crucial role of controller-selecting rules has gone little noticed. In a society replete with governments, private organizations, social forces, contractual arrangements, and individuals potentially capable of self-control, there must be rules that decide, for each domain of human activity, the division of social-control labor among the various controllers. Controller-selecting rules perform this function. They coordinate the social-control domains of, among others, the visible sovereigns that make and enforce laws and the invisible social forces that make and enforce norms.[84]

Professor Ellickson argues that "*[t]he content of controller-selecting norms will reflect general expectations about the comparative efficiencies of social forces and the state in generating and enforcing rules.*"[85] Any social control system gives rise to certain associated transaction costs and members of a social group must consider various factors to minimize their total costs.[86] This theory explains why there is "order without law"

[82] Robert Ellickson, *Order without Law: How Neighbors Settle Disputes* 126–127 (1991).
[83] *Id.*, at 240. [84] *Id.* at 134–135. [85] *Id.* at 249 [86] *Id.* at 242.

in Shasta County: A change in animal trespass law fails to affect resource allocation because "legal rules are costly to learn and enforce." In the particular setting of Shasta County, between parties with complex continuing relationships, the transaction costs of resolving minor disputes through social norms are lower than through formal legal rules.[87] The choice is thus made for the "social norms" controller.

Professor Ellickson's system of social control, and in particular controller-selecting norms, develops the Coase theorem and implicates more complicated and diverse relationships between law and social norms, as proved by the studies in the past two decades. It is also consistent with the Coase theorem and the dominating literature on legal enforcement. The most classic statement in economic analysis of legal enforcement remains that "the optimal amount of enforcement is shown to depend on, among other things, the cost of catching and convicting offenders, the nature of punishments – for example, whether they are fines or prison terms – and the responses of offenders to changes in enforcement."[88] This means that whether a person chooses to control his behavior through the legal system or other social-control systems depends on a comparison of the costs and benefits in different systems. The behavioral challenge to law and economics mostly targets the rationality hypothesis, but not the cost-benefit analysis part.[89]

As the Shenzhen case has revealed, law is layered and fragmented in China. In such situations, what is the law and when is it enforced? What is the controller choice of a village co-op, a main actor of the small-property market?

Following the cost-benefit analysis in law and economics, we could say that villagers would pursue the law that is most friendly to small property or would decide whether to comply with the legal prohibition on rural land development and transfer based on their calculations of their costs and benefits of complying with or disobeying the law. The problem is that with layering, fragmentation, and mutually conflicting laws, it is

[87] *Id.* at 242–249; Robert C. Ellickson (1986). Of coase and cattle: Dispute resolution among neighbors in Shasta County, 38 *Stan. L. Rev.* 623, 628–629.

[88] Gary S. Becker (1974). Crime and Punishment: An Economic Approach, in *Essays Econ. Crime & Punishment* 2.

[89] *See, e.g.*, Christine Jolls, Cass R. Sunstein and Richard Thaler (1998). A behavioral approach to law and economics, 50 *Stan. L. Rev.* 1471; Christine Jolls, *Behavioral Law and Economics*, National Bureau of Economic Research Working Paper No. w12879. (2007); Ryan Bubb and Richard H. Pildes (2014). How behavioral economics trims its sails and why, 127 *Harv. L. Rev.* 1593.

hard to conduct the cost-benefit analysis, which is premised on a static view of the mutually influencing and coevolving social-control systems. The basic idea is, what would happen if we add a third dimension, time, to Professor Ellickson's two-dimension system of social control?[90]

When I say the village co-op led by Pan was captured by the mafia system, it is not to say that there had been a mafia system of small property ready for Pan to adopt. It is the confluence between the small-property market and the mafia that conceived the mafia-style small-property business. Similarly, it is not to say that there had been a legal system for the transfer of rural land use rights ready for Z village's leader DYJ to adopt. Although the Shenzhen city government has provided various policies that serve as official channels for villages to get legal rights, all of which are responses to the emergence of the small-property market, whether a village co-op can get legal rights through such channels is also subject to its interactions with the government.

Imagine that you were a village co-op leader in Shenzhen – what are the costs and benefits of developing small-property houses? You would ask whether the government would demolish your small-property constructions and whether you would be sent to prison for "illegal transfer of land use rights." Or you would consider the question from the opposite angle – what are the costs and benefits of not developing small-property houses? What is the possibility of obtaining legal rights to develop the village land? There is no abstract answer to give. It all depends on the micro- and macro- economic situations, the internal governance of your village, the strategy you have taken in dealing with the local government, and other factors. In addition the above factors are changing and mutually influencing each other. Because a village co-op can, to some extent, actually influence what law is applied and when that law is applied, its cost-benefit analysis is influenced by its own choice.[91]

For the analysis of this *fluid* situation, we must understand that for any particular actor, behaviors are decided not only by the economic restraints, as Demsetz would argue, nor only by pure communal settings, which Ostrom would emphasize, nor solely by interest groups or other political factors, which Levmore and Wyman would argue, but by all the

[90] Adding a third dimension to Professor Ellickson's two-dimension table of the system of social control would transform the table to a cuboid, as each system would evolve across the time, during which they interact and influence each other. For Ellickson's two-dimension system of social control, *see* Ellickson, *supra* note 82, at 131.

[91] *See* Section 5.3 for more details.

above factors together. Simply speaking, there are not two[92] or three[93] stories about the evolution of property rights. It is one integrated and fluid story with all factors considered. Moreover, given particular economic, social, and political restraints, different actors still can choose different strategies. It is thus important to add actors into our discussion of institutions as well.

5.2.3 Multiple-Network Evolution

Two pieces of recent research are particularly helpful in this regard. One is a theoretical framework developed by Nee and Opper. In their multilevel causal model of institutional change, they discuss how private entrepreneurs under economic incentives developed market practices decoupled from the old communist regime, and then how formal institutions made changes promoted by private entrepreneurs' collective action and their own legitimacy seeking. The formal institutions also monitor the evolution of informal norms, and private entrepreneurs from time to time have to comply with a particular set of formal rules. Overall, a private entrepreneur behaves in response to market incentives, pressures from his fellow businessmen and partners, and micro- and macro-level changes in formal institutions. Both the community of private entrepreneurs and the political institutions have kept evolving together with the market.

Padgett and Powell develop a more delicate theory of the emergence of organizations and markets. They "hope to point the way toward a new path in new social science – namely, toward a theory of the co-evolution of social networks" through their "infrastructural work of synthesizing social science with biochemistry."[94] According to them, "[L]earning at the human level is equivalent to co-evolution of rules and protocols at the 'chemical' level. Actors thereby become vehicles through which autocatalytic life self-organizes."[95] Their mantra in the book is that, "[I]n the

[92] *See, e.g.*, Saul Levmore (2002). Two stories about the evolution of property rights, 31 *J. Legal Stud.* S421; Richard A. Epstein (2002). The allocation of the commons: Parking on public roads, 31 *J. Legal Stud.* S515.

[93] *See* Elinor Ostrom (1990). *Governing the Commons: The Evolution of Institutions for Collective Action*.

[94] John F. Padgett and Walter W. Powell (2012). *The Emergence of Organizations and Markets* 3. (I am grateful to Xiaohong Xu for recommending this literature.)

[95] *Id.*

short run, actors create relations; in the long run, relations create actors."[96]

They argue that most social science proceeds according to the logic of methodological individualism – taking as given some constitutive features of the hypothesized individual or actor. In contrast, they argue for a multiple-network perspective:

> Our social science disciplines usually segregate their intellectual activities by analyzing only one domain at a time, as if the other domains and disciplines did not exist. At best, external domains are conceptually black-boxed as reified 'environments' without examining their internal structures. In contrast, the whole point of a multiple-network perspective is to superimpose multiple domains, with their respective production and exchange networks, and to examine feedback dynamics.[97]

Together with other authors, Padgett and Powell present fourteen historical case studies to develop their theory, which can be divided into three clusters: European co-evolution of early capitalism and state formation; Communist economic reform and transition; and technologically advanced capitalism and science.[98] One case study is the multiple-network ensemble in Renaissance Florence, as the authors write: "In the economic domain, for example, the person may be a businessman; in the kinship domain, he may be a father; in the political domain, he may be a politician – all depending upon how he is attached to others in that domain. Properly speaking, individuals don't have goals; roles have goals. Consistency of motivations across roles should in no way be presumed for complicated persons."[99]

Going back to our Shenzhen case, a village co-op leader has three identities: economic actor, villagers' representative, and implementer of government policies. A change in one network influences his choices in the other two. These mutual and interactive networks are the key to understanding the relationship between small property and the related formal institutions in Shenzhen, and understanding what law is activated and why and when it is applied.

5.3 Village Leaders' Three Identities and an Integrated Explanation

In general, a village co-op leader in Shenzhen has three identities: operator of the village co-op company responsible for maximizing its

[96] *Id.* at 2 [97] *Id.* [98] *Id.* [99] *Id.* at 5.

economic performance; villagers' elected representative charged with taking care of villagers' interests[100]; and implementer of government policies. As a company operator, a village leader should respond to economic incentives, such as the demand for rural land development and transfer. But his leadership and capability is not the only factor that contributes to the economic performance of a village co-op; the specific macro- and micro-economic situations matter as well, among other factors. A village co-op leader has a choice to develop the village land illegally against the legal prohibition or to apply for legal rights from the government, in particular considering the adaptive government policies adopted after the formation of the small-property market.[101] As an elected village representative, a village co-op leader faces pressure for reelection and, thus, must satisfy villagers' demands for dividend payments and other economic benefits as much and as soon as possible. The source for dividend payments can range from a purely illegal small-property business to other more legal businesses of the village co-ops, such as renting factory space. As an implementer of government policies, a village leader is expected to implement government prohibition on rural land development and transfer as effectively as possible. In reality, he has the discretion to implement the prohibition to different degrees.

Choices in each arena are influenced by decisions in others. For example, economic choices and their effectiveness influence the other two arenas. Successful economic choices can increase a village co-op leader's capacity to negotiate with both the government and ordinary villagers. An economic failure, on the other hand, would make it hard for a village co-op leader to satisfy the demands of either the government or ordinary villagers. As a result, he or she would tend to choose to make quick money from short-term small-property business. In the long run, this further decreases the leader's capacity to implement government policies or take care of ordinary villagers' interests, and increases the risk of being captured by organized violence.

Of course, once an economic choice is made, it also has influence on its choices in the other two roles. For example, once the choice of going black is made, it would be hard for a village co-op leader to continue to implement government policies; rather, he would rely on bribery to

[100] Kinship is another factor that might influence village governance and property arrangements. However, as both are single-family-name villages, I assume that the kinship dynamics are not the reason for the difference between them.

[101] *See* Chapter 4.

continue his interactions with government agencies and officials. At the community level, being captured by the local mafia would damage a village co-op leader's ability to respond to ordinary villagers' interest demands; in the end, he would have to rely mainly on organized violence to discourage villagers from demanding economic interests and participation in village governance. The mutual influence between the political and community levels is also significant. Once a village co-op leadership is captured by organized violence, although a relationship with the government could still be maintained through bribery, the hope for that village to be incorporated into the new legal order, i.e., a system that would grant it legal rights to develop its land, diminishes. In contrast, village co-ops that are proactively implementing government policies, even though sometimes just rhetorically or under a radically different interpretation, might be rewarded by being given priority in entering into the legal system.

5.3.1 *Investment Failure, Village Crisis, and Mafianization*[102] *of W village*

The village co-op form originated in W village. In 1984, W village began to experiment with village co-ops as a way to collect money for village development. Villagers can buy shares from the village co-op. In the early years, shareholders had good returns and W village was depicted as a model of "socialist common ownership," which was said to provide a way to combine the advantages of market and socialism.[103] W village even held a conference on the so-called W village Model in the Grand People's Hall in Beijing, where important national activities are often held. For a while, W village seemed to exemplify a new future for rural China. National leaders, including Deng Xiaoping, toured W village, which was an indication of its success.[104]

As discussed in other parts of this book, village co-ops are responsible for the management of collective-owned land that is not allocated to individual households. They use such land to build factories to rent to

[102] In the existing literature, mafianization means "the pursuit of organized crime based on the privatization of physical security measures." Stuart Corbridge et al. (2005). *Seeing the State: Governance and Governmentality in India* 39; *see also Economic Liberalization and Political Violence: Utopia or Dystopia?* 331 (Francisco Gutierrez and Gerd Schonwalder, eds., 2010).

[103] Tian and Jing, *supra* note 31.

[104] Southern Metropolitan Daily, *supra* note 4, at 174.

outside investors. Although village co-ops could participate in many other kinds of economic activities, land rent is the main income for all of the village co-ops in Shenzhen. Village co-ops are responsible for issuing dividends to their shareholders/villagers each year. Dividends become the main indicator for the village co-op's performance in "representing villagers' interests." Villagers often cannot tell and even do not care how well the collective asset is managed by the village co-ops; what they really care about is how much dividend they are paid each year. Their support for the village co-op is also mainly based on the amount of dividends they are allocated. As the board of a village co-op is elected every three years, village co-op leaders care more about how much dividend they could pay to shareholders/voters than they care about the long-term performance of the village co-op. Additionally, shares are spread among villagers, rather than concentrated among a few villagers. Even members of the village co-op boards have no more shares than ordinary villagers. Thus, there are no controlling shareholders who might have enough incentives to monitor the long-term economic performance of the village co-op.

If a village co-op makes money, issuing dividends is not such a problem. But tensions often arise when a village co-op does not make enough money to issue dividends or even suffers a loss. Unsurprisingly, some village co-ops issue dividends to villagers even when they have suffered an economic loss in that year. They often borrow money from banks to do so. In particular, many village co-ops rely on small-property businesses to issue dividends. Although it might not be the best investment from a long-term perspective, selling a plot of land to an outside investor, or cooperating with a real estate developer to build a small-property compound and then using the sales money to issue dividends, makes perfect sense for village co-ops, as they are under pressure to issue dividends to their shareholders.

Unfortunately, the success of W village co-op did not last long. At its height, in 1992, the year Deng Xiaoping's tour, W village co-op began to buy land in Hainan, Jiangxi, Yunnan, and many other parts of China. All of these investments failed with the meltdown of the real estate bubble in the early 1990s.[105]

[105] 田加刚、刘丽琦、景剑峰："审计报告揭开南国第一村集资内幕"，"民主与法制时报" 2006年04月09日 [Tian Jiagang, Liu Liyi and Jing Jianfeng, *Audit Report Reveals the Inside Story of Fund Collection at the First Village of Southern China*, DEMOCRACY & RULE OF LAW NEWS, April 9, 2006], http://finance.sina.com.cn/g/20060409/15592485805.shtml.

The leader at the time, who was Pan's father, tried in 1996 to decrease the amount of the annual dividend payment. This triggered a crisis of confidence. Pan's father managed to remedy this crisis by asking for forgiveness from his villagers and promising better economic performance in the future.[106] Afterwards, he began to unseat members of the village co-op board who had disagreed with him during the crisis, and he consolidated control over the village co-op between himself and his close family members. Nevertheless, in 2002, the village co-op could not afford to pay dividends to shareholders anymore.[107] This ultimately led to a lasting village governance crisis.

In 2005 Pan's father decided to retire, but he nonetheless supported Pan in his campaign to become party secretary and co-op board chairman of the village. Pan won the positions amid complaints about the legitimacy of the election. Villagers were unhappy about this, and BD took advantage of this unhappiness. In 2007, a villager who was a little brother of BD stood out and demanded that Pan step down. He and his fellows in the village also mobilized others to go to the sub-district and district governments to report the problems in W village, including the abuse of power and corruption of Pan's father, the alleged cheating in elections, and nonpayment of dividends, etc. The Shajing sub-district government sent a working team to W village to investigate the problems. Pan panicked. Neither the villagers nor the sub-district government liked him. It seemed that he and his father would lose everything after the government's investigation.

In this situation, BD became a life-line. According to Pan:

> BD is from a nearby village. I knew him before that. I knew that he was very powerful in both the white and black worlds ... I knew that if I devoted myself to BD, villagers would not dare make trouble anymore and I would keep my position. So I went to BD and begged him to deal with the villagers. In about one month, the sub-district government asked me and the dissenting villagers to go to their office, and we made a deal there. Obviously BD can handle problems that the government cannot handle. Since then, I'm his little brother.

This village governance crisis not only explains why Pan was willing to become a little brother of BD and why W village co-op sold land to BD's

[106] Southern Metropolitan Daily, *supra* note 4, at 177. [107] *Id.* at 172.

companies so cheaply. It also influenced the interactions between W village and the local government.

First, it led to a relationship mainly based on corruption. Because small property is still technically "illegal," the W village co-op paid regular money to government officials not to enforce the legal prohibition.[108] In addition to participating in a mafia, Pan was also convicted of bribery. Each year, in spring festival and mid-autumn festival, the W village co-op sent money to party-secretary Liu of the Shajing subdistrict in the form of gifts. From 2005 to 2012, the total amount was 1.25 million RMB. In 2009 and 2011, when the Bao'An district government decided to demolish several small-property buildings in W village and even to remove Pan from the position of village party secretary, Pan sent money to Liu in the total amount of RMB 1.2 million to resolve the issues.[109] Regarding individual villagers' building of small property, W village co-op did not have the capacity to stop it. As these villagers would complain: "You still owe me dividends – how could you further stop me from making a living by building a small house?"

Second, the village governance crisis excluded W village from the Shenzhen government's village redevelopment plans. In the early 2000s, Pan and his father had been hoping to benefit from the Shenzhen government's village redevelopment policies. They made a plan for redeveloping the village and even showed their plan for a new village to reporters. As of 2014, Shenzhen government has approved over 300 village redevelopment projects, but W village has never been on the list. There are no details available for its application for redevelopment, but its village governance crisis might have caused reasonable concern from the local government about whether the village co-op could persuade villagers to accept the plan and thus to surrender their land for it.

Moreover, the presence of BD would also dissuade any village redevelopment. Because many plots of the village land had been sold to BD or in cooperation with BD, it would be costly to assemble the plots from BD's hands. The village redevelopment plan would grant legal rights to village land and thus required huge capital investment. BD, although rich enough to develop small-property buildings, did not have the billions of RMB required for a village redevelopment project. Village redevelopment projects have been done mostly by the top real estate developers in China, who are among the few that have the financial capacity to take on

[108] Shenzhen Court Decision, *supra* note 10, at 46. [109] *Id.*

such a project. A local mafia involved in organized crime is usually not a favorite business partner of such big companies, which are more sensitive to legal requirements.

In the end, W village was excluded from the legal world and captured by the illegal world of violence and corruption. It was just a matter of time before it became the target of legal enforcement.

5.3.2 *Increasing Dividends, Governing Capacity, and Legalization of Z village*

Z village co-op presents an opposite case. On one hand, as the representative of villagers' interests, it managed to be one of the first groups of villages that were incorporated into the Shenzhen government's village redevelopment plan, and thus one of the first to get legal rights to develop village land. On the other hand, as the implementer of government policies, it successfully controlled small-property development within the village.[110] This was an important factor that helped its application for village redevelopment.

Since becoming the head of Z village in 1999, DYJ demonstrated his talent in developing the economy. His experience in a big real estate company also gave him a new idea for developing the economy: rather than building more buildings, as many other village co-ops in Shenzhen did, he focused on improving the village environment, following which housing rents were raised. During his leadership, dividends paid to villagers increased at an average annual rate of 10 percent (Figure 5.1).[111]

Increasing dividend payments enabled the village co-op to behave on the basis of long-term considerations. The first thing DYJ did was to build a park to preserve 40,000 square meters of lychee forest. At that time, many village officials would have preferred to develop the land into buildings for sale or rent. But DYJ intentionally played the "sustainable development" card and pushed this project through.[112] Part of the

[110] This does not mean there were no small-property constructions – in fact the village co-op developed a small-property building, but the local government officials acquiesced in this illegal construction as a reward for the village coop's support for a government expressway project. 徐文阁: "水源保护区违建上千套房全卖光" ，"南方都市报" 2010年6月3日 [Xu Wenge, *Up to One Thousand Small-Property Apartments Were Sold Out*, SOUTHERN METROPOLITAN DAILY, June 3, 2010], http://focus.szonline.net/Channel/content/2010/201006/20100603/242134.html.

[111] Cheng, Liu and Yan, *supra* note 44, at 81–95.

[112] Southern Metropolitan Daily, *supra* note 4, at 86.

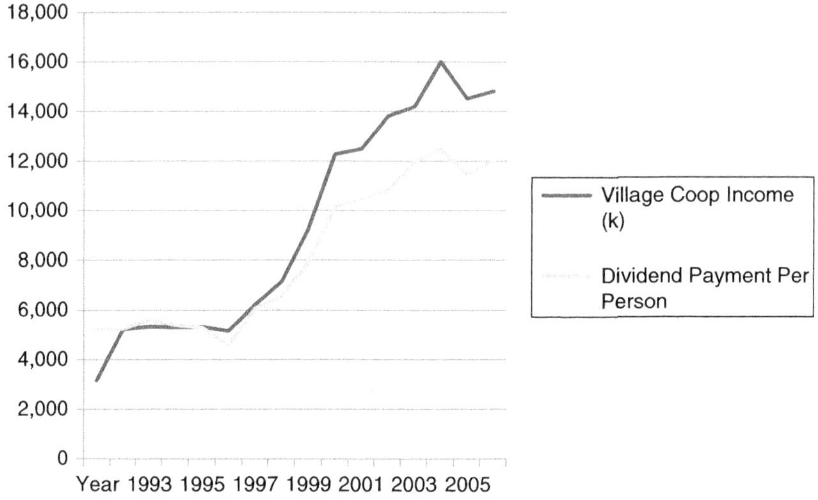

Figure 5.1 Z village co-op income and dividend payment per person: 1992–2007
Source: Author's compilation, data from Cheng, Liu and Yan, *supra* note 45, at 96.

success was attributable to the fact that the village co-op was not under much pressure to make money from this land to pay dividends to villagers.

Increasing dividend payments also won the village co-op leader support from the villagers to overcome the collective action problem. In 2000, a company that rented its factory space from the village co-op planned to move elsewhere because the original factory could no longer satisfy its manufacturing capacity. To expand the factory would involve moving dozens of individual households. DYJ successfully persuaded the households impacted by the expansion to move. As a result, the company paid three million more RMB per year to the village co-op for rental of the expanded factory space.[113]

DYJ also managed to successfully implement government policies on many occasions, even at the expense of short-term village interests. For example, in 2012 the city planned to build an expressway crossing the village and a transformer station. The two projects required over 40,000

[113] "深圳市十大杰出青年候选人：邓" [DYJ, *Candidate for Top Ten Outstanding Youth*], http://news.qq.com/a/20071107/003755.htm.

square meters of land from the village. DYJ persuaded his villagers to support both projects.[114]

Under the "sustainable development" umbrella, the Z village co-op leader successfully restrained villagers from building small-property constructions. It was such a success that Z village became an oft-cited case by government officials who were worried about the continuous spread of small property in the city.

All of the above facilitated Z village's application for village redevelopment. A leader of the Shenzhen city government said, "We should support villages like Z, which strictly control the construction of illegal buildings."[115] Another reason for this quick acceptance is that the restriction of small-property development also decreased the cost and difficulty of redevelopment. As DYJ said, "There will not be villagers who could become billionaires through village redevelopment. The top difficulty for village redevelopment is demolition. We don't have many illegal buildings and thus no complicated compensation problems."[116] This also made the Z village redevelopment an attractive deal for real estate developers. In the end, Z village co-op got WK, a top real estate developer in China, as its partner.

Good relations with the government and a partnership with a top real estate company increased the village co-op's capacity to negotiate with nailhouse owners in resolving the hold-out problem. Winning the case against the nailhouse owners gave the latter no choice but to accept the village co-op's offer. In this instance, the village co-op has actually benefited from the layering and fragmentation of law through its creative interpretation and use of different laws, which was supported by the local court largely because the village co-op had successfully made itself a model of compliance with the law and supporting government policies and projects. In the future, this village co-op's use of majority voting in village redevelopment might also influence the evolution of related formal institutions in Shenzhen.

In conclusion, Z village presents an example in which a village co-op made proactive use of the layering and fragmentation of law. It successfully created an advantage for itself in one system, and used it as leverage

114 *Id.*

115 龙岗区委办公室："第四次旧村改造工作会议纪要"（2003年8月26日）[OFF. OF THE PARTY COMM. OF LONGGANG DIST., SUMMARY OF THE FOURTH MEETING ON OLD VILLAGE REDEVELOPMENT (August 26, 2003).]

116 Southern Metropolitan Daily, *supra* note 4, at 87.

in other systems, the success of which in turn increased its leverage in the original system. This process went on continuously and not only did the village co-op win legal rights to develop and sell its land, but the accumulation of successful cases could also promote change in the whole system.

5.4 Conclusion

As emphasized in other chapters, I take an evolutionary approach in examining the small-property market in China and informal property rights in general. Legalization and mafianization represent two possible destinies of small property in Shenzhen. I hesitate somewhat in using the words "legalization" or "mafianization," as it is easy to imagine a legal system or a mafia system that a village co-op tries to enter or is forced to enter, without recognizing the fact that both systems are changing and evolving together with the small-property market. In addition, social norms always govern some spheres and will not be replaced by law, as evidenced by the prevalence of shadow economies in developed countries.[117] In Section 5.3, I highlighted the role of dividend payments in village governance and the chain effects in the other two systems, but this is not a story about how economic success/failure led to success/failure in politics and community governance. Dividend payments themselves are subject not only to the market, but also to the latter two factors. The three systems, market, community, and law, are mutually influencing.

There are also many other villages somewhere on the spectrum between legalization and mafianization. We can say that each village has its own distinct destiny that is determined by the co-evolution of the three systems and its own strategic choices, which are often made on an *ad hoc* basis.

To understand the evolution of property rights, traditional research emphasizes the definition of property rights at the beginning and at the end and compares efficiencies of different property arrangements. But the definition of property rights is the outcome rather than the cause of the evolution of property rights, and it is often unclear and ambiguous in an unsettled society. This chapter shifts the focus from investigating

[117] The ratio of shadow economy in GNP ranges from 8.8% in the United States to 28.6% in Greece in OECD countries; in developing countries, it can be as high as 67.3% in Georgia. *See* Friedrich Schneider, *Size and Measurement of the Informal Economy in 110 Countries*, Workshop of Australian National Tax Centre, ANU, Canberra. (2002).

different property arrangements to investigating the different roles of key actors that are negotiating for property rights, how they make use of the layering and fragmentation of law and other social-control systems to achieve their goals, and how such efforts result in changes in law and other social-control systems.

The mutual-influence and co-evolution of different social-control systems seem mysterious and are difficult to observe and predict. To understand these phenomena, we need to focus on the different roles of the key actors that play simultaneously in all the social-control systems, none of which are an external environment or isolated from the others. The key actors connect different systems and make their co-evolution possible. Ultimately, the goal is not "rooting property law in social contracts," but is instead a new kind of symbiotic relationship between different social control systems, in particular law and norms. Evolution of property rights is a systematic and integrated project.

6

All Quiet on the Judicial Front?

Property norms are more responsive to social change than is property law. Property law reform (statutory change) is difficult and time-consuming in China. Can the courts play a role in mediating between property law and norms? In the United States, Supreme Court decisions have marked different stages of social progresses, recently extending marriage rights to same-sex couples, for example. Should we have the same expectations of the Chinese judiciary or imagine its role in a similar way? Despite the strong party-state in China, the meaning of the law and its application are subject to the discretion of the judiciary to some extent. The judiciary's application and interpretation of the law are particularly crucial when the law-on-the-books lags development in reality. In the context of small property, implementing the legal prohibition on rural land development and transfer would jeopardize both economic development and social stability. However, the judiciary in China, a civil law jurisdiction, is supposed to apply (rather than make) the law. Does the Chinese judiciary then facilitate or hinder social and economic change? Can we rely on the Chinese courts to serve as an engine of social change? This chapter examines the Chinese judiciary's responses to small property, with a focus on how it addresses the tension between legality and social change.

At first glance, the local judiciaries of Shenzhen and Beijing adopt differing approaches: The former follows an approach of judicial minimalism, i.e., "leaving things undecided,"[1] whereas the latter follows an approach more akin to judicial entrepreneurialism. Intermediate and basic courts in Shenzhen, which are funded by local governments of the same level, choose either not to decide cases or to make decisions that uphold the law but intentionally leave the

[1] Cass R. Sunstein (2001). *One Case at a Time: Judicial Minimalism on the Supreme Court* preface, X.

consequences of illegality blank. In contrast, the local judiciary in Beijing invented a rule of reliance interest to adjudicate most of the surplus value of small property to the buyer in an effort to minimize a decision's negative impact on the buyer and, to a limited extent, deter small-property sellers from suing. Underlying these two seemingly different approaches, however, is the same bottom line: make no changes to the status quo or minimize the negative impacts of illegality when it must be confirmed.

As discussed in previous chapters, there are two major categories of disputes: property disputes and contract disputes. In Chinese judicial practices nationwide, the focal point is contract disputes. *De facto* possession is respected, and the violation of such possession often occurs in cases in which the *de facto* possessors use their small property as a pledge. Even in these cases, local courts in Shenzhen generally protect *de facto* possession. Such possession disputes are discussed below in the section on Shenzhen, but this chapter's main focus is contract disputes and the different approaches to them.

This chapter supplements the argument that social norms are more responsive to social development than is the law by extending the discussion from property laws and regulations to judicial decisions. Its conclusion is that the Chinese judiciary is reactive and responsive to social change rather than leading it. It thus represents neither a hindrance to nor engine of social change. The remainder of the chapter is structured as follows. Section 6.1 discusses judicial minimalism in the Shenzhen courts. Section 6.2 analyzes judicial entrepreneurialism in the Beijing courts, with a focus on the Artist Village case in which the court invented the rule of reliance interest. Section 6.3 examines the evolution of the responses of the Supreme People's Court (SPC) to small property, as well as high courts' attitudes nationwide, to present a comprehensive view of the Chinese judiciary's approach to small property. Section 6.4 concludes.

6.1 Judicial Minimalism in Shenzhen

The local judiciary in Shenzhen initially refused to adjudicate small property cases. As time has gone by, however, there have been an increasing number of cases directly or indirectly involving small property. The local courts have protected *de facto* possession against private trespass and chosen either not to decide whether small-property contracts are legal or to intentionally leave the consequences of illegal contracts unelaborated in cases requiring them to confirm the illegality of small-property contracts.

6.1.1 *Illegal Property, Valid Possession*

As noted, the local courts of Shenzhen have protected the *de facto* possession of small property against encroachment. In Shenzhen, such encroachment generally occurs in the context of private debt collection, with the encroacher taking possession of a small property to collect a debt owed by the small-property owners. In these cases, the Shenzhen courts have taken a clear standing to protect owners' right of possession. In Chinese legal terms, the original owner has no legal ownership, but rather valid possession. The following case serves to illustrate.

In 2006, a Ms. Han bought an apartment through a Cooperative Housing Construction (CHC) arrangement in Jianshang New Village in the Bao'An District of Shenzhen. She also filed an application with the Shenzhen government in 2009 to register her apartment as a "historical illegal housing." As mentioned in Chapters 2 and 4, registration of historical illegal housing is the preliminary requirement but not guarantee for legalization. A Mr. Huang moved into this apartment without Ms. Han's consent because her husband owed him money. Ms. Han filed a suit with the court to have Mr. Huang evicted.

Both the Bao'An Basic Court and Shenzhen Intermediate Court confirmed that Mr. Huang had a receipt stating that Ms. Han's husband had pledged a small-property house to him in return for borrowing RMB 100,000, but still made it very clear that Mr. Huang had violated Ms. Han's possession rights and ordered him to move out immediately. Mr. Huang's argument, however, is quite essential to our theoretical interests here. In the appellate writ, Mr. Huang argued as follows.

> The first instance decision on the one hand acknowledges that the property rights of the apartment are unclear while recognizing Ms. Han as the valid possessor on the other hand, resulting in an obvious contradiction. If it is unclear [in law] who is the property rights holder of the apartment, we cannot be sure that Ms. Han is the legal possessor. Clearly Ms. Han has no legal basis to occupy the apartment; therefore hers is also illegal possession. The appellant occupied the apartment on the basis that Ms. Han's husband has borrowed RMB 100,000 from him and agreed to use the apartment as a pledge. Therefore, the appellant's possession has a

> basis and is not illegal encroachment. If we followed the first-instance court's logic, [and] if we can assume Ms. Han's legal possession is based on so-called cooperative housing construction, which has neither legal effect nor legal clarification, then the pledge agreement between Ms. Han's husband and the appellant can also make the latter's possession legal.[2]

Mr. Huang also argued that because the status of small property is a policy question yet to be settled by the Shenzhen government the court should have declined to adjudicate the case, leaving it to government agencies to deal with.[3] The Shenzhen Intermediate Court did not buy that argument, however. It decided that possession is *de facto* per se. Ms. Han was able to provide solid evidence of a CHC contract to prove her *de facto* possession, which did not contradict the fact that she had no legal property rights to the apartment. Hence, her rights and interests in the apartment should be protected by law. Regarding Mr. Huang's pledge right, in contrast, even if one can be said to exist, he cannot take possession by himself. Furthermore, small property cannot be legally pledged. Accordingly, it was right for the first-instance court to confirm the illegality of Mr. Huang's possession. Hence, the Shenzhen Intermediate Court ordered Mr. Huang to move out of the apartment within ten days of its decision.[4]

This case can be understood only against the backdrop of small-property development, which is discussed in Chapter 2. CHC, although illegal, has been widely adopted throughout Shenzhen's history with the encouragement of and endorsement by the village collectives in which such real estate is located. So-called private pledge agreements, in contrast, enjoy no support from, and nor have they been confirmed by, the "network of institutional innovators" at whose center the village collectives lie, and therefore have no legal or *de facto* force. In other words, technically neither type of possession has any legal basis. However, their respective strengths in the social settings, of which the courts are part and recognize, are fundamentally different.

In cases such as that brought by Ms. Han, court recognition of valid possession often depends on a clear record, either in the shape of forms issued by village collectives or the official registration of historical illegal housing. An application for the status of "historical illegal housing" is

[2] 广东省深圳市中级人民法院民事判决书（2015）深中法民终字第546号 [Shenzhen Intermediate People's Court Civil Case Final Trial No. 546 (2015)].
[3] *Id.* [4] *Id.*

only the preliminary step of legalization. The whole process is long and unpredictable, resulting in only a small portion of housing ultimately being legalized relative to the numerous applications covering hundreds of thousands of small-property buildings filed. In other words, filing an application with the government is far from constituting legalization. However, in practice, government receipts, each of which has a unique number, become official documents on which the Shenzhen courts rely in deciding who has possession rights. Although such official receipts are not a guarantee for legalization, they save court costs by confirming the facts of possession and minimizing potential conflict between judicial and administrative decisions.

6.1.2 *Contracts*

The Shenzhen courts have adjudicated the validity of small-property contracts in two ways. The first is to confirm the illegality of the contracts without elaborating upon the consequences of voiding them. The second is to defer to government policies and to decline to adjudicate before the government clarifies the legal status of small property houses. It is unclear why two approaches are applied even to cases decided by the same division of the Shenzhen Intermediate Court within a given year. However, they are not fundamentally different in the sense that both are responsive and reactive.

6.1.2.1 Confirming Illegality without Adjudicating the Consequences

The Shenzhen Intermediate Court has confirmed the illegality of rural land transfers in a few cases while intentionally leaving the consequences of void contracts unelaborated. In the cases discussed below, neither party to the dispute in question sought to clarify those consequences because both wanted the court to make a decision that they could then use, not as final adjudication on who owned the property, but rather as strong legal evidence to either support their application to the government for legal titles, or to contest the other party's application within the government system. Because the court does not have the final say on small-property houses, it does not mind confirming the illegality of small-property contracts while leaving the real consequences to government policy and the bargaining of the parties involved.

In the first case considered here, Tongle village co-op had sold a 100-square-meter plot of land to a Mr. Liao to build a residential house in 1999. In 2013, it then sued Mr. Liao in court to void the contract on the basis of the illegality of rural land transfers. The first-instance court ruled for Tongle, citing the national legal prohibition on rural land development and transfer. It decided that although Mr. Liao had built a residential house and applied for the registration of historical illegal housing, the original rural land transfer contract was still illegal because there was no legal registration of either the land transfer or the house. Mr. Liao appealed, arguing that Tongle village co-op had not disputed the validity of the contract in the fourteen years since its signature. On the contrary, it had actually assisted Mr. Liao in preparing his application for historical illegal housing. Mr. Liao also presented his unique application number, indicating that his house was official, albeit illegal, i.e., officially illegal. Tongle village co-op's real motivation for filing its suit was to force Mr. Liao to sell his house for village redevelopment. The appellate court, i.e., the Shenzhen Intermediate Court, rejected Mr. Liao's argument, confirming the illegality and invalidity of the contract. It specified that simply filing an application with the government was insufficient to render the original contract legal.

The interesting part of the court's decision is that it intentionally left the consequences of declaring the contract illegal undecided. For reasons that remain unclear, both parties insisted that the court should not decide on the house built on the land in question. The court appeared quite relieved by such insistence, making it very clear that it was not deciding on the house, or, more specifically, who should have the house and what should be done with it. Instead, it declared only that the two parties could discover the results of the invalid contract by seeking other legal channels.[5]

In the second case, individuals named Liao and Li had signed a housing transfer contract in 2010 that involved the former selling the latter a 1600-square-meter building for RMB 2 million. The contract had been witnessed by a lawyer and registered with the village co-op. Again the seller sued the buyer to void the contract. The first-instance court asked both parties whether they would like the court to decide on the consequences of an invalid contract, and both replied that there was no need. Li had already applied to the government for the registration of illegal historical housing. The court confirmed the illegality of the contract and decided to leave the consequence thereof

[5] 广东省深圳市中级人民法院民事判决书（2014）深中法房终字第961号[Shenzhen Intermediate People's Court Civil Case Final Trial No. 961 (2014)].

unelaborated.[6] Li appealed to the Shenzhen Intermediate Court, making the two following arguments:

First, the court should defer to the government when dealing with illegal historical housing to avoid any conflicts between the government and the judiciary. In Li's lawyer's words:

> Whether such a building belongs to [the category of] historical illegal building or whether Li's property rights will be confirmed in the end must be decided by the administrative agency. This case lies in the sphere of administrative reform rather than in the jurisdiction of the court. If the court decided to invalidate the contract without clear laws, it would greatly increase the uncertainty and cost of reforms related to historical illegal buildings. If the court decided that all transfers of historical illegal buildings are invalid, it would create a situation in which the court's decisions contradicted the confirmation and titling of the administrative agency, which would not be good for the stability and seriousness of the law or the related reforms in Shenzhen. It would also create new social conflicts.[7]

Second, it was argued that Liao had signed the contract with the real intention and awareness of the legal uncertainty of rural land transfer and had sued to void the contract simply because housing prices had increased. Accordingly, the court should defend the good faith principle in contract law and discourage such speculative legal actions.[8]

Despite these powerful arguments, however, the Shenzhen Intermediate Court confirmed the illegality of the transfer with reference to national laws. Its decision did not elaborate on the consequences of the invalid contract.

6.1.2.2 Deferring to Governmental Policy

The Shenzhen courts have also taken the less controversial approach of deference to government policy. In a 2015 decision, for example, the first-instance court declined to decide on the validity of the contract in question, determining that the contract parties could sue again after the administrative agency had dealt with the illegal building concerned. One party appealed, with recourse to the same argument as that made by the Shenzhen Intermediate Court in the aforementioned case, that is, that there was no need for the administrative agency to deal with the illegal building first. However, in this case, the same court as the appellate court

[6] 广东省深圳市中级人民法院民事判决书（2014）深中法房终字第2025号[Shenzhen Intermediate People's Court Civil Case Final Trial No. 2025 (2014)].

[7] *Id.* [8] *Id.*

disregarded this very argument that itself had previously made, confirming the first-instance court's decision to defer to the administrative agency.[9]

However, this solution came with a cost, as illustrated by the argument made by one of the parties in another case:

> Shenzhen City started investigating and dealing with historical illegal buildings in 2009, but to date has not dealt with the applications effectively. The urbanization of rural areas is a very long process. The court's decision of deference leaves the property *res nullium*, which is against common sense and not good for dispute resolution or settling conflicts.[10]

Nevertheless, the Shenzhen Intermediate Court, again the appellate court in this case, adjudicated that without proper legal certificates or an administrative decision on historical illegal buildings, it had no way of determining the validity of the contract and thus had to reject the original seller's claim.[11]

Overall, the judicial practice of the Shenzhen Intermediate Court has not been consistent. This lack of consistency is probably due not to corruption but to the lack of clear guidance from the law and, more fundamentally, to the conflict between law and reality. In both of the approaches discussed above, the court has played a minimal role, neither departing from the law nor changing the status quo in reality. However, law and reality are in tension with each other, which is why the court confirmed illegality but refused to elaborate upon the consequences of invalid contracts. Deference to administrative decisions is an even safer choice. The cost, as some litigants have pointed out, is the continued uncertainty over small property. In response, the Shenzhen Intermediate Court can argue that such uncertainty is not its responsibility; what it can do is simply not exacerbate the situation. This approach can be called judicial minimalism with Chinese characteristics.

6.2 Judicial Entrepreneurialism in Beijing

Small property development and transactions play an important role in the economic and societal development of periurban areas in Beijing.

9 广东省深圳市中级人民法院民事裁定书（2015）深中法房终字第1965号 [Shenzhen Intermediate People's Court Civil Case Final Trial No. 1965 (2015)].

10 崔庆林广东省深圳市中级人民法院民事裁定书（2014）深中法房终字第658号 [Shenzhen Intermediate People's Court Civil Case Final Trial No. 658 (2014)].

11 *Id.*

Hundreds of thousands of such transactions have occurred since the 2000s. The Beijing City Departments of Land and Urban Planning have initiated quite a few demolition campaigns against small-property buildings.[12] However, as in Shenzhen, such legal enforcement efforts have had limited success, as evidenced by the continuing existence of the market. The local courts of Beijing have taken a more direct approach than their Shenzhen counterparts in adjudicating small property disputes. While confirming the illegality of small-property contracts, they have introduced the concept of reliance interest in defining the consequences of void contracts. As a result, small-property sellers need to pay most of the surplus value to the property buyers. The reliance interest principle thus reduces the negative impacts on small-property buyers and, to a limited extent, deters sellers from suing. As the following discussions will make clear, the Beijing approach has involved a coordinated effort in which the Beijing High Court has defined the principles while the lower-level courts have figured out the specific mechanism, i.e., the introduction of the concept of reliance interest in dealing with small property, in contrast to the individual decision-making we saw in the case of Shenzhen.

6.2.1 Beijing High Court: Mediating between Upholding the Law and Resolving Social Problems

The Chinese judiciary is not supposed to make laws; it is charged only with applying laws. Each provincial-level jurisdiction has one high court, which is the highest court within that jurisdiction and is tasked with the responsibility of maintaining the consistency of the judicial decisions reached by the lower courts it oversees. When a gap between reality and the law emerges, the lower courts cannot find a clear criterion for adjudicating cases, and inconsistency arises. Such a situation arose in 2004, leading the Beijing High Court to promulgate an opinion clarifying the validity of small property contracts and the principles of dealing with such cases.

12 *See*, e.g., 市国土局：加强农村集体土地管理，依法使用集体土地 [City Land Administration Bureau: Strengthening Rural Collective Land Administration and Use Collective Land in Accordance with Law],www.beijing.gov.cn/zfhf/jbdrd/t1322421.htm; “北京市禁止违法建设若干规定” (2011年1月10日)（北京市政府第228号令） [Beijing City Several Provisions on Prohibiting Illegal Construction, Beijing City Government Ordinance No. 228, January 10, 2011].

It first defined the nature of the disputes heard to date:

> These cases mainly concerned a house seller suing a house buyer to void the contract and get her house back. The seller was usually a rural village member, and the buyer was usually an urban resident or from another village; occasionally the buyer was also the village member. Such transactions were often made more than two years before the litigation, and [some] even more than ten years ago. Both parties fulfilled their contract obligations; payment was made, and the buyers moved into the houses in accordance with the contracts. However, in most cases there was no registration of the change in housing ownership or residential land use rights. The reason for the litigation was generally an increase in land value, land expropriation or housing demolition resulting in a much higher value of the house than the original contract price. [In a typical case], the seller sued the buyer to grab the surplus value. Many buyers had renovated, redecorated or even changed the original building.[13]

The Beijing High Court made it clear that its opinion was a summary of a meeting among judges from the first civil division, filing division, and division of supervision, and should be referred to by the lower courts. The meeting summary promulgated the majority opinion, indicating that there was a minority opinion that was not incorporated into the summary. The majority opinion held that small-property contracts should be deemed void. The main reasons for that opinion are as follows. First, small-property house transactions involve rural residential land transactions, which are prohibited by law. Second, residential land use rights are an entitlement enjoyed by the members of rural collectives and cannot be transferred. Selling rural houses constitutes selling rural land, which endangers the rights of village collectives and is explicitly prohibited by law. Third, there is no registration system for rural house transactions, and a buyer cannot obtain legal protections for property ownership. Fourth, recognizing the validity of small property contracts is not conducive to the protection of sellers' interests. In many cases, sellers are in a weak position, and their interest in survival is related to their demand for the return of their houses. All in all, the Beijing High Court concluded that such contracts should be deemed void as a principle.

The Beijing High Court also specified three operating principles. First, respecting history and considering the reality. This principle recognizes that

[13] 北京市高级人民法院关于印发农村私有房屋买卖纠纷、合同效力认定及处理原则研讨会会议纪要的通知（2004年12月15日京高法发[2004]391号）[Beijing City High People's Court Notice on Circulating Summary of the Meeting on Rural Private Housing Transaction Dispute and Contract Effect Adjudication, December 15, 2004, No. 391.]

small-property transactions occur against the backdrop of a burgeoning migrant population and ongoing urbanization. On the one hand, the legal prohibition is a reality; on the other, judges should recognize the complicated nature of such cases and settle conflicts of interests properly. Second, emphasizing both legal effect and social impact. Decisions must be made in a way that facilitates dispute resolution, guides behaviors of the parties' concerned, and constrains farmers' behavior in dealing with their houses. Third, comprehensively evaluating both parties' interests. In particular, after deciding to return a house to the seller, the court should also make proper arrangements for the house buyer, including allowing sufficient time for her to relocate.[14]

The Beijing High Court tackled the small property issue in another meeting summary in 2006. This time, it published the minority opinion from the 2004 meeting, which emphasized the uncertainty of the law and the lack of explicit legal prohibition and argued that recognizing the validity of small-property contracts could constrain farmers from selling their houses and also be conducive to stabilizing the current housing possession relationship. Moreover, restricting farmers from voiding small-property contracts would be consistent with the principle that parties should not profit from their own mistakes, and serve to protect the bona fide reliance of buyers. It is also a requirement of estoppel and the principle of good faith. This 2006 meeting summary also clarified the allocation of liabilities in the case of void contracts, with the seller and buyer assuming the major and minor liabilities, respectively.[15]

6.2.2 The Artists' Village Case: Ma v. Li

Xindian Village is located in Songzhuang Township in Tongzhou District, a periurban district of Beijing. In the 1990s, the township government implemented a development-by-culture policy, which attracted hundreds of artists, including an artist whose last name is Li, to base themselves in Songzhuang. In the years since, artists and the accompanying industry have become important pillars of the Songzhuang society and economy. Most of the artists bought houses from farmers. Li, for example, paid a farmer named Ma RMB 45,000 for a rural house. Both parties signed the contract, which also bore the signature of a middleman

[14] *Id.*

[15] 北京市高级人民法院民事审判实务疑难问题研讨会会议纪要（2006年9月14日）[Beijing City High People's Court Meeting Summary on Difficult Cases in Civil Trial, September 14, 2006].

and the seal of the villagers' committee. The villagers' committee even recorded the transaction on Ma's land use rights certificate, which he delivered to Li along with the house. Li subsequently redecorated the house and added three new rooms with the approval of the villagers' committee.[16]

However, in 2007 Ma sued Li in the Tongzhou District Court seeking to void the sales contract. Ma was not alone in taking such action, with a growing trend among farmers to file such suits in an attempt to profit from rising land values.[17] This particular case drew widespread attention nationwide and prompted the Beijing local judiciary to implement the aforementioned principles outlined by the Beijing High Court. The national media coverage also made the judges aware of the *de facto* guiding effect of their decision in the case. Given that the judges subsequently published commentaries to explain their decisions, it is also plausible that the local judiciary intended to make the case a *de facto* guiding case.

In the first instance, the Tongzhou District Court ruled that contracts in violation of the law and administrative regulations were void. As an urban resident, Li was not permitted to buy a rural resident's house. The result of the void contracts was that Li would have to return the house to Ma, whereas Ma would have to compensate Li "according to the current value of the house."[18] With the Tongzhou District Court's authorization and an application by Ma, a real estate company appraised the value of the house and the other structures that Li had added to the property at RMB 93,808, which did not include the value of the residential land use rights. Therefore, the court adjudicated that Ma should pay Li compensation in that amount.[19]

Li appealed to the No. 2 Intermediate Court of Beijing, which followed the two meeting summaries issued by the Beijing High Court and confirmed both that the contract was void and that Ma was entitled to the value of the house and additional structures.[20] Such compensation

[16] 北京市第二中级人民法院民事判决书(2007)二中民终字第13692号 [Beijing City No. 2 Intermediate People's Court Civil Case Final Trial No. 13692].

[17] 李馨(Li Xing), 城镇居民购买农村私有房屋的合同无效 [Contracts through which Urban Residents Bought Rural Private Houses Are Invalid], "人民司法（案例）" [People's Judiciary: Cases], 2008年第10期，第25页 [No. 10 (2008), page 25].

[18] 北京市通州区人民法院民事判决书（2007）通民初字第1031号 [Beijing City Tongzhou District People's Court Civil Case First Trial No. 1031 (2007)].

[19] *Id.*

[20] 北京市第二中级人民法院民事判决书(2007)二中民终字第13692号[Beijing City No. 2 Intermediate People's Court Civil Case Final Trial No. 13692].

obviously did not take into account the increased land value. The No. 2 Court introduced a new concept to tackle the imbalance in interests between the two parties that the Tongzhou court's decision would cause:

> Considering that the seller knew that the house and residential land was inalienable and argued for the voiding of the contract many years later, he should bear the main responsibility for the void contract. Regarding compensation for the buyer's loss of reliance interest (信赖利益), we should comprehensively consider the increase in land value or benefits to the seller in the case of demolition and compensation, as well as the buyer's loss due to the difference between the current house value and the original price.[21]

In short, although rural residential land use rights are inalienable, the seller's compensation to the buyer should consider the increased land value because of the violation of the buyer's reliance interest. The latter principle was the creation of the Beijing No. 2 Court, as Li never mentioned reliance interest. Procedurally, the Beijing No. 2 Court cannot adjudicate additional compensation to Li because she appealed on the basis of the effectiveness of the contract rather than the inadequacy of the compensation. Following this decision, Li initiated another suit in the Tongzhou District Court in 2008. With the court's authorization, a real estate company appraised the value of the residential land at RMB 264,700. The Tongzhou District Court awarded 70 percent of the residential land value to Li, confirming the Beijing No. 2 Court's judgment that Ma should bear the main responsibility for the void contract.[22]

What happened afterwards is also interesting. The enforcement of judicial decisions has been problematic in China. It was thus questionable whether Li would return the house voluntarily. Also recall that the Beijing High Court requires a balance between legal effect and social impact in such decisions. The Tongzhou District Court postponed the enforcement of the first case decision confirming the invalidity of the contract. Instead it waited until the second case, i.e., the compensation case, had been decided and persuaded Ma to pay compensation first. However, Li still maintained that she could not return the house without a place to relocate. To avoid any element of "social instability," the Tongzhou District Court coordinated with the government of Songzhuang Township, where the house was located, which agreed to find a

[21] *Id.*

[22] 北京市通州区人民法院民事判决书（2008）通民初字第02041号[Beijing City Tongzhou District People's Court Civil Case First Trial No. 02041 (2008)].

place for Li to live and create art. As a result, Li voluntarily returned the house to Ma.[23]

As noted, the judges of both the Beijing No. 2 Intermediate Court and Tongzhou District Court subsequently published commentaries providing more background details on their decisions. First, Judge Li Xing of the former court, who handled the appellate decision introducing the concept of reliance interest, suggested that judges should explicitly explain the consequences of void contracts to the parties concerned, directly ask whether the losing party would like to sue for compensation, and explain to her the legal basis of such a suit, i.e., reliance interest. Judge Li essentially called for this judicial entrepreneurialism approach to be used in dealing with similar cases in the future. This is very different from the Shenzhen courts, which avoided giving a clear opinion on the consequences of void contracts.

A more important question is, what does reliance interest mean? The main consequence of a void contract is pre-contractual liabilities, which are designed to protect the special relationship of trust between the two parties involved in the process of communication, negotiation, and the revocation or voiding of contracts.[24] The party at fault should pay compensation to the other party for her loss of reliance interest, which comprises the direct and indirect losses that she suffers owing to her belief in the effectiveness of the contract. The direct losses include the costs of signing and fulfilling the contract, whereas the indirect loss is the opportunity cost.[25] Both parties to small-property contracts know that the buyer is buying the right to live in a particular area in exchange for paying the seller the contract price. With a shift in the market, the current value of the house combined with the residential land use rights far exceeds the original contract price. That difference in value means that the buyer benefits from voiding the contract, and therefore that the buyer's reliance interest is lost. Recognizing the difference as the buyer's indirect loss is also convenient for the courts. To be clear, this was the

[23] 北京市通州区人民法院(Beijing City Tongzhou District People's Court), 通州区法院经多方协调妥善执结画家村房讼案件(Tongzhou District People's Court Settled the Enforcement of the Artist's Village Case well through Negotiations with Multiple Parties), on file with the author.

[24] 陈汉东 (Chen Handong), 农村房屋买卖协议被确认无效后，出卖人要承担缔约过失责任赔偿买受人信赖利益损失 (Sellers Should Take the Pre-Contractual Liabilities Compensating Buyer's Reliance Interest Loss after Rural Housing Contracts Being Confirmed Invalid).

[25] Li, *supra* note 17.

first time that pre-contractual liabilities, including reliance interest compensation, were applied to a contract that was rendered void due to a violation of the law.

Second, according to Judge Chen Handong of the Tongzhou District Court, who handled the specific compensation of reliance interest, pre-contractual liabilities have five criteria: (1) the contract in question must be signed, (2) one party must violate the legal obligations generated by the good faith principle, (3) one party must be at fault, (4) the party that is not at fault must suffer a loss of reliance interest, and (5) there must be causality between one party's fault and the other party's reliance interest loss.[26] The aforementioned small property case arguably falls into the sphere of pre-contractual liabilities, but only arguably. Most importantly, it is difficult to say which party should have borne the main responsibility for signing an illegal contract because both parties knew it was illegal. Nevertheless, by introducing a relatively reasonable legal principle in hearing the case, the Beijing No. 2 Intermediate Court and Tongzhou District Court found a way to consider both the history and reality of small-property transactions, to maximize both the legal and social impacts, and to achieve a balance between the interests of both parties. This case clearly illustrates the more entrepreneurial and proactive approach adopted by the Beijing local judiciary relative to its Shenzhen counterpart.

6.3 Supreme People's Court and High Courts Nationwide

The SPC is the highest judicial authority in China. It has generally been consistent in its deference to national law and governmental policies on the small property issue. Early in 2007, for example, then SPC Vice President Huang Songyou commented on the issue in his speech at the National Civil Case Adjudication Work Meeting:

> According to Article 6 of the General Principles of Civil Law, civil activities must obey the law and national policies in the absence of related laws. Therefore, when we adjudicate cases, if the law is unclear about a particular kind of disputes, we should look to national policies: if there are national policies, we should adjudicate in accordance with those policies rather than [leaving the matter to] judges' individual discretion. For example, [say that an] urban and rural resident have signed a contract involving the sale of rural residential land or housing but the rural

[26] Chen, *supra* note 24.

resident refuses to deliver the land or house [and], the urban resident files a suit in court requesting that the rural resident fulfill the contract. How [should we] deal with such cases? Current laws, including the Property Law, do not explicitly state whether urban residents can buy residential land or houses in rural areas; therefore, adjudication must apply national policies. Considering that our country's social welfare system has not been fully established and that residential land use rights and houses are the foundation of farmers' livelihood, it is not yet the right time to allow the transfer of rural residential land use rights and housing. As a result, national policies prohibit urban residents from buying rural residential land or houses. The Office of the State Council promulgated the Notice on Strengthening Land Transfer Administration and Strictly Prohibiting Overselling Land on May 6, 1999. Article 2, Section 2 of the Notice states that "houses in the rural area cannot be sold to urban citizens." On December 24, 2004 the State Council emphasized this again in the Decision on Deepening Reform and Tightening Land Administration: "Strengthen rural residential land administration; strictly prohibit urban residents from buying residential land in rural areas." Therefore, according to current national policies, the people's courts should not support urban citizens' litigation claim concerning the buying of rural residential land or houses.[27]

This extract from Huang's speech offers clear evidence of the SPC's deferential approach. In China, the judiciary has not traditionally been an engine or center of social reform.[28] Judges are expected to apply the law and implement government policies rather than to make laws. As the country's highest court, the SPC is particularly aware of its position and function within the wider political structure. For the SPC, adhering to political boundaries is more important than resolving problems. Or, in other words, it can resolve problems and disputes only within the boundaries of its powers, which do not include making laws that go against clear policies set by the administrative branch. This political constraint explains the series of guidelines the SPC has issued in relation to small property, as outlined in the following.

[27] 黄松有(Huang Songyou), 2007年4月9日在全国民事审判工作座谈会上的讲话（节选）[Excerpts from the Speech at the National Civil Adjudication Affairs Forum dated at 4th September 2007], 最高人民法院民事审判第一庭编《民事审判指导与参考》）[Guidance and Reference on Civil Adjudications, edited by the Civil Adjudication Tribunal No.1 of the Supreme People's Court]，2007年第2集，总第30集[2nd Series of 2007, 30th Series in total].

[28] *See* Shitong Qiao and Frank Upham, China's Changing Property Law Landscape. See in Graziadei, M. and Smith, L. (Eds.), Comparative Property Law: Global Perspectives. Cheltenham, UK: Edward Elgar Publishing, 2017.

In 2008, the SPC issued "Several Opinions on Providing Judicial Protection and Legal Service to Promote Rural Reform," the title of which also reveals the function of the Chinese judiciary within the overall political structure. The Opinions state:

> Residential land use rights shoulder the social function of ensuring that all farmers have housing in which to reside and are an important part of rural land administration. We should adjudicate the invalidity of the transfer of rural residential land, which is against laws, administrative regulations and related national policies, and . . . would result in farmers losing their residential land use rights.[29]

The SPC showed some responsiveness to reality in its 2011 Summary of National Civil Case Adjudication Work Meeting. Similar to the Beijing High Court's 2008 opinion, this summary incorporates fault into the allocation of losses. It stipulates that "in considering allocating losses as a result of void contracts, we should consider the parties' fault and avoid imbalance in the parties' interests." It is unclear what brought about this apparent change in attitude.[30]

However, we have found no case in which the SPC has made a decision in accordance with this principle of balancing interests. Instead, in the two most recent National Civil Case Adjudication Work Meetings, the SPC reemphasized its deference-based approach. In its Summary of the 2015 Meeting, held on April 19–20, for example, it states:

> In the current period, our country's urbanization is still at a relatively low level and the social welfare system in rural society is not yet well-functioning. Therefore, residential land still plays the role of social security and social welfare, and as a result the country is not ready to completely lift the restrictions on the transfer of rural residential land use rights. In those areas that have been designated as experimenting with residential land transfer, we can adjudicate disputes concerning mortgages and the transfer of rural residential land in accordance with relevant national policies. In non-experimental areas, we should generally

29 最高人民法院印发 "关于为推进农村改革发展提供司法保障和法律服务的若干意见" 的通知（法发[2008]36号）[Supreme People's Court Notice on Circulating of Several Opinions Regarding the Supply of Judicial Assurance and Legal Service in Advancing Rural Development & Reform, No.36 of 2008] See at: www.law-lib.com/law/law_view.asp?id=291525, latest access: January 7, 2017.

30 最高人民法院关于印发 "全国民事审判工作会议纪要" 的通知，法办[2011]442号 [Supreme People's Court Notice Regarding Circulation of the National Civil Adjudication Affairs Meeting Summary, No.442 of 2011] See at: http://china.findlaw.cn/lawyers/article/d457741.html, latest access on January 7, 2017.

> adjudicate the invalidity of housing sale contracts between rural and urban residents or rural residents from different village collectives. The buyer can sue for the return of the contract price and interests calculated according to the rates of the People's Bank in the same period. The buyer can also claim compensation for added structures or the costs of renovation and rebuilding.[31]

This foregoing statement constitutes a quite comprehensive elaboration of the SPC's approach to rural land transfer. It also reflects the country's most recent policy change, i.e., the central government's designation of thirty-three counties and urban districts as areas authorized to experiment with rural land transfer, and instructs lower courts to adjudicate in accordance with the authorized reform policies in those areas. At the same time, it also reiterates the social security function of rural residential land and clearly reconfirms the invalidity of transaction contracts. More importantly, the statement for the first time clarifies the main consequence of void contracts. If the 2011 meeting summary conveys a positive signal for following or endorsing the Beijing local judiciary's practices, this summary actually goes against local practices and preempts any future local judicial innovation. Now that the SPC has spoken, local practices inconsistent with this guideline can no longer be maintained. Regardless of whether the Chinese courts void or confirm the validity of small-property contracts, adjudication both within and outside the experimental areas should defer to national policies.

This deferential approach is reflected in the most recent, and more important, work meeting. The Eighth National Court Civil and Commercial Adjudication Work Meeting on November 30, 2016 was attended not only by judges, but also by officials from the national legislature and the State Council. Most significantly, Meng Jianzhu, a member of the Political Bureau of the CCP Central Committee and Secretary of the Central Political and Legal Committee, sent important instructions, and SPC President Zhou Qiang attended and delivered an important speech. In comparison, only SPC vice-presidents attended the meetings discussed in previous paragraphs. The 2016 meeting again decided to "provide judicial protection" for the government's development goals, and the meeting summary elaborates in more detail how to adjudicate cases related to rural residential land transfer. It includes one paragraph dedicated to the allocation of the benefits of rural land transfer contracts,

[31] 2015年全国民事审判工作会议纪要 [2015 National Civil Adjudication Affairs Meeting Summary] See at: www.66law.cn/laws/128045.aspx, latest access on January 8, 2017.

specifying that, with respect to rural collective land that has not been converted to state-owned land at the end of a trial, all contracts should be deemed void. Moreover, it clearly states that dealing with illegal buildings is a function of the administrative agencies and that the people's courts should avoid the *de facto* titling of illegal buildings through civil adjudication. The people's courts should not accept cases in which the parties involved are requesting the adjudication of the ownership of and rights to illegal buildings.[32]

Overall, the SPC is a follower rather than a driver of China's social and policy reforms. Its guidelines also impose constraints on local judicial entrepreneurialism. A survey of the high people's courts across the country also reflects such a deferential approach. The Guangdong People's High Court stipulated in its 2012 Provincial Civil Adjudication Work Meeting Summary that "[i]f parties' litigation claims involve illegal land use or illegal buildings and need administrative agencies to make decisions to clarify property relationships, courts should not accept such case and should tell parties to apply to administrative agencies for their decisions first."[33] This stipulation reflects the Guangdong judiciary's deference to the administrative agencies in dealing with rural real estate transfer. Such a deferential approach can both reduce the information costs of investigating informal property and contract relationships and avoid conflicts with the administrative agencies.

The Shanghai People's High Court has promulgated a quite progressive guiding opinion on disputes concerning rural residential land and housing transactions that outlines four principles. First, it confirms the validity of rural housing transactions between members of the same township, breaking the connection between rural house and village membership to some extent. Second, the contracts by which rural houses are sold to buyers from outside of a township can be valid if the related government agency has approved the transaction. However, it is unclear from which level of government approval would be sufficient. If the

[32] 第八次全国法院民事商事审判工作会议（民事部分）纪要（2016年11月30日）[Summary of the 8th National Court Civil & Commercial Adjudication Affairs Meeting (Civil Edition), 30th November 2016] See from Supreme People's Court: www.chinacourt.org/article/detail/2016/11/id/2361616.shtml, latest access on January 7, 2017.

[33] 广东省高级人民法院[Guangdong Province High People's Court], 全省民事审判工作会议纪要，第六十九条 (2012年6月26日)[Provision 69 of the Civil Adjudication Affairs Meeting Summary of Guangdong Province issued on26th June 2012], available at: www.66law.cn/laws/117186.aspx, latest access on January 8, 2017.

approval of a township-level government is meant, that would constitute a big green light. Third, unapproved transaction contracts, if not yet fulfilled and the buyer has yet to move in, should be deemed void. Fourth, the court should not express its attitude toward the effectiveness of an unapproved but fulfilled contract, particularly if the buyer has already occupied the house. However, the Shanghai courts should respect history, reality, and the buyer's *de facto* right to occupy, live in, and use the disputed house. In the third situation, the seller only needs to return the contract price and interests. In the fourth situation, if redevelopment has occurred, the Shanghai People's High Court emphasizes that buyers are generally entitled to 70 percent of the compensation.[34]

As of December 13, 2016, high courts of only Beijing, Shanghai, and Guangdong had promulgated special guidelines on the adjudication of disputes arising from the transfer of rural land and/or housing. A few other provincial high courts have included guidelines on how to deal with such disputes in their instructions to the courts within their jurisdictions, albeit only in the form of a few sentences or paragraphs. For example, the Shandong People's High Court stipulated in 2005 that contracts transferring rural houses should be deemed void unless agreed between members of the same village.[35] The Hubei People's High Court has issued only one sentence about the transfer of rural residential land: "In our country rural land belongs to collective ownership; if villagers sell their houses but the transfer of rural residential land is not approved by village collectives, such transactions are void."[36] This stipulation makes village approval a requirement, but it is unclear whether it is a sufficient or necessary requirement. If the former, it would render all such transaction contracts agreed in Shenzhen effective if a similar stipulation applied to Shenzhen. The An'Hui People's High Court, probably following the SPC's 2011 balance-of-interests principle, adopted the Beijing People's High Court's approach in 2012: small-property contracts

[34] 上海市高级人民法院[Shanghai City High People's Court] "关于审理农村宅基地房屋买卖纠纷案件的原则意见"（沪高法民－[２００４]４号）[General Principle and Opinions Regarding Adjudication of Rural Homestead Transaction Dispute Cases, Civil Division No.4 of 2004].

[35] 山东省高级人民法院[Shandong Province High People's Court]关于印发 "全省民事审判工作座谈会纪要" 的通知(鲁高法[2005]201号) [Notice on Circulation of the Shandong Civil Adjudication Affairs Meeting Summary, No.201 of 2005].

[36] "湖北省高级人民法院民事审判若干问题研讨会纪要"（２００４年１０月３０日）[Hubei Province High People's Court Civil Adjudication Affairs Meeting Summary, dated at 30th October 2004].

are void, but the contract parties are responsible for pre-contractual liabilities.[37]

Because most of the country's provincial high courts promulgated their opinions on small-property transactions before the SPC elaborated its opinion systematically and comprehensively in 2015, it is unclear whether they will follow the SPC's lead. Nevertheless, currently available data reveal quite a decentralized approach to such transactions, with differences among high courts likely due to differing local situations. In Beijing and Shanghai, China's two largest metropolitan areas, simply rejecting the validity of small property transactions without any mechanism to deter farmers from voiding the related contracts risks jeopardizing both the stability and economic development in both cities. As a result courts in both cities have elaborated relatively sophisticate rules to adjudicate small-property contract disputes. In Guangdong, the government has been proactive in the design of land reform policies, including the relaxation of rural land transfer requirements to varying degrees. However, the downside of these policies is that they are too complicated for the judiciary to apply and have resulted in wide between-city variation within the province. In such a situation, deference to local governments is probably the best strategy for minimizing both the cost of clarifying land rights and potential conflicts with the rapidly changing land administration system. The high courts of Shandong, An'Hui, and Hubei appear to have made decisions based on their information on local economic and societal needs and the particulars of the small-property markets in their jurisdictions.

In summary, both the SPC and high courts across China have adopted a deferential approach to small property transactions. For the SPC, that approach involves deference to national laws and policies, whereas for the high courts it is deference to local policies and situations. Overall, the Chinese judiciary is constrained by its role of applying the law rather than making it, and is at best reactive and responsive to social change.

[37] "安徽省高级人民法院关于审理房屋买卖合同纠纷案件适用法律问题的指导意见" [Guidance and Opinions from Anhui Province High People's Court Regarding Application of Law in Adjudicating Real Estate Transaction Contract Dispute Cases]（安徽省高级人民法院审判委员会民事执行专业委员会2012年3月5日第1次会议通过）[Passed by the First Meeting of the Professional Committee of Civil Execution of the Anhui Province High People's Court Adjudication Committee, dated at 5th March 2012].

6.4 Conclusion

Small property is often assumed to have sparked a war between law and social norms, but no such war can be seen on the judicial front. At most, as in the local Beijing courts, we have seen a low-intensity confrontation because of the limitation inherent to the functioning of the Chinese judiciary and its relatively weak position within the overall political structure. That is why most of this book focuses on conflicts between statutory laws and regulations and small-property norms. In China, various institutional actors proceed sequentially in the co-evolution of law and social norms: first, the administrative agencies and local governments, then the central government and legislature, and, finally, the judiciary, which follows. However, this chapter does not paint an entirely pessimistic picture of the Chinese judiciary. As revealed in the Artists' Village case, Chinese judges are adept at finding middle ground owing to their expertise in maneuvering judicial doctrines and principles. Such compromises are not ideal – just as the reliance interest concept does not fully resolve the issues discussed herein, but they do reduce the intensity of the aforementioned war and the casualties thereof and afford room for the evolution of both laws and norms. In that sense, doing little is not entirely a bad move.

Conclusion

Market Transition: Sticky Norms or Sticky Law?

The Shenzhen government called small-property constructions an urban cancer, but failed to erase them. Worldwide, countries strived to formalize the informal property sector and did not succeed. The idea underlying these disparate efforts is that informal property is a sticky norm that needs to be changed by law. But the question is: Which is the problem in market transitions – sticky norms or sticky law?

As the small-property case in Shenzhen, China has shown, what is sticky is not the norms, but the law. The law is an easy target for manipulation by interest groups during market transition. In contrast, property norms are more responsive to the market and social changes.

Professor Ellickson calls for invigorating social norms by law;[1] here I call for invigorating legal change by social norms, at least in the context of developing countries like China, where formal institutional building is full of uncertainty and redundant to social and market needs.

C.1 The Residual Legal Centralism in Law and Social Norms

The existing research on law and social norms focuses mainly on the evolution of social norms and how law can change social norms, but not how social norms can change law and the *co-evolution* of law and social norms.[2]

In the law and social norms literature, the evolution of social norms has been at center stage. In a bird's eye view of the literature, Professor Ellickson proposes a model for the change of social norms, but not for law.[3] He does

[1] Robert Ellickson (1991). *Order without Law: How Neighbors Settle Disputes* 284.

[2] "The recent law and economics literature on social norms focuses on two issues. The first issue concerns the conditions under which norms should be expected to be efficient . . . The second issue concerns the attitude the state should take toward norms." Eric A. Posner (1996). Law, economics, and inefficient norms, 144 *U. Pa. L. Rev.* 1697, 1697. *See also* Richard H. McAdams (1997). The origin, development, and regulation of norms, 96 *Mich. L. Rev.* 338, 347–49.

[3] Robert C. Ellickson (2001). The market for social norms, 3 *Am. Law & Econ. Rev.* 1, 13.

discuss the politics of ranchers in Shasta, and in particular, how different groups lobby to change the legal rules.[4] But the interplay between law and norms in Shasta presents an incomplete picture in that both the norms and the law are clear-cut rules: "open-range" or "closed-range."[5] The rules here do not have the depth and flexibility that accommodates changing social situations and corresponding institutional innovation. In short, it is a picture of a mature society in which law is clearly defined by a centralized government authority.

The same can be said about Eric Posner and Richard McAdams's classic exploration of social norms. Their main focus is why people obey social norms and how law can change social norms.[6] For example, Richard McAdams discusses the expressive function of law, mainly targeting social norms.[7] Other members of the new Chicago School, represented by Sunstein and Kahan, investigate various ways through which law can influence social norms, refreshing our understanding of the ways that law can influence people's behaviors.[8] Scholars like Sunstein do recognize that the impact of law on human behavior "has everything to do with social norms"; however, Sunstein does not bother to investigate how social norms can promote legal change, not to mention the co-evolution of law and social norms.[9] Cooter examines three effects of social norms on law: expression, deterrence, and internalization, but he does not address the effect of social norms on law from the perspective of institutional change.[10]

A more generous recognition of the positive contribution of property norms is presented in *Property Outlaws*. Penalver and Katyal discuss the crucial functions of property outlaws to the development and

[4] Ellickson, *supra* note 1, at 29–39.

[5] To determine whether an owner of cattle is liable for damages stemming from unintentional cattle trespass on unfenced land, "open range" means territory where a cattleman is not liable for trespass damages; "closed range" means territory where a cattleman is strictly liable for any damage his livestock might cause while trespassing within the area. Robert C. Ellickson (1986). Of coase and cattle: Dispute resolution among neighbors in Shasta County, 38 *Stan. L. Rev.* 623, 626.

[6] *See, e.g.*, Eric A. Posner (2002). *Law and Social Norms*; McAdams, *supra* note 2.

[7] Richard H. McAdams (2000). A focal point theory of expressive law, 86 *Va. L. Rev.* 1649.

[8] *See* Richard H. Thaler and Cass R. Sunstein, (2008). *Nudge: Improving Decisions about Health, Wealth, and Happiness*; Dan M. Kahan (2000). Gentle Nudges vs. Hard Shoves: Solving the Sticky Norms Problem, 67 *U. Chi. L. Rev.* 607.

[9] Cass R. Sunstein (1996). Social Norms and Social Roles, 96 *Colum. L. Rev.* 903.

[10] Robert D. Cooter (2000). Three Effects of Social Norms on Law: Expression, Deterrence, and Internalization, 79 *Or. L. Rev.* 1.

progress of our society, including expressive and redistributive functions.[11] In another paper on a similar topic, Edwards develops a theory of law to explain why property outlaws always exist. He writes:

> Sometimes law is enforced, sometimes it isn't; sometimes law is complied with, sometimes not . . . I have referred to the limits of socially acceptable deviance around law as 'parameters of acceptable deviance.' Within these parameters are behaviors that are illegal but socially acceptable; their boundaries are the point at which law is actually enforced. Those boundaries become, in a sense, the informal but real law.[12] Law functions as an anchor on behavior, providing stability, but also space for deviance which permits the evolution of property rights.[13]

But the above researchers still do not address one crucial question: Why do some property outlaws lead to changes in the legal system and thus advance social progress, while others lead to conflicts between property outlaws and property laws?[14] Answering this question is the first step to explore the co-evolution of law and social norms.

Even in addressing the inherent limits of property law, Edwards still recognizes that "law functions as an anchor on behavior."[15] This comfort with law in discussing the relationship between law and social norms decreases when the setting is shifted to developing countries. In discussing the evolution and chaos of property rights in developing countries, Fitzpatrick investigates the *conflicts* between law and norms, with more focus on the incapacity of law than the above approaches that focus on the role of law in changing norms. As he argues, "Unless social order is established, most commonly through legitimate and capable government, the process of allocating and enforcing property rights will tend to cause conflict because different claimants will resort to competing legal, normative, and coalitional enforcement mechanisms."[16]

This argument is based on his observation that "in most Third World societies, nonstate resource governance mechanisms have evolved

[11] Eduardo Moisés Peñalver and Sonia K. Katyal (2007). Property outlaws, 155 *U. Pa. L. Rev.* 1095.

[12] Mark A. Edwards (2010). Acceptable deviance and property rights, 43 *Conn. L. Rev.* 43 457, 459–460.

[13] *Id.*

[14] For a related discussion, *see* Naomi R. Lamoreaux (2011). The mystery of property rights: A US perspective, 71 *J. Econ. Hist.* 275.

[15] Edwards, *supra* note 12.

[16] Daniel Fitzpatrick (2006). Evolution and chaos in property rights systems: The third world tragedy of contested access, 115 *Yale L.J.* 996,1010.

separately from, and often in contradiction to, state institutions." The idea is that law and norms are exogenous rather than endogenous to each other. Thus when the government's effort to build a unitary property law system creates a confrontation, the result is that "state law has either overridden nonstate governance mechanisms or failed to facilitate adaptation to new circumstances of urbanization, migration, and commodification of rights to land."[17] This echoes de Soto's argument rooting the law in social contracts, and this belief is widely shared by people concerned about law and development. This "law or norms" choice reflects another drawback of the existing research: Too much of the literature views law in developing countries as a unitary system, which is not true at least in China, and probably in many other countries.[18] Fitzpatrick did notice the "polynormative system of official law," but he regards it as the *result* of the government's efforts to replace the informal system with a unitary state law.[19] This research treats the layering and fragmentation of law as an inherent characteristic of legal systems in developing countries, an endogenous situation we must consider in understanding property rights in developing countries. The layering and fragmentation of law does not necessarily lead to conflicts between law and norms, but it in fact leads to more possibilities.

The more comprehensive typology on the relationship between formal and informal institutions developed by political scientists can be applied to the relationship between law and norms: This typology includes complementary, accommodating, substitutive, and competing relationships.[20] Social norms can be a catalyst to change law. Nevertheless, even such a typology ignores the fact that the relationship between law and norms is changing over time as both law and norms are changing. When a particular social norm arises, it might challenge and compete with the corresponding law; it might substitute law in regulating the particular social or market relations; law might make adaptive changes to accommodate it; in the end, they may complement each other. We need a more comprehensive and dynamic understanding of the co-evolution of law and social norms.

[17] *Id.* at 1012.

[18] *See, e.g.*, Karen Clay and Gavin Wright (2005). Order without law? Property rights during the California gold rush, 42 *Explorations Econ. Hist.* 155; Annette M. Kim (2004). A market without the 'right' property rights, 12 *Econ. Transition* 275.

[19] Fitzpatrick, *supra* note 16, at 1012.

[20] Gretchen Helmke and Steven Levitsky (2004). Informal institutions and comparative politics: A research agenda, 2 *Persp. Pol.* 725, 728. (The author thanks John Yasuda for recommending this literature.)

C.2 Property Norms Are More Responsive to Social Change Than Property Law

The conventional view seems to be that law changes much more swiftly than norms. For example, North argues that:

> Changes in informal constraints–norms, conventions, or personal standards of honesty, for example–have the same originating sources of change as do changes in formal rules; but they occur *gradually* and sometimes quite *subconsciously* as individuals evolve alternative patterns of behavior consistent with their newly perceived evaluation of costs and benefits.[21] [emphasis added]

> The process of change is overwhelmingly incremental . . . The incremental change may come *from a change in the rules via statute or legal change.* For informal constraints there may be *a very gradual withering away* of an accepted norm or social convention or the gradual adoption of a new one as the nature of the political, social, or economic exchange gradually changes.[22] [emphasis added]

North does not explain in detail why informal constraints such as norms tend to change more gradually than law.

Ellickson elaborates systematically on why "inefficient social norms tend to be weeded out too slowly."[23] Reasons include the cognitive biases in favor of the status quo, the costliness of displacing internalized norms, and the costliness of moving away from a local optimum.[24]

The small-property case does not fit in either of the analyses above. In Shenzhen, people favor "reform and change" rather than the status quo, cannot wait to displace the old communist norms that prohibit land alienation, and successfully moved away from the old situation.

Both North and Ellickson write about the interest group problem in social change. North writes that "the larger the number of rule changes, the greater the number of losers and hence opposition."[25] Ellickson criticizes the interest-group theories of norms, which hold that "members of powerful interest groups manipulate the content of norms to serve their own selfish interests."[26] He argues instead that, "One can readily understand how concentrated lobbies might be able to influence the legal

[21] Douglass C. North, *Institutional Change: A Framework of Analysis* 6 (1994), http://dlc.dlib.indiana.edu/dlc/handle/10535/4102.
[22] *Id.* [23] Ellickson, *supra* note 3, at 32. [24] *Id.* at 32–34.
[25] North, *supra* note 21, at 6.
[26] Robert C. Ellickson (1987). A critique of economic and sociological theories of social control, 16 *J. Legal Stud.* 67, 95.

system. The informal control system, by contrast, is much more diffuse, and norms seem stubbornly resistant to deliberate influence."[27]

Their discussions on interest groups do not address directly the question of whether law or norms change more quickly. But starting from their idea that law is more susceptible to interest group pressure, we can argue that social norms tend to be more responsive to social change compared to law that is hijacked by interest groups. The change of the power structure often takes a long time, which is often as unmovable as a mountain. Meanwhile, the emergence of a market is often a natural response of individuals to new profit opportunities, which is as easy as the downward flow of water.

The formation and operation of social norms can be triggered by social change apart from interest group politics. Such market norms are often self-enforcing in the absence of political interference.[28] Social norms, at least, reflect the politically disadvantaged groups' demand for rule change, and thus provide another discourse on institutional change, while the politically advantaged groups favor the status quo of "sticky" law.

Here I do not try to make a general argument that social norms change more swiftly than law, but instead I try to raise the possibility that in certain cases, particularly against the backdrop of post-communist transition, interest groups can hijack the legal change while the market provides plenty of opportunities and incentives for bottom-up institutional exploration.[29]

It is also worthwhile to point out that property norms in such situations are different from norms such as foot-binding, dueling, the diamond industry in New York City, and even the informal resolution of property disputes among rancher neighbors in Shasta County. The crucial distinction is that property norms in my case are not built on a close-knit community. Rather they are supported by a network of institutional innovators, including local villagers, lawyers and real estate brokers, and are open to anyone who is willing to adopt them. They are more similar to and more encompassing than what Strahilevitz calls

[27] *Id.* at 96.

[28] "Some norms are self-enforcing (the incentive to obey comes from the fact that obedience confers private benefits) because they are constitutive of advantageous transactions." Richard A. Posner (1997). Social norms and the law: an economic approach, 87 *Am. Econ Rev*. 365, 366.

[29] The existing discussion on sticky norms, based on the assumption that social norms have been internalized, is well-grounded. *See* Kahan, *supra* note 8. However, internalization is not an inherent characteristic of social norms. *See* Ellickson, *supra* note 3, at 3; McAdams, *supra* note 2, at 394–397.

norms of "intermediate-knit groups," which are characterized by a mixture of familiars and strangers. "An intermediate-knit group member anticipates having repeat-player interactions with his proximate companions, but not with the strangers who are also members of the group."[30] The network of institutional innovators in the small-property case consists of villagers who know each other, the village co-ops which keep and transmit information, real estate brokers and lawyers who know the villagers, and other buyers and sellers who connect to villagers and to each other through the village co-ops. Such social norms provide another society-wide way of rearranging property rights in defiance of the sticky formal property order. As a result, it also has bigger potential in promoting legal change.

C.3 Reconstitution of Law and Social Norms

This research does not propose a pure bottom-up institutional change approach. As seen from the small-property case, law also plays an important role in the formation, operation, and institutionalization of the small-property market. This research presents a more nuanced interaction and co-evolution of property law and norms. The layering and fragmentation of law requires government officials to engage in the *reconstitution of law* to determine what law, the meaning of the law, and its application, and leaves room for ordinary citizens and organizations to engage in the reconstitution of law to serve their own interests. In the small-property case, villagers in Shenzhen developed widespread norms of rural land development and transfer despite the legal prohibition and government monopoly on rural-urban land conversion. The unsanctioned bottom-up reconstitution of law is often labeled as illegal and might face the risk of legal enforcement. However, the layering and fragmentation of law also leave room for discretion in legal enforcement. Enforcement officials can decide what and how to enforce according to their ideological preference, operational goals of that particular government department, and even career goals and personal interests of particular government officials.[31] Reconstitution of law at local settings is

[30] Lior Jacob Strahilevitz (2003). Social norms from close-knit groups to loose-knit groups, 70 *U. Chi. L. Rev.* 359, 360.

[31] Ryken Grattet and Valerie Jenness (2005). The reconstitution of law in local settings: Agency discretion, ambiguity, and a surplus of law in the policing of hate crime, 39 *Law & Soc'y Rev.* 893, 894.

also a bargaining process in which government officials and actors in the informal sectors such as village co-ops in Shenzhen negotiate to define the law at stake.[32]

During the formation and operation of the small-property market, the 1988 constitutional amendment played an important role. Although the official stance was that the actualization of the right to transfer land use rights should rely on the follow-up promulgation and reform of particular land administration laws, the amendment provided the literal basis on which ordinary people can reasonably claim that the transfer of (both *rural* and urban) land use rights is consistent with the Chinese constitution and that the 1998 LAL and other administrative ordinances that prohibits the transfer of rural land use rights are actually unconstitutional.[33] Even if many villagers in Shenzhen and other actors of the small-property market might not grasp the legal details, the market-orientated atmosphere and the encouragement of institutional exploration, with endorsements from Deng Xiaoping and other national leaders, and the 1988 constitutional amendment as a concrete and highly visible milestone, do shape the reconstitution of layered and fragmented laws toward the social consensus and norm of rural land development and transfer.

At the beginning, the reconstitution of laws at local villages was tolerated to a great extent by the formal institutional actors. As institutional building is fraught with uncertainties, the formal institutional architects, such as Deng Xiaoping and other national leaders in the 1980s, sought inspiration from the informal institutions and tolerated their deviation from the formal laws, in particular if such bottom-up reconstitution served higher goals of the government, such as economic development and social stability, though in conflict with particular lower laws.

At a certain point, property norms grow big enough that the challenge they pose to property law can no longer be ignored. As a result, formal institutional actors have to respond to the property norms. Due to the preference for the status quo and other reasons, their first response is often to suppress the property norms, which usually fails. After that, and sometimes even concurrent with the suppression, more accommodating

32 *Id.*

33 *See, e.g.*, 刘连泰："集体土地征收制度变革的宪法空间"，《法商研究》2014年第3期。[Liu Liantai, *The Constitutional Dimension of Reforming the Requisition Regime of Collective-Owned Land*, STUD. LAW & BUS., No. 3 (2014)].

responses are often made, which means alterations to the formal institution. There is, in this sense, a long and bumpy road toward the convergence of property law and norms. In such a transition, different institutional actors, formal or informal, would reconstitute the laws at particular settings according to their needs. Some succeed, and some fail. But this apparent chaos should not dampen our cautious optimism. This chaotic process can also be viewed as a process for institutional experiments and competition. Those rules that reduce conflicts between law and social norms prevail over rules that intensify the conflicts.

The following institutional change is a process I would like to call the reconstitution of law and social norms, as it is based on both the existing laws and the emergent norms, which are products of the bottom-up reconstitution of the existing laws. The spread of the small-property constructions and their important function in the local economy prompted the Shenzhen city government's engagement with and creation of accommodating amendments to its land law and policies. In the end, the small-property market also prompted the Chinese central government to set an agenda for an integrated market for urban and rural land use rights. Though this process involved the gradual adaptation and eventual convergence with the property norms, it is not a simple informalization of the formal system, or formalization of the informal system. The parallels between property law and norms and the interactions between the systems exist in all societies and time periods.

Property law and norms could be either in harmony or in conflict. If changes in one system are in harmony with the other, their interaction will tend to reduce transaction costs to society; if changes in one system are in conflict with the other, their interactions will tend to increase transaction costs to society. Such transaction costs include the costs of making an exchange and the cost of maintaining the structure of both property law and norms.[34] During the market transition, social change causes change in property norms; while property law might fail to follow such changes due to hindrance by interest groups. As a result, transaction costs to society increase. Such increased transaction costs could lead to changes in property law, though not necessarily. If

[34] *See* Svetozar Pejovich (2012). The effects of the interaction of formal and informal institutions on social stability and economic development, 2 *J. Markets & Morality* 164, 171.

adaptive legal change is made, and the accompanying reconstitution of law and social norms occurs, transaction costs can be reduced. When both social surroundings and institutional infrastructure settle, transaction costs would be reduced to a low level until new social change brings another round of significant frictions and conflicts between property law and norms.

C.4 De Soto Revisited

I am frequently asked how the Chinese example augments our understanding of the vitality of informal property systems as presented by de Soto's works on Peru.

The first is the relationship between modern market economy and property law. In an interview, de Soto said: "I'm not saying . . . that other reforms aren't necessary. I'm simply saying that a property rights system is a principal reform, without which other reforms are difficult to manage. It's quite clear that property law does not resolve the other problems. But to me, what is also quite clear is that without property law, you will never be able to accomplish other reforms in a sustainable manner."[35] The small-property market in Shenzhen and China's land law reform prove that property norms often move ahead of property law in market transition. Thus, it is unrealistic to make creating a property law a precondition of market transition.

The second, and I believe more important, point is how the Chinese example provides a dynamic perspective and, as a result, helps us focus on the interaction mechanism between existing law and norms. De Soto, though recognizing and praising without hesitation the vitality of the informal economy in Peru, compares it to an ideal world with "good law." My research compares two systems that both exist in the real world and strives to explore the mechanisms of such an interactive system. De Soto focuses on the inadequacy of the informal system and argues for the *demand* for a "good" legal system. My research focuses more on the supply side – why is there "bad" rather than "good" law? How can we transform bad law to good law? The answer actually lies in the informal property systems that de Soto laments. Property norms would trigger a

[35] Jeremy Clift, *Hearing the Dogs Bark*, FIN. & DEV. 11 (December 2003).

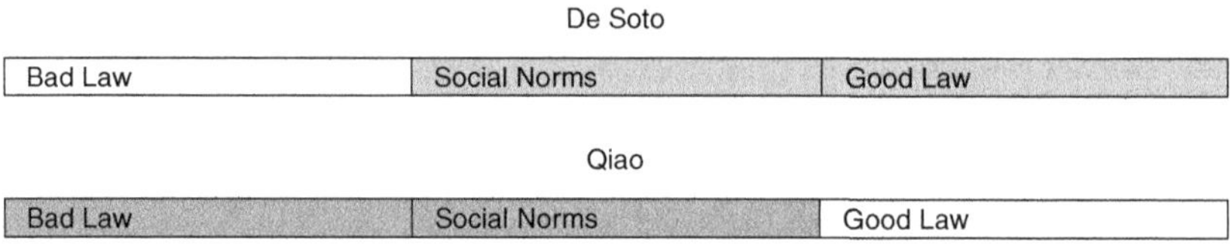

Figure C.1 What de Soto and Qiao compare

series of reconstitution of law processes, through which the legal system could be improved. This reconstitution thesis differs from de Soto's formalization argument in that it emphasizes the co-evolution and symbiotic relationship between property law and property norms (Figure C.1).

Appendix 1

Research Methods

My understanding of Shenzhen and its small-property market is based on my eleven-month fieldwork in China. I spent the first twenty days (August 9–26, 2011) in Beijing doing interviews and collecting materials on the evolution of national laws and central government policies related to the nationwide phenomenon of small-property markets and meeting with people for contacts in Shenzhen. From August 27, 2011 to July 5, 2012, I spent all of my time in Shenzhen doing fieldwork except for two short academic trips.

The forms of my interviews vary. The majority were in-depth interviews, typically a one to two-hour conversation on the small-property market in Shenzhen. Some were half or a whole-day road trips to villages located in different districts of Shenzhen, including visits to a couple of small-property neighborhoods, during which I usually had conversations with multiple persons. I took several of these road trips with Lao Zhang, a retired government official who had been in charge of issuing export permits to village factories in the 1980s and an expert of the small-property market in Shenzhen. From Lao Zhang, I learnt to how to identify small-property buildings from their appearance and how to communicate with local villagers, real estate brokers, etc. After several road trips with Lao Zhang, I learned how to do the on-site observations and interviews by myself. I also made friends with several village co-op leaders, who provided valuable internal information and data on rural land development and transfer within their villages.

To understand the history of Shenzhen villages, I hired four research assistants from the Shenzhen University, a local college with a concentration of local students. I got to know their villages through conversations with them, their parents and other relatives, and elders in their villages. I also did interviews with journalists and lawyers, who not only discussed cases they reported or represented with me, but also introduced me to their clients on several occasions. I was even invited to advise on one case and to attend the court trial. I also collected case files from lawyers.

One form of my interviews was participation in local salons, which were attended by both intellectuals and persons related to the small-property market in various ways. For example, the first one I attended was on how to deal with the illegal buildings in Shenzhen, hosted by a lawyer acquaintance. The participants included a university-based sociologist, CEOs of top real estate companies in Shenzhen, local villagers, lawyers, a street-level government official, and real estate brokers. In addition to the information provided in the salon, I was able to establish contacts with the participants for further conversations. Another form of interviews was academic exchange. For example, a friend at the Urban Planning, Land and Resources Commission of Shenzhen City helped me get an invitation to give a lecture on the American land regime to her colleagues, after which I was granted opportunities to ask questions to the audience.

My fieldwork depended on contacts and network. Although I was not able to randomly select my interviewees, I did pay attention to their representativeness. My interviewees include not only real estate brokers, developers, and speculators but also low- and middle-income tenants and buyers of small-property apartments; not only village co-op leaders but also ordinary villagers; not only villagers that owned eleven small-property buildings or more but also villagers that had been deprived of their land for various reasons; not only city government officials but also grassroots-level government employees; not only lawyers but also judges, etc. Neither did I use a standardized survey because each person would know different things about the small-property market. I usually drafted an outline for an in-depth interview and kept the conversations open for any direction the interviewee might take.

At the end of my fieldwork, I participated in a research project commissioned by the Shenzhen city government to draft policies on rural land development and transfer. The project was led by a Peking University professor I knew. I was accepted as a member of the professor's research team after giving his team a presentation of my fieldwork. The Shenzhen city government granted our team full access to government employees and government data. In addition, the research team covered many more villages than I could do alone. All the interviews were well taped and recorded in the form of three volumes of transcripts, totaling 401,770 words. I use "Interview Transcript" in the book to refer to interviews done by the team.

In addition to the interviews, I also collected various materials, including government investigation reports and other documents, court files, village maps and records, transaction documents, and news reports.

Appendix 2

Pictures of Small-Property Constructions in Shenzhen

Note: All the following pictures were taken by the author during his fieldwork in Shenzhen.

Figure A2.1 An intracity village of small property in Shenzhen

(a)

(b)

Figure A2.2(a and b) Small-property constructions in intracity villages
Note: The Chinese characters are covered to avoid unwanted attention to the neighborhood.

Figure A2.3 Inside view of a small-property building

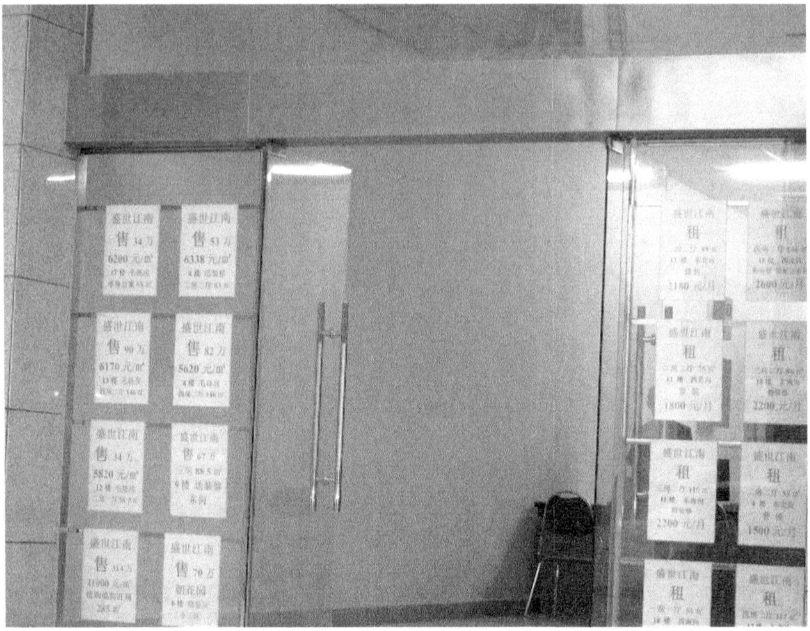

Figure A2.4 A real estate broker's office, with prices of small-property apartments listed on the door

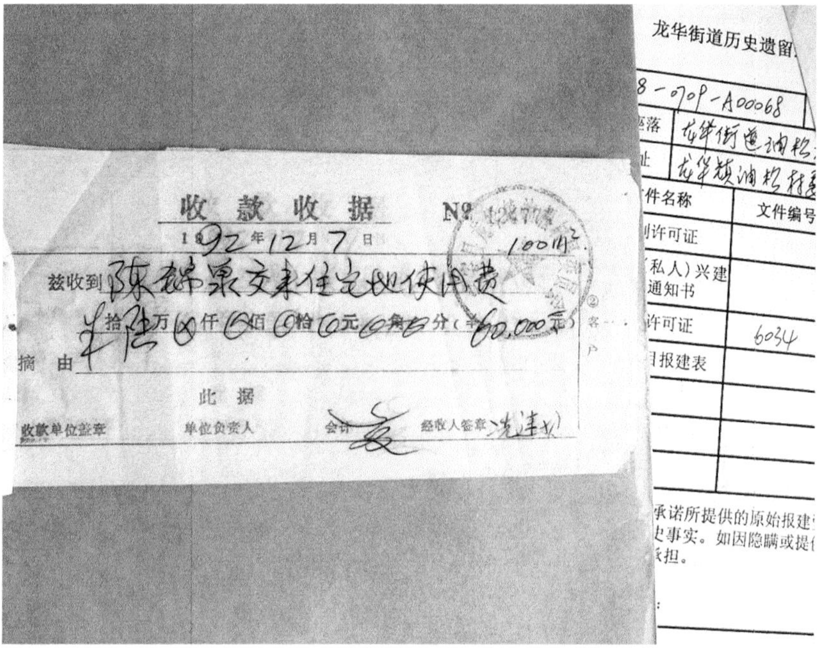

(a)

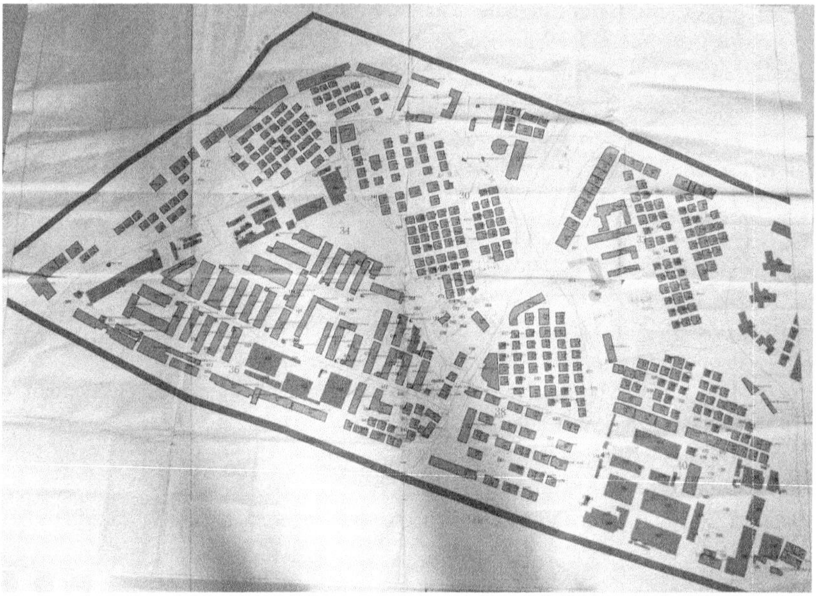

(b)

Figure A2.5(a and b) Recording map and receipts of small-property transactions

REFERENCES

English

Ackerman, W. G., & Johnson, S. T. (1996). Outlaws of the past: A Western perspective on prescription and adverse possession," *Land & Water Law Review, 31*, 79–112.

Ahdieh, R. (2011). Beyond individualism in law and economics. *Boston University Law Review, 91*(1), 43–85.

Alston, L. J., & Libecap, G. D. (1996). The determinants and impact of property rights: Land titles on the Brazilian frontier. *Journal of Law, Economics, and Organization, 12*(1), 25–61.

Alston, L. J., Libecap, G. D., & Mueller, B. (1999). *Titles, Conflict, and Land Use: The Development of Property Rights and Land Reform on the Brazilian Amazon Frontier*. Ann Arbor: University of Michigan Press.

Alston, L. J., Libecap, G. D., & Schneider, R. (1995). Property rights and the preconditions for markets: The case of the Amazon frontier. *Journal of Institutional and Theoretical Economics, 151*(1), 89–107.

Anderson, T. L., & Hill, P. J. (1978). An American experiment in anarcho-capitalism: The not so wild, wild West. *Journal of Libertarian Studies, 3*(1), 9–29.

(2002). Cowboys and contracts. *Journal of Legal Studies, 31*(2), S489–514.

Ayres, I. (1997). Protecting property with puts. *Valparaiso University Law Review, 32*, 793.

(2005). *Optional Law: The Structure of Legal Entitlements*. Chicago, IL: University of Chicago Press.

Ayres, I., & Balkin, J. M. (1996). Legal entitlements as auctions: property rules, liability rules, and beyond. *Yale Law Journal, 106*, 703–750.

Ayres, I, & Talley, E. (1995). Solomonic bargaining: Dividing a legal entitlement to facilitate Coasean trade. *Yale Law Journal, 104*, 1027–1117.

Baird, D. G., Gertner, R. H. & Picker, R. C. (1994). *Game Theory and the Law*. Cambridge, MA: Harvard University Press.

Banner, S. (2002). Transitions between property regimes. *Journal of Legal Studies, 31*(4), S359.

Bardsley, N., Mehta, J., Starmer, C., & Sugden, R. (2010). Explaining focal points: Cognitive hierarchy theory versus team reasoning. *Economic Journal, 120* (543), 40–79.

Barros, D. B. (2010). *Hernando de Soto and Property in a Market Economy.* Burlington, VT: Ashgate Publishing Company.

Becker, Gary S. (1968) Crime and Punishment: An Economic Approach. *Journal of Political Economy 76*(2), 169–217.

Bernstein, L. (1992). Opting out of the legal system: Extralegal contractual relations in the diamond industry. *Journal of Legal Studies, 21*(1), 115–157.

(1996). Merchant law in a merchant court: Rethinking the Code's search for immanent business norms. *University of Pennsylvania Law Review,* 144, 1765–1821.

(2001). Private commercial law in the cotton industry: Creating cooperation through rules, norms, and institutions. *Michigan Law Review,* 99, 1724–1790.

Besley, T. (1995). Property rights and investment incentives: Theory and evidence from Ghana. *Journal of Political Economy, 103*(5), 903–937.

Bromley, D. W. (2009). Formalising property relations in the developing world: The wrong prescription for the wrong malady. *Land Use Policy, 26*(1), 20–27.

Bubb, R., & Pildes, R. H. (2014). How behavioral economics trims its sails and why. *Harvard Law Review, 127,* 1593–1678.

Calabresi, G., & Melamed, A. D. (1972). Property rules, liability rules, and inalienability: One view of the Cathedral. *Harvard Law Review, 85,* 1089–1128.

Carbonara, E., Parisi, F., & von Wangenheim, G. (2008). Lawmakers as norm entrepreneurs. *Review of Law and Economics, 4*(3), 779–799.

Chang, Y. (2012). Property law with Chinese characteristics: An economic and comparative analysis. *Brigham-Kanner Property Rights Conference Journal, 1,* 345–372.

(in press). Optional law in property: A theoretical critique. *New York University Journal of Law & Liberty,* Retrieved from http://ssrn.com/abstract=2351651.

Chen, R. (2010). *Informal sales of rural housing in China: property, privatization and local public finance.* Retrieved from ProQuest Digital Dissertations. (AAT 3408511).

Chin, J. (2010). China's blood-stained property map. *Wall Street Journal.* Retrieved from http://blogs.wsj.com/chinarealtime/2010/10/29/chinas-blood-stained-property-map/ (last visited 2013, February 15)

Clarke, D. C. (2003). Economic development and the rights hypothesis: The China problem. *American Journal of Comparative Law, 51*(1), 89–111.

Clay, K., & Wright, G. (2005). Order without law? Property rights during the California Gold Rush. *Explorations in Economic History, 42*(2), 155–183.

Clift, J. (2003, December). Hearing the dogs bark. *Finance & Development,* 8–11.

Coase, R. H., & Ning, W. (2012). *How China Became Capitalist*. Basingstoke, Hampshire: Palgrave Macmillan.

Cooter, R. D. (1998). Expressive law and economics. *Journal of Legal Studies*. *27* (S2), 585–607.

Cooter, R. D., & Landa, J. T. (1984). Personal vs. impersonal trade: The size of trading groups and the law of contracts. *International Review of Law and Economics*, *4*, 15–22.

Cooter, R, & Schafer, H. (2012). *Solomon's Knot: How Law Can End the Poverty of Nations*. Princeton, NJ: Princeton University Press.

Corbridge, S., Williams, G., Srivastava, M., & Veron, R. (2005). *Seeing the State: Governance and Governmentality in India*. Cambridge, United Kingdom: Cambridge University Press.

Crawford, V. P., Gneezy, U., & Rottenstreich, Y. (2008). The power of focal points is limited: Even minute payoff asymmetry may yield large coordination failures. *American Economic Review*, *98*(4), 1443–1458.

Davis, K. E., & Trebilcock, M. J. (2008). The relationship between law and development: Optimists versus skeptics. *American Journal of Comparative Law*, *56*(4), 895–946.

Demsetz, H. (1967). Toward a theory of property rights. *American Economic Review (Papers and Proceedings)*, *57*(2), 347–359.

De Soto, H. (1989). *The Other Path: The Invisible Revolution in the Third World*. New York, NY: Harper & Row Publishers.

(2000). *The Mystery of Capital: Why Capitalism Triumphs in the West and Fails Everywhere Else*. New York, NY: Basic Books.

Di Taranto, G. (2012). Towards a renewed development theory: Hernando De Soto and institutionalist contractualism. *Journal of European Economic History*, *41*, 81–99.

Dixit, A. K. (2004). *Lawlessness and Economics: Alternative Modes of Governance*. Princeton, NJ: Princeton University Press.

Economist. China's economy: Bamboo capitalism. (2011, March 10). *Economist*. Retrieved from www.economist.com/node/18332610.

China's state capitalism: Not just tilting at windmills. (2012, October 4). *Economist*. Retrieved from www.economist.com/node/21564235.

Edwards, M. A. (2010). Acceptable deviance and property rights. *Connecticut Law Review*, *43*(2), 459–460.

Ellickson, R. C. (1986). Adverse possession and perpetuities law: Two dents in the libertarian model of property rights. *Washington University Law Quarterly*, *64*, 723–737.

(1986). Of Coase and cattle: Dispute resolution among neighbors in Shasta County. *Stanford Law Review*, *38*, 623–687.

(1987). A critique of economic and sociological theories of social control. *Journal of Legal Studies*, *16*(1), 67–99.

(1991). *Order without Law: How Neighbors Settle Disputes*. Cambridge, MA: Harvard University Press.

(1993). Property in land. *Yale Law Journal, 102*, 1315–1400.

(2001). The market for social norms. *American Law & Economic Review, 3*(1), 1–49.

(2012). The costs of complex land titles: Two examples from China. *Brigham-Kanner Property Rights Conference Journal*, 1, 281–302.

Ellickson, R., & Been, V. (Eds.). (2005). *Land Use Controls: Cases and Materials* (3rd edn.) New York, NY: Aspen Publishers.

England, V. (2007, September 17). Mega-city plans for Hong Kong. *BBC News*. Retrieved from http://news.bbc.co.uk/2/hi/asia-pacific/6989473.stm.

Epstein, R. A. (1996). Babbitt v. Sweet Home Chapters of Oregon: The law and economics of habitat preservation. *Supreme Court Economic Review, 32*, 1–57.

(2002). The allocation of the commons: Parking on public roads. *Journal of Legal Studies, 31*(2), S515–544.

Epstein, R. C. (1997). Protecting property with legal remedies: A common sense reply to Professor Ayres. *Valparaiso University Law Review, 32*, 833–853.

Fennell, L. A. (2012). Options for owners and outlaws. *Brigham-Kanner Property Rights Conference Journal, 1*, 239.

Field, E. (2003). Property rights, community public goods, and household time allocation in urban squatter communities: Evidence from Peru. *William and Mary Law Review, 45*, 837–887.

(2004). Property rights, community public goods and household time allocation in urban squatter communities: Evidence from Peru. *William and Mary Law Review, 45*(3), 837–888.

(2005). Property rights and investment in urban slums. *Journal of the European Economic Association, 3*(2–3), 279–290.

(2007). Entitled to work: Urban property rights and labor supply in Peru. *The Quarterly Journal of Economics, 122*(4), 1561–1602.

Field, E., & Torero, M. (2006). Do property titles increase credit access among the urban poor? Evidence from a nationwide titling program. Unpublished research. Harvard University.

Fitzpatrick, D. (2006). Evolution and chaos in property rights systems: The third world tragedy of contested access. *Yale Law Journal, 115*, 996–1048.

French, H. W. (2006, December 19). Chinese success story chokes on its own growth. *New York Times*. Retrieved from www.nytimes.com/2006/12/19/world/asia/19shenzhen.html?pagewanted=2&_r=0&ex.

Galiani, S., & Schargrodsky, E. (2010). Property rights for the poor: Effects of land titling. *Journal of Public Economics, 94*(9–10), 700–729.

Garnaut, R., & Ligang, S. (Eds.). (2004). *China's Third Economic Transformation: The Rise of the Private Economy*. Abingdon, Oxon: RoutledgeCurzon.

Grattet, R., & Jenness, J. (2005). The reconstitution of law in local settings: Agency discretion, ambiguity, and a surplus of law in the policing of hate crime. *Law & Society Review 39*(4), 893–942.

Grief, A. (1994). Cultural beliefs and the organization of society: A historical and theoretical reflection on collectivist and individual societies. *Journal of Political Economy, 102*(5), 912–950.

(2004). Impersonal exchange without impartial law: The community responsibility system. *Chicago Journal of International Law, 5*(1), 109–138.

Gutierrez, F., & Schonwalder, G. (Eds.). (2010). *Economic Liberalization and Political Violence: Utopia or Dystopia?*. London, England: Pluto Press.

Hadfield, G. K., & Weingast, B. R. (2012). What is Law? A coordination model of the characteristics of legal order. *Journal of Legal Analysis, 4*(2), 471–514.

Haggard, S., MacIntyre, A., & Tiede, L. (2008). The rule of law and economic development. *Annual Review of Political Science, 11*, 205–234.

Heller, M. A. (1998). The tragedy of the anticommons: Property in the transition from Marx to markets. *Harvard Law Review, 111*(3), 621–688.

Heller, M., & Hills, R. (2008). Land assembly districts. *Harvard Law Review, 121* (6), 1465–1527.

Hellman, J. (1998). Winners take all: The politics of partial reform in postcommunist transitions. *World Politics, 50*(2), 203–234.

Helmke, G., & Levitsky, S. (2004). Informal institutions and comparative politics: A research agenda. *Perspectives on Politics, 2*(4), 725–740.

Ho, P. (2001). Who owns China's land: Policies, property rights, and deliberate institutional ambiguity. *China Quarterly, 166*, 404–405.

Jacobs, A. (2012, February 2012). Residents vote in Chinese village at center of protest. *New York Times.* Retrieved from www.nytimes.com/2012/02/02/world/asia/residents-vote-in-chinese-village-at-center-of-protest.html.

Jolls, C. (2007). Behavioral law and economics. National Bureau of Economic Research. No. w12879.

Jolls, C., Sunstein, C. R., & Thaler, R. (1998). A behavioral approach to law and economics. *Stanford Law Review, 50*, 1471–1550.

Kahan, D. M. (2000). Gentle nudges vs. hard Shoves: Solving the sticky norms problem. *University of Chicago Law Review, 67*, 607–645.

Kennedy, David (2011). Some caution about property rights as a recipe for economic development. *Accounting, Economics, and Law, 1*(1). www.degruyter.com/downloadpdf/j/ael.2011.1.1/ael.2011.1.1.1006/ael.2011.1.1.1006.pdf

Kennedy, D., & Stiglitz, J. (Eds.). (2013). *Law and Economics with Chinese Characteristics: Institutions for Promoting Development in the Twenty-First Century.* Oxford, United Kingdom: Oxford University Press.

Kim, A. M. (2004). A Market without the 'right' property rights - Ho Chi Minh City, Vietnam's newly-emerged private real estate market. *Economics of Transition, 12*(2), 275–305.

King, W. (2003). Illegal settlements and the impact of titling programs. *Harvard International Law Journal*, 44, 433–471.

Krier, J. E., & Schwab, S. J. (1995). Property rules and liability rules: The Cathedral in another light. *New York University Law Review*, *70*, 440–483.

Kung, J. K. (2000). Common property rights and land reallocations in rural China: Evidence from a village survey. *World Development*, *28*(4), 701.

Kung, J. K., & Lin, J. Y. (2003). The causes of China's great leap famine, 1959–1961. *Economic Development and Cultural Change*, *52*(1), 51–73.

Kuran, T. (1989). Sparks and prairie fires: A theory of unanticipated political revolution. *Public Choice*, *61*(1), 41–74.

Lamoreaux, N. R. (2011). The mystery of property rights: A US perspective. *Journal of Economic History*, *71*(2), 275–306.

Landa, J. (1981). A theory of the ethnically homogeneous middleman group: An institutional alternative to contract law. *Journal of Legal Studies*, *10*(2), 349–362.

Lau, L. J., Yingyi Q., & Roland, G. (2000). Reform without losers: an interpretation of China's dual-track approach to transition. *Journal of Political Economy*, *108*(1), 120–143.

Le, Z. (2010). *The Path of Shenzhen*. Beijing, China: People's Press.

Leeson, P. T. (2009). The laws of lawlessness. *Journal of Legal Studies*, *38*(2), 471–503.

Levmore, S. (2002). Two stories about the evolution of property rights. *Journal of Legal Studies*, *31*(2), S421–451.

(2003). Property's uneasy path and expanding future. *University of Chicago Law Review*, *70*, 181.

(2009). Interest groups and the problem with incrementalism. *University of Pennsylvania Law Review*, *158*, 815.

Li, L. (2012). Land titling in China: Chengdu experiment and its consequences. *China Economic Journal*, *5*(1), 47–64.

Lieberthal, K. G. (1992). The 'Fragmented Authoritarianism' model and its limitations. In Lieberthal, K. G., & Lampton, D. M. (Eds.), *Bureaucracy, Politics, and Decision Making in Post-Mao China*. Berkeley: University of California Press.

Lin, J. (1988). The household responsibility system in China's agricultural reform: A theoretical and empirical study, *Economic Development and Cultural Change*, *36*(3), S199-S225.

Macaulay, S. (1963). Non-contractual relations in business: A preliminary study. *American Sociological Review*, *28*(1), 55–67.

McAdams, R. (1997). The origin, development, and regulation of norms. *Michigan Law Review*, *96*, 338–433.

(2000). A focal point theory of expressive law. *Virginia Law Review*, *86*(8), 1649–1729.

(2001). Signaling discount rates: Law, norms, and economic methodology [Review of Law and Social Norms, by Eric A. Posner]. *Yale Law Journal, 110*, 625.

(2008). Beyond the prisoner's dilemma: Coordination, game theory, and law. *Southern California Law Review, 82*(2), 209–258.

McAdams, R. H., & Nadler, J. (2005). Testing the focal point theory of legal compliance: The effect of third – party expression in an experimental hawk/dove game. *Journal of Empirical Legal Studies, 2*(1), 87–123.

Mehta, J., Starmer, C., & Sugden, R. (1994). The nature of salience – an experimental investigation of pure coordination games. *American Economic Review, 84*(3), 658–673.

Myerson, R. B. (2004). Justice, institutions, and multiple equilibria. *Chicago Journal.of International Law, 5*, 91–107.

Merrill, T. W. (1985). Property rules, liability rules and adverse possession. *Northwestern University Law Review, 79*, 1122–1154.

Merill, T. W. (2002). Introduction: The Demsetz Thesis and the evolution of property rights, *Journal of Legal Studies, 31*(2), S331–338.

Miceli, T. J., & Segerson, K. (2007). A bargaining model of holdouts and takings. *American Law and Economics Review, 9*(1), 160–174.

Milhaupt, C. J., & West, M. D. (2000). The dark side of private ordering: An institutional and empirical analysis of organized crime. *University of Chicago law review, 67*(1), 41–98.

(2004). Justice, institutions, and multiple equilibria. *Chicago Journal of International Law, 5*, 91–107.

Nee, V., & Opper, S. (2012). *Capitalism from Below: Markets and Institutional Change in China*. Cambridge, MA: Harvard University Press.

Nissim, R. (2008). *Land Administration and Practice in Hong Kong*. Hong Kong, China: Hong Kong University Press.

North, D. C. (1990). *Institutions, Institutional Change, and Economic Performance*. Cambridge, United Kingdom: Cambridge University Press.

(1994). Institutional change: A framework of analysis. Working paper. Retrieved from http://dlc.dlib.indiana.edu/dlc/handle/10535/4102.

O'Brien, K. J. (1996). Rightful resistance. *World Politics, 49*, 31–55.

Ostrom, E. (1990). *Governing the Commons: The Evolution of Institutions for Collective Action*. Cambridge, United Kingdom: Cambridge University Press.

Padgett, J. F., & Powell, W. W. (2012). *The Emergence of Organizations and Markets*. Princeton, NY: Princeton University Press.

Paoli, L. (2003). *Mafia Brotherhoods: Organized Crime, Italian Style*. Oxford, United Kingdom: Oxford University Press.

Parchomovsky, G., & Siegelman, P. (2004). Selling Mayberry: Communities and individuals in law and economics. *California Law Review, 92*, 75–146.

Payne, G., Durand-Lasserve, A., & Rakodi, C. (2009). The limits of land titling and home ownership. *Environment and urbanization*, *21*(2), 443–462.

Pejovich, S. (2012). The effects of the interaction of formal and informal institutions on social stability and economic development. *Journal of Markets & Morality*, (2)2, 164–181.

Peñalver, E. M., & Katyal, S. K. (2007). Property outlaws. *University of Pennsylvania Law Review*, *155*, 1095–1186.

Picker, R. C. (1997). Simple games in a complex world: A generative approach to the adoption of norms. *University of Chicago Law Review*, *64*(4), 1225–1288.

Posner, E. A. (1996). Law, economics, and inefficient norms. *University of Pennsylvania Law Review*, *144*(5), 1697–1744.

(1998). Symbols, signals, and social norms in politics and the law. *Journal of Legal Studies*, *27*(S2), 765–797.

(2002). *Law and Social Norms*. Cambridge, MA: Harvard University Press.

Posner, R. A. (1997). Social norms and the law: An economic approach. *American Economic Review*, *87*, 365–369.

Poulsen, A., & Sugden, R. (2010). *Understanding Focal Points in Bargaining Situations: An Experimental Investigation* (RES-000–22-3322). ESRC End of Award Report. Swindon: ESRC.

(2011). *Understanding Focal Points in Bargaining Situations: An Experimental Investigation* (RES-000–22-3322). ESRC End of Award Report. Swindon: ESRC.

Putterman, L. (1997). On the past and future of China's township and village-owned enterprises, *World Development*, *25*(10), 1639–1655.

Qiao, S. (2011) Preventing Land Grabbing by Privatization: Illusion or Reality?. Unpublished manuscript. On file with the author.

(2012). Governing the post-socialist transitional commons: a case from rural China. *Colorado Journal of International Environmental Law and Policy*, *24*, 115.

(2014). Planting houses in Shenzhen: A real estate market without legal titles. *Canadian Journal of Law and Society*. 29 (2), 253–272.

(2015). Small property, adverse possession and optional law. In Chang, Yun-chien (Ed.), *Law and Economics of Possession*. Cambridge University Press, pp. 290–319.

(2015). Small property, big market: A focal point explanation. *American Journal of Comparative Law*. 65 (1), 197–238.

Qu, F., Heerink, N., & Wanmao, W. Land administration reform in China: It's impact on land allocation and economic development. *Land Use Policy*, *12*(3), 193–203.

Rapaczynski, A. (1996). The roles of the state and the market in establishing property rights. *Journal of Economic Perspectives*, *10*(2), 87–103.

Ramzy, A. (2009). "Runners-Up: The Chinese Worker," *TIME*. www.time.com/time/specials/packages/article/0,28804,1946375_1947252_1947256,00.html.

Rose, C. M. (1998), The several futures of property: Of cyberspace and folk tales, emission trades and ecosystems. *Minnesota Law Review, 83*, 129–182.

Rose, C. (2013). Psychologies of property (and why property is not a hawk-dove game). In Penner, J. E., & Smith, H. E. (Eds.), *The Philosophical Foundations of Property Law*, Oxford, United Kingdom: Oxford University Press.

Schelling, T. C. (1960). *The Strategy of Conflict*. Cambridge, MA: Harvard University Press.

Schneider, F. (2002). Size and measurement of the informal economy in 110 countries. Workshop of Australian National Tax Centre. ANU, Canberra.

Scott, J. (1985). *Weapons of the Weak: Everyday Forms of Peasant Resistance*. New Haven, CT: Yale University Press.

Smart, A. (1986). Invisible real estate: Investigations into the squatter property market. *International Journal of Urban and Regional Research, 10*(1), 29–45.

(2001). Unruly places: Urban governance and the persistence of illegality in Hong Kong's urban squatter areas. *American Anthropologist, 103(*1), 30–44.

Smith, H. E., & Merrill, T. W. (2010). *The Oxford Introductions to U.S. Law: Property*. Oxford, United Kingdom: Oxford University Press.

Strahilevitz, L. J. (2003). Social norms from close-knit groups to loose-knit groups. *University of Chicago Law Review, 70*, 359–372.

Stubborn as a nail: China residents who refuse to move. *ABC News*. Retrieved from http://abcnews.go.com/International/photos/stubborn-nail-china-residents-refuse-move-19827908/image-19828396.

Sugden, R. (1996). *The Economics of Rights, Cooperation and Welfare* (2nd edn.). New York, NY: Palgrave Macmillan.

Sunstein, C. R. (1996). On the expressive function of law. *University of Pennsylvania Law Review, 144*(5), 2021–2053.

(1996). Social norms and social roles. *Columbia Law Review, 96*(4), 903–968.

Thaler, R. H., & Sunstein, C. R. (2008). *Nudge: Improving Decisions about Health, Wealth, and Happiness*. New Haven, CT: Yale University Press.

Thomas, C. (2011). Law and neoclassical economic development in theory and practice: Toward an institutionalist critique of institutionalism. *Cornell Law Review, 96*(4), 967–1024.

Trebilcock, M., & Veel, P. (2008). Property rights and development: The contingent case for formalization. *University of Pennsylvania Journal of International Law, 30*, 397–481.

Tsai, K. S. (2006). Adaptive informal institutions and endogenous institutional change in China. *World Politics, 59*(1), 116–141.

Upham, F. K. (2009). From Demsetz to Deng: Speculations on the implications of chinese growth for law and development theory. *NYU Journal of International Law and Politics, 41*(3), 551–602.

Wang, L., Tieshan S., & Sheng, L. (2014). Legal title, tenure security, and investment: An empirical study in Beijing. *Housing Studies*, 1–22.

Wang, Q., Miao Z., & Kee-Cheok, C. (2014). Stakeholder perspectives of China's land consolidation program: A case study of Dongnan Village, Shandong Province. *Habitat International*, *43*, 172–180.

Weiner, J. R. (2003). The global epidemic of illegal building and demolitions: Implications for Jerusalem. *Jerusalem Letter*. Retrieved from www.jcpa.org/jl/vp498.htm.

Weingast, B. R. (1997). The political foundations of democracy and the rule of law. *American Political Science Review*, *91*(2), 245–263.

Weiping, W. (2002), Migrant housing in urban China: Choices and constraints, *Urban Affairs Review*, *38*(1), 90–119.

Wenhong, C. (2007). Does the colour of the cat matter? The red hat strategy in China's private enterprises. *Management and Organization Review*, *3*(1), 55–80.

Wines, M. (2011). A village in revolt could be a harbinger for China. *New York Times*. Retrieved from www.nytimes.com/2011/12/26/world/asia/in-china-the-wukan-revolt-could-be-a-harbinger.html?pagewanted=all.

Wu, W. (2002). Migrant housing in urban China: Choices and constraints. *Urban Affairs Review*, *38*(1), 90–119.

Wyman, K. M. (2013). Problematic private property: The case of New York taxicab medallions. *Yale Journal on Regulation*, *30*(1) 125–277.

(2005). From fur to fish: Reconsidering the evolution of private property. *New York University Law Review*, *80*, 117.

Chinese

1. 韩俊主编： “中国农村土地问题调查” ，上海远东出版社2009年版。[HAN JUN ED. SURVEY ON CHINA'S RURAL LAND ISSUES 89 (2009).]
2. 程瑜、刘思霆、严韶：“一个客家村落的都市化——深圳樟树布村改革开放30年的发展与变迁” ，广东人民出版社2010年版。[YU CHENG, SITING LIU & SHAO YAN, URBANIZATION OF A HAKKA VILLAGE: THREE DECADES OF DEVELOPMENT AND CHANGE IN ZHANGSHUBU OF SHENZHEN 115 (2010).]
3. 北京大学国家发展研究院： “深圳市土地产权制度改革与二次开发利用机制创新研究报告” (2013)。[NATIONAL SCHOOL OF DEVELOPMENT, REPORT ON LAND REFORM IN SHENZHEN 33 (2013)]
4. 折晓叶：“村庄的再造：一个“超级村庄“的社会变迁” ，中国社会科学出版社1997年版。[ZHE XIAOYE, THE VILLAGE REMAKING (1997)]
5. 深圳市统计局、国家统计局深圳调查队：“深圳统计年鉴（2011）” ，中国统计出版社2012年版。[Shenzhen STATISTICAL YEARBOOK 2011,

STATISTICS BUREAU OF SHENZHEN CITY & SHENZHEN SURVEY OFFICE OF THE STATE STATISTICS BUREAU (2011).]

6. 乐正主编："深圳之路"，人民出版社2010年版。[ZHENG LE, THE ROAD OF SHENZHEN (2010)]
7. 陈锡文等："中国农村制度变迁60年"，人民出版社2009年版。[XIWEN CHEN ET AL., SIX DECADES OF THE EVOLUTION OF CHINESE RURAL INSTITUTIONS, PEOPLE'S PUBLISHING HOUSE (2009).]
8. 许崇德："中华人民共和国宪法史"，福建人民出版社2005年版。[XU CHONGDE, THE HISTORY OF CHINESE CONSTITUTIONAL LAW, FUJIAN PEOPLE'S PRESS (2005).]
9. 张五常："中国的经济制度"，中信出版社2009年版。[STEVEN N.S. CHEUNG, THE ECONOMIC SYSTEM OF CHINA, CITIC PRESS GROUP (2009)]
10. 深圳市查处违法建筑领导小组办公室："深圳市农村城市化历史遗留违法建筑信息普查申报数据统计报告"（2010年）。[SHENZHEN CITY GOVERNMENT. 2010. INVESTIGATION REPORT ON ILLEGAL BUILDINGS IN SHENZHEN.]
11. 田雪杨、朱道林："从"使用费"到"年租金"–抚顺市实行国有土地租赁制的发展历程"，"中国土地" 2004年第6期。[Tian Xueyang and Zhu Daolin, *From Land Use Fee to Annual Rents: The History of Implementing Renting of State-Owned Land in Fushun*, China Land, Vol. 6, June 2004, at 27–28].
12. 黄小虎："新时期中国土地管理研究"，当代中国出版社2006年版。[Huang Xiaohu, *Research on New Era Land Administration in China Vol 2*, Modern China Publishing House (2005)].
13. 王先进："城镇土地使用制度改革回顾"，"中国国土资源报" 2008年8月1日第5版。[Wang Xianjin, *Review of the Urban Land Use Reform*, China Land and Resources Newspaper, Aug. 1, 2008.]
14. 张清勇："纵向财政竞争、讨价还价与中央-地方的土地收入分成——对我国20世纪80年代以来土地收入的考察"，来源于www.unirule.org.cn/xiazai/200711/69.pdf. [Zhang Qingyong, *Vertical Fiscal Competition, Bargaining, and the Land Revenue Sharing Relationship between Central and Local Governments in China*], available at www.unirule.org.cn/xiazai/200711/69.pdf.]
15. 卞耀武主编："中华人民共和国土地管理法释义"，法律出版社1998年版。[BIAN YAOWU, INTERPRETATION OF PRC LAND ADMINISTRATION LAW, LEGAL PRESS (1998)].
16. 周诚主编："中国房地产市场年鉴（1996）"，中国计划出版社1997年版。[ZHOU CHENG, CHINA REAL ESTATE MARKET YEARBOOK 1996].
17. 甘藏春："重温<土地管理法>的全面修訂"，"中国法律发展评论" 2011年第6期。[Gan Cangchun, *The Comprehensive Revision of Land Administration Law*, China Law Development Commentary, Vol. 6, 2011.]
18. 国土资源部土地利用司调研组："创新制度、规范流转：集体建设用地流转调研报告"，"国土资源通讯" 2002年第3期。[Ministry of Land Resources Bureau of Land Use, *Investigation Team of the MLR Bureau of*

Land Use, Innovate Institutions and Regulate Transfers: Investigation Report on Transfer of Rural Construction Land, State-Owned Land Letters, State Land Resources Dispatch No. 3 (2002).]

19. 李丁财： "'三来一补'在宝安农村的实践" ，海天出版社1999年版。[DINGCAI LI, THE PRACTICES OF SANLAI YIBU IN BAO'AN, SHENZHEN (1999).]
20. 张仲林："特区早期的生活"，"深圳文史" 2009年第11期。[Zhang Zhonglin, Life in the Early Period of the SEZ, *Shenzhen Humanities and History* 11 (2009): 1.]
21. 黄珽主编： "深圳房地产年鉴（2011）" ，海天出版社2012年版。[SHENZHEN REAL ESTATE YEAR BOOK 2011 151 (Huang Ting ed., 2011).]
22. 刘连泰："集体土地征收制度变革的宪法空间"，"法商研究" 2014年第3期。[Liu Liantai, *The Constitutional Dimension of Reforming the Requisition Regime of Collective-Owned Land*, STUD. LAW & BUS., No. 3, 2014].

INDEX